A student's guide to Group Accounts

by Tom Clendon

KAPLAN

PUBLISHING

Thank you to the many people who have helped me in producing
this book. There is one, Sally Baker, to whom I owe a special debt
of gratitude, for this book is a far better one than I could have
achieved on my own or without her help.

British library cataloguing-in-publication data
A catalogue record for this book is available from the British Library.
Published by:
Kaplan Publishing UK
Unit 2 The Business Centre
Molly Millars Lane
Wokingham
Berkshire
RG41 2QZ

ISBN 978-1-84710-916-3

© Tom Clendon

First edition published 2009

Printed and bound in Great Britain.

All quotations at the beginning of chapters are Oscar Wilde's.

Contents

Technical corners

Technical corners contain an explanation discussion, analysis and sometimes examples of theoretical issues and areas of common concern.

contents A student's guide to Group Accounts

About this book

Why do you need this book?

This book was written to help you pass your accountancy exams. It will enable you to understand the most complex group accounting issues and to be able to apply them in the exam.

It is comprehensive and up to date in an area where there have been some recent and radical changes following the revisions to both IFRS3 Business Combinations and IAS27 *Consolidated and Separate Financial Statements* in January 2008 (effective from July 2009). These revisions have made dramatic changes in the way that all group accounts are prepared using international financial reporting standards.

The book deals with the practicalities as well as the theory of this crucial area. It is written in a relaxed but authoritative style reflecting the approach of a top tutor. A glossary provides assistance with understanding any unfamiliar terms.

How to use this book

Each chapter starts with a **What's new** section before going on to walk you through a worked **Example**.

Technical Corners provide discussion, analysis and sometimes examples of the theoretical areas that some students can find challenging. (For example, on provision for unrealised profits with transactions with associates and reverse acquisitions.)

Each chapter also contains **Mind Maps** and a **Double Entry** section that will reinforce your understanding. Essential to your understanding of group accounts is having the opportunity to practise what you have just learnt, so each chapter contains practice **Questions** with comprehensive easy to follow answers at the back of the book.

The chapters are ordered in a logical sequence and grouped together in colour-coded sections. Each section has a **Recap Chapter** to consolidate the key messages learnt as well as useful proformas. These recap chapters will prove invaluable revision aids.

All the workings for the preparation of group accounts and the necessary adjustments are laid out in simple proformas, adopting a plus minus approach. No T accounts are used and there is no need to be familiar with double entry bookkeeping. However for those of you who do like double entry each chapter does provide a double entry explanation of the latest consolidation adjustment introduced. There is also a double entry section to enable anyone who is a little rusty on their double entry to refresh themselves.

You should check the syllabus to the exam that you are studying for – or ask your tutor – to find out exactly what is relevant for you. If you are just starting your studies you may find that the latter chapters are not examined until the later stages – so you can pick up the book again and study those topics when they become relevant.

The book follows the convention of examinations in using the $ as the currency when applying international financial reporting standards. Of course when real companies publish their group accounts in accordance with international financial reporting standards the currency they report in is generally the one in which they trade. A UK company usually uses £s, for example.

Recent changes

IFRS3 Business Combinations and IAS27 Consolidated and Separate Financial Statements were both revised in January 2008 with changes being effective from July 2009.

The profound effect that these once in a generation revisions have made, in changing the way that all group accounts are prepared using international financial reporting standards, are fully reflected and integrated in this book.

The revisions make several changes to the measurement of the cost of the investment (chapter 4). More fundamentally though the revisions create a new measurement of the basic figures of goodwill and the non controlling interest (NCI and formally known as the minority interest). As a result where the NCI is measured at fair value at the date of acquisition, goodwill is calculated gross (chapter 5). Consequently the gross goodwill has a revised process of impairment review (chapter 7).

Accounting for the disposal of subsidiaries has changed (chapter 16). There is also a new approach to buying and selling investments in subsidiaries where control does not change, rather there is an increase or decrease in the NCI (chapter 15 and 16). As an accidental bi-product of these revisions there are some interesting new consequences to accounting for both vertical and mixed group structures (chapters 17 & 18).

The consequences of the revisions are not just considered in isolation because they impact on the preparation of every set of group accounts.

For example in accounting the impairment loss on gross goodwill in the NCI in the group income statement (chapter 11) and the exchange difference on gross goodwill in an overseas subsidiary (chapter 20).

The concluding chapter of the book draws together a theoretical overview of these changes (chapter 21).

section 1

Introducing the group statement of financial position

chapter 1

Introducing the big five!

> "We are all in the gutter, but some of us are looking at the stars."

What's new?

Well everything as is the first chapter!

This book is about learning how to prepare consolidated financial statements. That is to say to be able to aggregate the financial statements of a parent company together with its subsidiary company accounts. The best way of learning about this technique is to start with a relatively simple example of consolidating the statement of financial position of the parent and the subsidiary.

Two quick things to pick up on; firstly a subsidiary is a company that is controlled, and the parent company is the company that is doing the controlling! The parent and the subsidiary together therefore form a group. The idea of preparing consolidated accounts is to aggregate the accounts of the parent and the subsidiary as if the group were a single entity.

And just in case, secondly, a statement of financial position is what it says it is, i.e. a statement that shows the financial position of the company at a moment in time. It is like a photograph showing at the year-end a snap shot of the company's assets, liabilities and equity.

Assets are the resources of the company like plant and inventory and they are all listed in the top half of the statement of financial position. Assets are split between non-current and current on the basis of whether they are expected to still be there in one year's time.

Liabilities are the obligations of the company e.g. trade payables and loans and they are listed in the bottom half of the statement of financial position. Liabilities are split between non-current and current on the basis of whether they are expected to still be there in one year's time.

Equity is the owners' interest in the company. It will comprise the original capital contributed by the shareholders in the form of share capital and share premium and also the accumulated retained profits of the company.

In case you are unfamiliar with the look of the statement of financial position here is one!

Statement of financial position   *This used to be called the balance sheet.*

	$
Non current assets	
Intangibles	X
Tangibles	X
Investments	X
Current assets	
Inventory	X
Receivables	X
Cash at bank	X
	X
Ordinary share capital	X
Share premium	X
Other reserves	X
Accumulated profits	X
Equity	X
Non current liabilities	X
Current liabilities	X
	X

These are all DR balances.

These are all CR balances.

So, let's set about an example of preparing the group statement of financial position by consolidating the parent company's and subsidiary company's statements of financial position.

Example

The statements of financial position of two companies are as follows.

	Ghana $m	Accra $m
Non current assets		
Tangible	100	100
Investment in Accra	300	
Current assets		
Inventory	40	200
Receivables	60	100
Cash at bank	200	200
	700	600
Ordinary shares ($1)	160	100
Accumulated profits	240	200
Equity	400	300
Non current liabilities	100	200
Current liabilities	200	100
	700	600

Additional information;

Ghana has today acquired all the shares in Accra for $300m.

Required

Prepare the consolidated statement of financial position for the Ghana group.

Now let us step back and consider what the situation is here.

Firstly, Ghana is the parent company of Accra as it controls Accra by virtue of owning a majority, in fact a 100%, of the shares of Accra. This means that Accra is the subsidiary company. Because Ghana, the parent owns 100% of the shares of Accra this means there is no non controlling interest in the subsidiary's net assets. If the subsidiary was not 100% owned, then the minority of the shares in the subsidiary that are not owned by the parent are referred to as the non controlling interest (NCI) in the group accounts.

This conclusion should be expressed and summarised in the following working.

W1 Group structure

Ghana

↓ Parent interest 100%
   Non controlling interest nil   The acquisition was today

Accra

Secondly, let us consider what the net assets of Accra really are at the date of acquisition by using the accounting equation.

| Assets | minus | Liabilities | = | Share capital | plus | Reserves | = | Equity |

Which can also be expressed as

| Net assets | | = | Share capital | plus | Reserves |

From the figures in the statement of financial position at the date of acquisition, which is also the same as the year-end, we can see that the net assets are $300m. This is calculated as the ordinary share capital of $100m added to the reserves of $200m.

This conclusion should be expressed and summarised in the following working.

W2 Net Assets of the subsidiary

	At acquisition $m	At year-end $m
Share capital	100	100
Accumulated profits	200	200
	300	300

Thirdly, let us compare what Ghana paid for Accra with the share of the net assets that were acquired to see if any premium arose on acquisition i.e. what goodwill arose on acquisition. Goodwill will arise on consolidation if the parent company has paid a premium over and above the net assets of the subsidiary because it believes that the subsidiary's business has something special about it, perhaps in terms of reputation that means it will be a profitable acquisition.

Ghana has recorded the investment in Accra at $300m. In return it has acquired 100% of the net assets of Accra at the date of acquisition. The net assets of the subsidiary at acquisition have been determined in column 1 of w2 and are also $300m. This means that in this preliminary example no goodwill arose on acquisition.

This conclusion should be expressed and summarised in the following working.

W3 Goodwill

		$m
Cost of the parent's investment		300
Less the parent's % of the net assets at acquisition from w2 column 1	(100% x 300)	(300)
Goodwill		Nil

If any goodwill had arisen then it would have been capitalised as an intangible asset and then subject to an impairment review to see if any needs to be written off – but more of all that in later chapters!

Fourthly, we should consider what the non controlling interest is in the subsidiary's net assets at the year-end. The net assets of the subsidiary at acquisition have been determined in w2 column 2 at $300m. Now in this preliminary example as the subsidiary is 100% owned there will be no non controlling interest.

This conclusion should be expressed and summarised in the following working.

W4 Non controlling interest

		$m
NCI % of the subsidiary's net assets at the year end from w2 column 2	(0% x 300)	Nil

Next let us consider what the group accumulated profits should be. The accumulated profits in the group statement of financial position will be the profits that belong to the shareholders of the parent company. Ghana as the parent company has profits of $240m. Since Ghana owns 100% of the subsidiary Accra, Ghana's shareholders may also own some of Accra's profits. However, Accra has only just been acquired and so whilst a subsidiary it has not had the opportunity to earn any profits.

This conclusion should be expressed and summarised in the following working.

W5 Group accumulated profits

	$m
Parent's accumulated profits	240
Plus the parent % of the subsidiary's post acquisition profits	Nil
	240

Finally the group statement of financial position can be prepared. It should be noted that Ghana's investment in the subsidiary has been cancelled out with the share capital and pre acquisition profits of the subsidiary and so the share capital of the group is that of the parent company only.

Ghana Group statement of financial position

The parent's cost of investment in the subsidiary never appears as an asset of the group as it is cancelled in the goodwill calculation against the subsidiary's share capital and reserves.

	Ghana $m	Accra $m		Group $m
Non current assets				
Goodwill			none arises w3	Nil
Tangible assets	100	100	cross cast (100 + 100)	200
Investment in Accra	300		cancelled out in w3	Nil
Current assets				
Inventory	40	200	cross cast (40 + 200)	240
Receivables	60	100	cross cast (60 + 100)	160
Cash at bank	200	200	cross cast (200 +200)	400
	700	600		1,000
Ordinary shares ($1)	160	100	parent only	160
Accumulated profits	240	200	w5	240
Non controlling interest	—	—	w4	Nil
Equity	400	300		400
Non current liabilities	100	200	cross cast (100 + 200)	300
Current liabilities	200	100	cross cast (200 +100)	300
	700	600		1,000

The assets are cross cast in full.

The share capital of the group will be that of the parent company only.

The liabilities are cross cast in full.

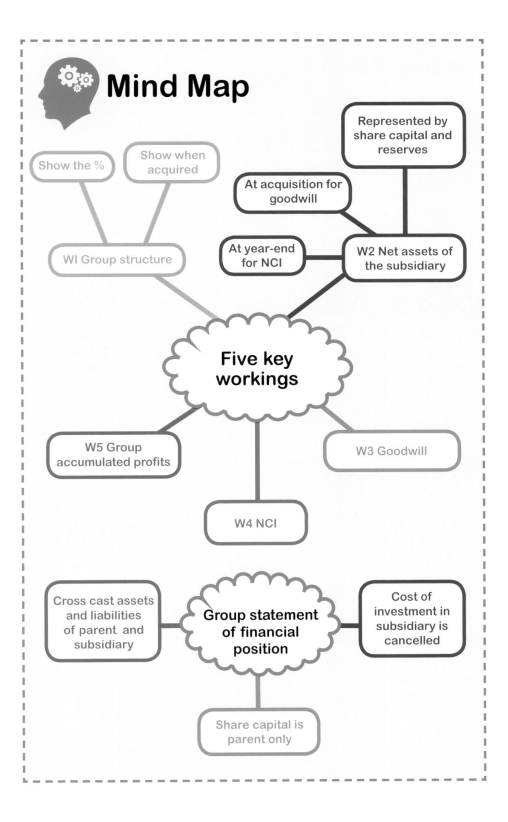

Mind Map

Show the %

Show when acquired

WI Group structure

Represented by share capital and reserves

At acquisition for goodwill

At year-end for NCI

W2 Net assets of the subsidiary

Five key workings

W5 Group accumulated profits

W3 Goodwill

W4 NCI

Cross cast assets and liabilities of parent and subsidiary

Group statement of financial position

Cost of investment in subsidiary is cancelled

Share capital is parent only

>> Double entry

The consolidation adjustments that will be made during the preparation of group accounts can be thought of and will be explained in terms of double entry.

If you are rusty regarding double entry then you may wish to refer to the recap on double entry bookkeeping found at the back of this book that sets out the basic double entry principles. Or you may wish to avoid double entry terms and that is OK as all the primary explanations and all the workings will be done in proformas with numbers being added and subtracted. This book is not about T accounts!

However, the only consolidation adjustment in the above example relates to the parent's investment in the subsidiary ($300m) and the equity of the subsidiary ($300m). All the other numbers have been cross cast.

The investment is an asset and thus a DR balance, and the share capital and accumulated profits of the subsidiary are equity and thus a CR balance. Accordingly when in w3 they are offset against each other the result is a perfect cancellation.

✿ Technical corner

Substance over form

There is a concept in accounting known as "substance over form". Accounting concepts are ideas and assumptions that are generally accepted.

Substance over form means that when preparing accounts it is assumed that we are striving to reflect the true economic substance of events and transactions i.e. to account for the truth rather than reflect the strict legal situation.

The preparation of group accounts is often quoted as an example of substance over form. You see strictly the parent company and the subsidiary company are two separate legal entities but we prepare the group accounts as if they were a single entity to reflect the fact that the parent company is in sole control. Because the parent controls the subsidiary's assets and liabilities it is appropriate to fully cross cast them to ensure that the shareholders of the parent company can appreciate the total resources that are controlled, even if the parent does not hold 100% of the shares in the subsidiary.

I suppose preparing a statement of financial position for the group is a bit like preparing one for a marriage! It maybe useful to aggregate the assets and liabilities of a husband and wife in a single statement but legally the husband and wife have separate legal personalities.

The parent company is not responsible for the liabilities of its subsidiary company, after all the parent is simply a shareholder in the subsidiary, which is a limited liability company. To that extent the preparation of the group accounts could appear misleading to a casual user as the group accounts aggregate all the assets and liabilities of the parent and its subsidiary companies together. This is because a lender to a highly geared and potentially insolvent subsidiary company needs to be reviewing the individual company's financial statements to assess the likelihood of recovering its money, rather than the overall group accounts.

Question Zambia

The statements of financial position of two companies are as follows.

	Zambia $m	Lusaka $m	
Investment in Lusaka	500		*Assets will be cross cast.*
Assets	600	650	
	1,100	650	
Ordinary shares ($1)	400	200	
Accumulated profits	400	300	
Equity	800	500	
			Liabilities will be cross cast.
Liabilities	300	150	
	1,100	650	

Additional information

Zambia has today acquired all the shares in Lusaka for $500m.

So it is a 100% subsidiary.

Required

Prepare the consolidated statement of financial position for the Zambia group.

Remember to do all five workings.

chapter 2

Goodwill and the non controlling interest (NCI)

> 66 Consistency is the last refuge of the unimaginative. 99

What's new?

Let us now consider an example where the cost of the parent company's investment in the subsidiary exceeds the share of the net assets of the subsidiary it has acquired. In these circumstances goodwill (w3) will arise on consolidation in the group accounts. Goodwill will be treated as an intangible asset in the group accounts.

Simultaneously let us also consider the situation where control is exercised by the parent owning a majority of the shares, rather than 100% so that a non controlling interest (NCI) will arise (w4).

Example

The statements of financial position of two companies are as follows.

	Jamaica $m	Kingston $m
Investment in Kingston	350	
Assets	500	500
	850	500
Ordinary shares ($1)	100	200
Accumulated profits	250	100
Equity	350	300
Liabilities	500	200
	850	500

Additional information

Jamaica has today acquired 160m of Kingston's 200m shares.

Required

Prepare the consolidated statement of financial position for the Jamaica group.

Once again, firstly we shall show the group structure, then calculate the net assets of the subsidiary (as represented by the share capital and reserves) at acquisition and year-end (which are again the same date), then calculate goodwill and the non controlling interest, before finally calculating the accumulated profits and preparing the group statement of financial position.

W1 Group structure

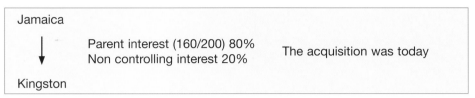

Jamaica

Parent interest (160/200) 80%
Non controlling interest 20%

The acquisition was today

Kingston

Jamaica is the parent company of Kingston as it controls Kingston by virtue of owning a majority (80%) of the shares of Kingston. Therefore there is a 20% non controlling interest in the net assets of Kingston.

W2 Net assets of the subsidiary

	At acquisition	At year-end
	$m	$m
Share capital	200	200
Accumulated profits	100	100
	300	300
	These are the net assets at acquisition that are used to calculate goodwill in w3	These are the net assets at the year end that are used to calculate the non controlling interest in w4

The net assets at acquisition and at the year-end are the same again but only because the acquisition has occurred at the year-end, so there has been no chance for the subsidiary to make any post acquisition profits.

Now let us compare the cost of the investment made by Jamaica, with the share of Kingston's net assets that were acquired, to calculate the goodwill on acquisition.

W3 Goodwill

		$m
Cost of the parent's investment		350
Less the parent's % of the subsidiary's net assets at acquisition from w2 column 1	(80% x 300)	(240)
Goodwill		110

The goodwill is capitalised as an intangible asset. Because of the transaction of purchasing the subsidiary there is a reliable measure of the goodwill. It is recognised as an intangible asset because it does not have a physical presence.

Let us now consider the non controlling interest in the subsidiary's net assets.

W4 Non controlling interest

		$m
NCI % of the subsidiary's net assets at the year end from w2 column 2	(20% x 300)	60

Then let us consider what the group accumulated profits should be. The subsidiary Kingston has only just been acquired and so whilst a subsidiary it has not had the opportunity to earn any profits that belong to Jamaica's shareholders.

W5 Group accumulated profits

	$m
Parent is accumulated profits	250
Plus the parent's % of the subsidiary's post acquisition profits from w2	Nil
	250

Finally the group statement of financial position can be prepared.

It should be remembered that

- the assets and liabilities of the parent and its subsidiary are still simply cross cast even though the subsidiary is not wholly owned by the parent

- the goodwill arising per w3 has to be included as an extra intangible asset but the cost of the investment in the subsidiary is not included

- the group equity comprises the parent's share capital, the accumulated profits per w5 and the non controlling interest per w4.

Jamaica group statement of financial position

		$m
Goodwill	w3	110
Assets	(500 + 500)	1,000
		1,110
Ordinary shares ($1)	parent only	100
Accumulated profits	w5	250
Non controlling interest	w4	60
Equity		410
Liabilities	(500 + 200)	700
		1,110

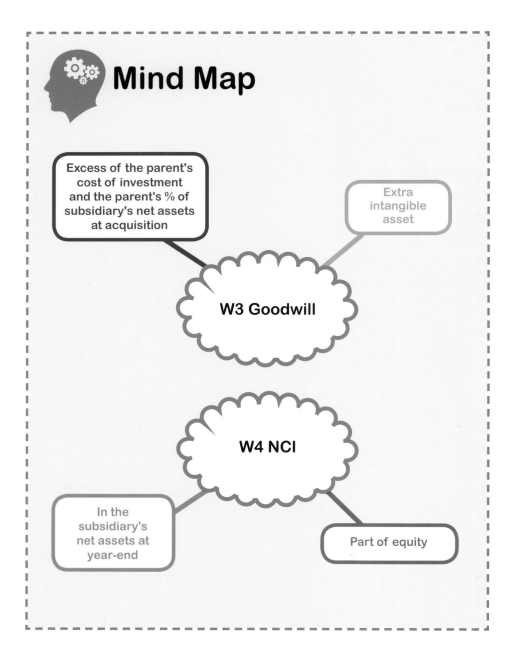

Mind Map

Excess of the parent's cost of investment and the parent's % of subsidiary's net assets at acquisition

Extra intangible asset

W3 Goodwill

W4 NCI

In the subsidiary's net assets at year-end

Part of equity

» Double entry

Let's look again at the calculation of goodwill of Kingston through the eyes of double entry and check that the goodwill arising on consolidation is really an asset i.e. a debit balance.

W3 Goodwill

		$m
Cost of the parent's investment		350
Less the parent's % of the subsidiary's net assets at acquisition	(80% x 300)	(240)
Goodwill		110

The investment in the subsidiary, $350m is a debit balance from the parent's statement of financial position, and the parent's share of net assets of the subsidiary at acquisition of $240m derives from the share capital and reserves at acquisition of the subsidiary, which are credit balances.

So with a debit of $350m having a credit of $240m offset against it we can see that the resultant balance is a debit balance of $110m.

As a debit balance, the goodwill is therefore an asset in the group statement of financial position.

Let's also look again at the calculation of the NCI w4 of Kingston through the eyes of double entry and check that the NCI arising on consolidation is really a credit balance i.e. to be included in the lower half of the statement of financial position.

W4 Non controlling interest

		$m
NCI % of the subsidiary's net assets at the year-end	(20% x 300)	60

At the year-end the net assets of the subsidiary of $300m is the share capital and reserves of the subsidiary, which are credit balances. Thus 20% of that $300m will also be a credit balance. In the statement of financial position all credit balances are reported in the lower half.

⚙ Technical corner

Negative goodwill

In exam questions – and in real life – goodwill almost inevitably arises on the acquisition of a subsidiary because it is normal that the consideration that the parent pays is a premium over and above the net assets that are acquired. As we have seen this goodwill arises in the group accounts and is treated as an intangible asset. As we shall see in Chapter 7 *Impairment revew of goodwill*, it will then be subject to an annual impairment review.

Thus for example if the parent pays $200m for 100% of a subsidiary with net assets of $150m then the goodwill arising is $50m.

		$m
Cost of the parent's investment		200
Less the parent's % of the subsidiary's net assets at acquisition	(100% x 150)	(150)
Goodwill "positive = an asset"		50

This positive goodwill is an asset and arguably is attributable to the general reputation of the business, its prospects of making future profits, and reflects a strong loyal customer base and a skilled workforce.

But there is a very unusual situation where on the consolidation of a subsidiary the goodwill that arises is not an asset. Let us consider the situation where instead of the parent paying a premium for the investment in the subsidiary it is able to acquire the subsidiary at a discount. Thus for example, if the parent pays $140m for 100% of the $150m net assets of the subsidiary the goodwill arising is a negative $10m.

		$m
Cost of the parent's investment		140
Less the parent's % of the subsidiary's net assets at acquisition	(100% x 150)	(150)
Goodwill "negative = a profit"		(10)

This is negative goodwill. It arguably arises because the future prospects of the business are poor. This negative goodwill is really a discount arising on consolidation. It comes about where there has been a bargain purchase if you like. Negative goodwill is therefore treated as a profit and as such the accounting treatment is to immediately recognise it in the income statement.

Question Trinidad

The statements of financial position of two companies are as follows.

Use this investment in the goodwill calculation w3.

	Trinidad $m	Tobago $m
Investment in Tobago	800	
Assets	1,000	900
	1,800	900
Ordinary shares ($1)	400	300
Accumulated profits	500	400
Equity	900	700
Liabilities	900	200
	1,800	900

Additional information

Trinidad has today acquired 225m shares of Tobago's 300m shares.

Use the number of shares bought in the w1 group structure working to show the parent's interest and NCI.

Required

Prepare the consolidated statement of financial position for the Trinidad group.

chapter 3
Post acquisition profits

> " Experience is the name everyone gives to their mistakes. "

What's new?

In the examples we have looked at so far, we have prepared the group accounts on the day the parent acquires control of the subsidiary. In these circumstances the subsidiary has had no opportunity to earn profits whilst being a group company i.e. there are no post acquisition profits of the subsidiary to be included in the group accumulated profits in w5.

In future the subsidiary will have been acquired prior to the reporting date so there will be post acquisition profits that can be included in the group accumulated profits. The pre acquisition profits form part of the net assets of the subsidiary at acquisition (w2) and are cancelled in the calculation of goodwill in w3.

Example

The statements of financial position of two companies are as follows.

	Cyprus $m	Nicosia $m
Non current assets		
Tangible	100	250
Investment in Nicosia	400	
Current assets	300	350
	800	600
Ordinary shares ($1)	250	200
Accumulated profits	250	100
Equity	500	300
Non current liabilities	140	170
Current liabilities	160	130
	800	600

Additional information

Cyprus acquired 150m shares in Nicosia one year ago when the reserves of Nicosia were $60m.

Required

Prepare the consolidated statement of financial position for the Cyprus group.

As always we start by establishing the group structure.

W1 Group structure

Cyprus

↓

Parent's interest (150/200) 75%   The acquisition was one year
Non controlling interest 25%   ago

Nicosia

What is new here is that the subsidiary was acquired one year ago. As such the $100m profits of Nicosia will have partly arisen before it joined the group i.e. will be regarded as pre acquisition and partly will have arisen after it joined the group i.e. will be post acquisition. The group will only be able to account for the parent's % of the post acquisition profits in the group accumulated profits (w5).

W2 Net assets of the subsidiary

	At acquisition $m	At year-end $m
Share capital	200	200
Accumulated profits	60	100
	260	300
	Used to calculate goodwill in w3	Used to calculate the non controlling interest in w4

The increase in the net assets of $40m ($300m – $260m) represents the profits of the subsidiary made since acquisition and the parent's % of this will be taken to group accumulated profits in w5.

W3 Goodwill

		$m
Cost of the parent's investment		400
Less the parent's % of the subsidiary's net assets at acquisition from w2 column 1	(75% x 260)	(195)
Goodwill		205

W4 Non controlling interest

		$m
NCI% of the subsidiary's net assets at year-end from w2 column 2	(25% x 300)	75

The non controlling interest in the subsidiary's net assets will be part of the group equity.

W5 Group accumulated profits

		$m
Parent's accumulated profits		250
Plus the parent's % of the subsidiary's post acquisition profits from w2	(75% x 40)	30
		280

The post acquisition profits of the subsidiary are represented by the increase in the net assets of the subsidiary between the date of acquisition and the year-end date i.e. the difference between column 1 and column 2 in w2.

Cyprus group statement of financial position

		$m
Goodwill	w3	205
Tangible non current assets	(100 + 250)	350
Current assets	(300 + 350)	650
		1,205
Ordinary shares ($1)	Parent only	250
Accumulated profits	w5	280
Non controlling interest	w4	75
Equity		605
Non current liabilities	(140 + 170)	310
Current liabilities	(160 + 130)	290
		1,205

In preparing the group statement of financial position, the assets and liabilities of the parent and its subsidiary are simply cross cast.

The goodwill arising has to be included.

The group equity comprises the parent's share capital, the group accumulated profits as calculated in w5 and the non controlling interest per w4.

» Double entry

This chapter has introduced the idea that the subsidiary had been acquired before the year-end. In these circumstances the profits of the subsidiary attributable to the parent at the year-end partly comprise profits at the date of acquisition (pre acquisition profits) and partly profits that have been generated in the post acquisition period (post acquisition profits).

The subsidiary's year-end accumulated profits are not cross cast in the group statement of financial position as in the process of consolidation the subsidiary's profits are allocated three ways!

The allocation of the CR balance of Nicosia's accumulated year-end profits could be expressed in double entry as follows

		$m	$m	
DR	Subsidiary's year-end accumulated profits	100		
CR	NCI		25	(25% x 100)
	The NCI share in the subsidiary's profits is part of the NCI in the net assets at the year-end in w4.			
CR	Parent's share of the pre acquisition profits		45	(75% x 60)
	The parent's share of the pre acquisition profits, together with their share of the subsidiary's share capital represents the parent's share of the net assets of the subsidiary at the date of acquisition, which are taken into the goodwill working in w3.			
CR	Parent's share of the post acquisition profits		30	(75% x 40)
	The parent's share of the post acquisition profits increase the group accumulated profits in w5.			

Mind Map

Accumulated profits belonging to parent shareholders

W5 Group accumulated profits

Parent company profits

Plus the parent's % of the subsidiary's post acquisition profits

As represented by the change in net assets

⚙ Technical corner

NCI as part of equity - the economic entity approach

The current accounting theory places the NCI as part of the ownership interest of the group and so it is required to be included as part of the equity of the group. That is to say that, whilst the parent company shareholders control the group, the group is considered as being partly owned by the parent shareholders and partly by shareholders owning the minority holdings in the subsidiaries i.e. the NCI. This modern attitude to the NCI in the group accounts can be referred to as the economic entity approach.

Historically the NCI – or minority interest as it used to be called – were often regarded as a second-class type of equity or even as a liability, a provider of finance if you like. The old fashioned approach of treating the NCI as a quasi liability can be referred to as the parent company or proprietary approach. This simply regarded the preparation of the group accounts exclusively from a parent company shareholders' perspective.

The adoption of the economic entity approach, and so placing the NCI within equity and treating them as co-owners of the group, has practical consequences, as we shall see later. For example when it comes to allocating gains and losses that relate to the subsidiary the NCI will participate in such adjustments.

Determining the acquisition date

Determining the exact date of acquisition of a subsidiary is very important as it is at that date that goodwill is determined as well as being the date from which the profits of the subsidiary start to be consolidated.

The date of the acquisition of a subsidiary is the date on which the acquirer obtains control of the subsidiary.

In all of our examples this date has been simply stated. It is generally presumed to be the date on which the parent company acquires control of the assets, assumes responsibility for the liabilities and pays for the shares (though the timing of the payment of deferred consideration and contingent consideration is not relevant).

The parent should consider all the pertinent facts and circumstances in identifying the acquisition date e.g. there might be a written agreement, which specifies the acquisition date. Other factors to consider include the date that the parent commences directing the operating and financial policies and the date of the appointment of the parent's majority on the board of directors.

Question Croatia

The statements of financial position of two companies are as follows.

	Croatia $m	Zagreb $m
Not a group asset – but used to calculate goodwill.		
Non current assets		
Tangible	1,000	800
Investment in Zagreb	600	
Current assets	400	200
	2,000	1,000
Ordinary shares ($1)	800	100
Accumulated profits	750	400
Equity	1,550	500
Non current liabilities	250	300
Current liabilities	200	200
	2,000	1,000

Use the 60m to work out the parent's % and hence the NCI %.

Additional information

Croatia acquired 60m shares in Zagreb one year ago when the reserves of Zagreb were $60m.

These are the pre acquisition reserves w2 column 1

Subsidiary bought last year! Net assets at acquisition and year-end will be different!

Required

Prepare the consolidated statement of financial position for the Croatia group.

recap

of the first section

What's new?

Absolutely nothing!

Let's take this opportunity to recap on the key messages and proformas that we have learnt in the first three chapters. It is important that we can remember these messages and proformas as we shall be reusing them in subsequent chapters as we build our knowledge.

🔑 Key messages

- A group of companies comprises, as a minimum, a parent company and its subsidiary.

- A subsidiary is an entity that is controlled by the parent.

- Control will normally be achieved by the parent owning a majority of the ordinary shares in the subsidiary.

- Group accounts are prepared as if the group were a single entity and this reflects substance over form.

- The assets and liabilities of the parent and the subsidiary are cross cast in full.

- The parent's investment in the subsidiary is not a group asset, rather it is cancelled out in determining the goodwill arising on consolidation.

- Goodwill arising is accounted for as a group intangible asset and is subject to an annual impairment review (though we have not done the impairment review yet!).

- The share capital of the group is that of the parent only.

- The group accumulated profits will be those of the parent company plus the parent's share of the subsidiary's post acquisition profits less any goodwill impaired (although we haven't seen any goodwill impaired yet!).

- The non controlling interest (NCI) in the net assets of the subsidiary will be presented as part of the equity of the group.

W1 Group structure

Parent		
↓	Parent's interest XX% Non controlling interest (NCI) XX%	The acquisition was XX ago
Subsidiary		

W2 Net assets of the subsidiary

	At acquisition $	At year-end $
Share capital	XX	XX
Accumulated profits	XX	XX
	XX	XX
	↓	↓
	The net assets of the subsidiary at the date of acquisition is used to calculate goodwill in w3	The net assets of the subsidiary at the year-end is used to calculate the NCI in w4

The difference between the net assets in the post acquisition period represents the profits of the subsidiary made since acquisition and the parent's % of this will be taken to group accumulated profits in w5.

W3 Goodwill

		$
Cost of the parent's investment		XX
Less the parent's % of the subsidiary's net assets at acquisition	(Parent % x w2 column 1)	(XX)
Goodwill		XX

The goodwill arising is an intangible asset in the group accounts.

W4 Non controlling interest

		$
NCI% of the subsidiary's net assets at the year-end	(NCI% x w2 column 2)	XX

The NCI in the net assets will be part of the group equity.

W5 Group accumulated profits

The accumulated profits of the group will comprise those of the parent, plus the parent's % of the subsidiary's post acquisition profits. The post acquisition profits are represented by the increase in the net assets of the subsidiary between the date of acquisition and the year-end date i.e. the difference between column 1 and column 2 in w2.

		$
Parent's accumulated profits		XX
Plus the parent's % of the subsidiary's post acquisition profits from w2	(P% x difference in columns at w2)	XX
		XX

section 2
Introducing fair values

chapter 4

Recording the fair value of the investment in the subsidiary

What's new?

As we have seen so far the parent's cost of the investment in the subsidiary has been given to us in the question. However it is important to understand where this figure comes from and what it comprises as it can be necessary to have to work out the cost of the investment. In principle this must be at the fair value of the consideration that has been given. By definition fair value of an asset is the amount that it can be exchanged for in an arm's length transaction between informed and willing parties.

The consideration given by the parent company for the shares in the subsidiary can comprise:

- cash
- shares
- deferred consideration
- contingent consideration.

Cash paid

The fair value of the cash paid is simply the amount of cash.

Shares issued

Where the parent company issues shares as consideration for acquiring the shares in the subsidiary this is known as a share for share exchange. The shares being issued are those of the parent company. Shares have a nominal value (often $1) and when they are issued for consideration in excess of this the excess is taken to the share premium account. The fair value of the shares is their market value.

Deferred consideration

Where the parent has consideration to pay in the future, this will represent either a liability or equity.

Where the parent company has an obligation to pay cash in the future it will have to record a liability. If you were selling something would you rather be given $1,000 in cash now or a $1,000 in cash in one years time? Well, I know that I would prefer to receive the cash now rather than wait for a year. In other words cash in the future in today's money terms is worth less. Therefore it is necessary to discount the deferred consideration to its present value to reflect the time value of money. The fair value of the liability is therefore measured at the present value of the future cash flow.

Where the parent company will issue shares in the future this is also deferred consideration and it will be recorded as equity. The fair value of those shares to be issued in the future is the market value of the shares at the date of acquisition.

Contingent consideration[1]

Where the consideration will be paid in the future and is dependant on an uncertain future event (e.g. a profits target being met) then it is known as contingent consideration. At the date of acquisition the fair value of such consideration may in practice be difficult to determine and accordingly in questions should be given.

Where the contingent consideration will be paid in cash then a provision for the contingent liability will be recognised. If that liability is subsequently paid at a different amount than originally recorded then the difference that arises is recognised as a gain or loss in income. In other words if it transpires that in fact the contingent liability does not have to be paid at all (for example the profit target is not achieved) then at that time the liability is derecognised (removed from the accounts) and a corresponding gain is recorded in income.

Where the contingent consideration is to be settled in shares then an equity reserve is recorded at the value of the shares at the date of acquisition. Regardless of the share price when the shares are actually issued no gain or loss will arise. If the shares are not issued then there is no change in the equity of the company.

---

1   Before IFRS3 *Business Combinations* was revised in January 2008 contingent consideration was only accounted for if it was probable. Now contingent consideration is always accounted at its fair value.

Let's look at a comprehensive example.

Example

Malawi has made an acquisition of 100% of the shares in Blantyre. The consideration that Malawi gave for the investment in the subsidiary Blantyre comprised:

1 Cash – Malawi paid $25,471 to the shareholders of Blantyre.

2 Shares - Malawi issued 10,000 shares to the shareholders of Blantyre, each with a nominal value of $1 and a market value of $4.

3 Deferred consideration - $20,000 is to be paid two years after the date of acquisition. The relevant discount rate is 10%.

4 Contingent consideration – Further monies may be payable at a later date subject to performance targets being met. The fair value of this consideration is $38,000.

At the date of acquisition Blantyre's net assets were $80,000.

Required

(i) Determine the fair value of the consideration that Malawi has given in buying its investment in Blantyre.

(ii) Determine the goodwill arising on the consolidation of Blantyre in the Malawi group accounts.

(iii) Show the subsequent accounting for the deferred consideration.

(iv) Show the subsequent accounting for the contingent consideration on the basis that the performance targets were not met.

(i) The cost of the investment that Malawi made in Blantyre can be ascertained by aggregating the fair value of the consideration given.

Cost of Investment in Blantyre

		$
Cash	There is no problem ascertaining the fair value of cash!	25,471
Shares	The fair value of the 10,000 shares that the parent issued is the market value of $4 each	40,000
Deferred consideration	The fair value of the $20,000 cash that is payable in two year's time is the present value – thus it is discounted to its present value by multiplying it by $\dfrac{1}{1.1^2}$	16,529
Contingent consideration	The contingent consideration must also be at fair value	38,000
		120,000

(ii) Having ascertained the correct fair value of the consideration given by the parent, and since the value of the subsidiary's net assets at acquisition is given we can move straight on to working 3 to ascertain the goodwill arising.

		$
Cost of the parent's investment (at fair value)		120,000
Less the parent's % of the net assets at acquisition	(100% x 80,000)	(80,000)
Goodwill		40,000

(iii) Subsequent accounting for the deferred consideration.

The recognition of the liability of deferred consideration will result in further accounting entries.

At the date of acquisition Malawi recorded a liability to pay the shareholders of Blantyre $20,000 in two year's time, which because of the time value of money was discounted and measured at the present value of $16,529. Now whenever a liability has been discounted that discounting will be need to be subsequently unwound to reflect the increase in the present value as each year passes. This unwinding of the discount creates a finance charge (interest cost) that is charged to the income statement.

In two year's time Malawi will have to pay the liability at the agreed amount of $20,000 whilst it has only initially measured the liability at $16,529, so the difference is the finance cost of $3,471. However this finance cost is not simply charged equally over the two years of the liability because we have the actual relevant interest rate given (at 10%). So in the first year the finance cost will be calculated as 10% x $16,529 = $1,653. This will be charged to the income statement and will increase the liability.

One year after the acquisition the liability of deferred consideration will therefore be measured at $18,182 (being $16,529 plus $1,653). In the following year there will another 10% finance charge before the liability is finally settled at $20,000. This is all best summarised in the following working.

	Opening balance	Plus the finance cost charged to income statement at 10%	Less the cash paid	Closing balance
	$	$	$	$
Year 1	16,529	1,653	(Nil)	18,182
Year 2	18,182	1,818	(20,000)	Nil

(iv) Subsequent accounting for the contingent consideration, where the performance targets were not met.

The recognition of the contingent consideration resulted in a provision for a liability at the date of acquisition that was measured at the fair value of $38,000. This will only be actually paid if certain performance targets are met e.g. a future level of profit is achieved.

If those targets are not met then the liability to pay the $38,000 has been extinguished. This would mean that the parent company and hence the group is better off! There is therefore a gain of $38,000 recorded in the income statement. The same principle would apply by recording a loss in the event that the liability was settled for more than the estimate of the original fair value.

In the unlikely circumstances that the amount of consideration changes because of new information about the fair value of the amount of consideration at the acquisition date (rather than because of a post-acquisition event) then retrospective restatement is required. In the above example if this meant that the $38,000 was not payable then no gain would arise, rather the fact that the liability is extinguished results in the original cost being revised downwards to $82,000 ($120,000 - $38,000) and so the goodwill is reduced to $2,000 ($82,000 – (100% x $80,000)).

» Double entry

Let's look again at the recording of the fair value of the consideration that Malawi gave on the purchase of the shares in Blantyre – through the eyes of double entry – and check that the entry to record the investment really is a DR entry, so that all the considerations that were given have created CR entries.

Paying cash out of $25,471 will decrease the asset of cash. When assets go down this is a CR. The entry in cash is CR Cash $25,471.

Issuing 10,000 $1 shares with a market value of $4 each will increase equity. When equity goes up this is a CR. Shares will be recorded at their nominal value of $10,000 in share capital and the excess consideration of $30,000 will be taken to share premium. The entry in equity is CR Share Capital $10,000 CR Share Premium $30,000.

Deferred consideration is agreeing to pay cash in the future so will increase liabilities. When liabilities go up this is a CR. The entry is CR Liabilities $16,529.

Contingent consideration creates a provision, a liability of uncertain timing or amount, so will increase liabilities. When liabilities go up this is a CR. The entry is CR liabilities (provision) $38,000.

All these CRs mean that Malawi is acquiring the asset of investment in Blantyre. When assets go up this is a DR. The entry is DR investment in Blantyre $120,000.

		$	$
DR	Investment in Blantyre (balancing figure)	120,000	
CR	Cash		25,471
CR	Share Capital		10,000
CR	Share Premium		30,000
CR	Liability - Deferred consideration		16,529
CR	Liability – Provision for contingent consideration		38,000

Mind Map

Fair value is the amount that an asset can be exchanged for in an arm's length transaction between informed and willing parties.

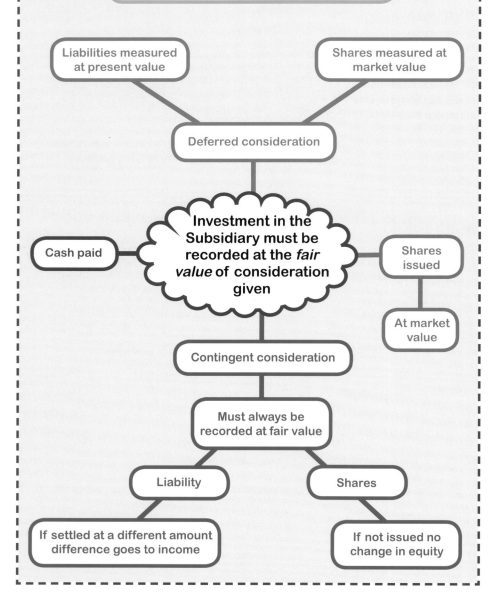

Liabilities measured at present value

Shares measured at market value

Deferred consideration

Cash paid

Investment in the Subsidiary must be recorded at the *fair value* of consideration given

Shares issued

At market value

Contingent consideration

Must always be recorded at fair value

Liability

Shares

If settled at a different amount difference goes to income

If not issued no change in equity

⚙ Technical corner

Accounting for professional fees on acquisition

Legal fees and other associated professional fees incurred by the parent company as part of the acquisition of the subsidiary are immediately written off to income. Following the revision of IFRS3 *Business Combinations* in January 2008 such costs are no longer to be capitalised (added) as part of the cost of the investment. This is because the fair value of the investment is being considered from the perspective of what the seller receives and not what the buyer has paid out.

However, arguably the immediate write off of professional fees on the acquisition of an investment in a subsidiary is inconsistent with treatment of such costs when buying property plant and equipment. IAS16 *Property Plant and Equipment* requires that when measuring the initial cost of these assets their cost includes all costs necessary to bring the asset into working condition for its intended use. This would include not only its original purchase price but also costs of related professional fees e.g. architects and legal fees.

Accounting for issue costs and share premium

When shares are issued for consideration in excess of their nominal value the excess consideration is recognised and credited to the share premium account. The share premium account, like ordinary share capital is part of equity. On the issue of shares the associated issue costs can be written off to the share premium account. Thus if 10,000 $1 shares are issued for $3 each, cash of $30,000 will be received. The initial recognition of the share premium will be $20,000, being $2 a share on 10,000 shares. However, if the costs of issue are $1,000 then this is written off to the share premium account reducing it to $19,000. To summarise, in double entry terms.

DR	Cash	$30,000	
CR	Share capital		$10,000
CR	Share premium		$20,000
DR	Share premium	$1,000	
CR	Cash		$1,000

Question Russia

Remember that the shares issued must be recorded at fair value.

Russia has made an acquisition of 100% of the shares in Moscow. Moscow has a share capital of 50,000 shares with a nominal value of $1 each. The consideration that Russia gave for the investment in the subsidiary included a 2 for 1 share for share exchange. The market value of Russia shares is $3. The shareholders of Moscow are also paid cash immediately of $62,963. In addition Russia will also pay cash of 80 cents per share in one year's time. Assume a relevant discount rate of 8%.

Remember to discount the deferred consideration.

At the date of acquisition the net assets of Moscow were $150,000.

Required

(i)   Determine the fair value of the consideration that Russia has given in buying its investment in Moscow.

(ii)   Determine the goodwill arising on the consolidation of Moscow in the Russia group accounts.

chapter 5

Non controlling interest (NCI) at fair value and gross goodwill

> ❝ If you want to tell people the truth, make them laugh, otherwise they'll kill you. ❞

What's new?

In the exercises we have looked at to date we have calculated the goodwill arising on the acquisition of the subsidiary by comparing the fair value that the parent has given with the parent's share of the subsidiary's net assets acquired. Strictly the goodwill of the subsidiary that arises from this calculation is the goodwill that is attributable to the parent only. This method is known as the proportionate method of calculating goodwill.

There is an alternative way of measuring goodwill whereby goodwill is calculated by reference not only to the fair value of the parent's cost of investment but also to the fair value of the NCI at acquisition. Thus the value of the whole subsidiary at acquisition is compared with the whole of the net assets at acquisition to ascertain the whole of the goodwill. This will have the effect of both increasing the goodwill arising and the NCI. This method means goodwill is calculated gross i.e. in full.

It is a matter of accounting policy, on an acquisition by acquisition basis, as to whether goodwill is to be calculated on a proportionate basis or gross basis.

Example

Libya acquires 80% of Tripoli's share capital in a share for share exchange. The subsidiary Tripoli has 100 $1 nominal value shares. Libya makes a 2 for 1 share issue when the share price of each Libya share is $5. At the date of acquisition the net assets of Tripoli are $600.

Required

(i) At the date of acquisition calculate the goodwill arising that is attributable to the parent i.e. using the proportionate method and calculate the NCI

(ii) Given the market value of a Tripoli share is $8 at the date of acquisition, calculate the fair value of the NCI at acquistion and gross goodwill.

(i) To calculate goodwill we need the cost of the parent's investment, and this sees us repeat the earlier exercise of having to ascertain the fair value of the consideration that the parent has given to acquire its interest in the subsidiary.

The cost of the investment that Libya, the parent, has made in Tripoli, the subsidiary, is the fair value of the consideration given. This is the market value of the shares that Libya has issued.

Libya issues two shares for every one share that it acquires	Libya is acquiring 80% of the Tripoli's shares	Libya is having to issue 160 shares	Libya's shares are each worth $5	The fair value of the consideration given by Libya is $800
2/1 x	(80% x 100) =	160	x $5	= $800

In working 3 the goodwill therefore that is attributable to the parent company is:

		$
Cost of the parent's investment (at fair value)		800
Less the parent's % of the net assets at acquisition	(80% x 600)	(480)
Goodwill (attributable to the parent)		320

The NCI at acquisition is based on the net assets of the subsidiary only.

		$
NCI % in the net assets	(20% x 600)	120

In passing it is relevant to note that the goodwill of $320 is the difference between what the parent has paid and what the parent has acquired. In other words this goodwill is wholly attributable to the parent and none is attributable to the NCI. Now this is inconsistent with the way that the other assets of the subsidiary are consolidated. The plant and inventory of the subsidiary for example are aggregated in full and then a NCI in the net assets is reported. The calculation of goodwill gross will mean that this inconsistency is corrected and the NCI at acquisition will also be at fair value.

(ii) Now, in order to answer the second part of the exercise i.e. to calculate goodwill gross we need to know the fair value of the NCI at the date of acquisition. This is calculated as the market value of Tripoli's shares not acquired by Libya i.e. value of the shares owned by the NCI shareholders.

The number of shares of Tripoli that are not acquired by Libya is 20	The market value of each Tripoli share at acquisition is $8	So the fair value of the NCI is $160
20% x 100 = 20	x $8	= $160

Now we can proceed to calculate gross goodwill and the NCI. First, as before, we calculate the goodwill attributable to the parent company, then we can add the difference between the fair values of the NCI at acquisition with their share of the net assets at acquisition.

Goodwill calculation

		$	$
Cost of the parent's investment (at fair value)		800	
Less the parent's % of the net assets at acquisition	(80% x 600)	(480)	
Goodwill (attributable to the parent)			320
Fair value of the NCI at acquisition		160	
Less the NCI % of the net assets at acquisition w2	(20% x 600)	(120)	
Goodwill (attributable to the NCI)			40
Gross (or full) goodwill at acquisition			360

The calculation of the NCI would now increase by $40 i.e. the goodwill of the NCI. In this way both the asset of goodwill increase by $40 in the top half of the group statement of financial position and the NCI increase by $40 in the bottom half of the group statement of financial position.

Alternatively the calculation of the gross goodwill could be presented by aggregating the fair value of the consideration paid by the parent (the shares in the subsidiary that were bought) with the fair value of the NCI (the shares that were not bought) and then comparing that with 100% of the net assets at acquisition.

This presentation emphasises that it is consistent to have the parent's cost of investment and the NCI at acquisition both at fair value. It is usually quicker as well!

		$
Cost of the parent's investment (at fair value)		800
Fair value of the NCI at acquisition		160
		960
Less 100 % of the net assets at acquisition w2	(100% x 600)	(600)
Gross (or full) goodwill at acquisition		360

The NCI at acquisition is based on the fair value – which will comprise both the NCI % of the net assets but also includes the goodwill attributable to the NCI.

		$
NCI % in the net assets w2	(20% x 600)	120
Plus the goodwill attributable to the NCI w3		40
		160

Because when gross goodwill is determined the NCI at acquisition must be at fair value, it is no co-incidence that this working shows the NCI at acquisition is $160 – which is the fair value of the NCI at acquisition that we had worked out earlier.

It is fair to say that in the majority of cases

- goodwill will be calculated gross

- the fair value of the NCI at acquisition will be given

- presenting the gross goodwill calculation by aggregating the fair value of the consideration paid by the parent with the fair value of the NCI and subtracting 100% of the net assets will be quicker.

Because these are such important principles let's have a look at an example of the NCI at the year-end. In this example we shall see there is an alternative way of calculating the year-end NCI when the fair value of the NCI has been given at the date of acquisition.

Example

Amazon acquires 60% of River's share capital for consideration of $900. River has 200 shares and the market value of each share is $5. At the date of acquisition the net assets of River were $800, and are $950 at the year-end.

Required

(i) Calculate the gross goodwill arising at acquisition (w3).

(ii) Calculate the NCI at the year-end (w4).

(i)   In this example, the NCI will be 40%.

If we are to calculate the gross goodwill we need to have the fair value of the NCI at acquisition. Now, whilst in later examples this may well be given (like the fair value of the cost of the investment in the subsidiary is often given) it can be worked out as the value of the shares at acquisition that are not purchased by the parent company. Once this has been calculated we can move straight to w3 goodwill to answer the question.

40% x 200 = 80	x $5	= $400
The number of shares that are not acquired by Amazon is 80	The value of each River share at acquisition is $5	So the fair value of the NCI at acquisition is $400

W3 Goodwill calculation

		$	$
Cost of the parent's investment		900	
Less the parent's % of the net assets at acquisition	(60% x 800)	(480)	
Goodwill (attributable to the parent)			420
Fair value of the NCI at acquisition		400	
Less the NCI % of the net assets at acquisition	(40% x 800)	(320)	
Goodwill (attributable to the NCI)			80
Gross (or full) goodwill at acquisition			500

Or W3 Goodwill

		$
Cost of the parent's investment		900
Fair value of the NCI at acquisition		400
Less 100% of the net assets at acquisition	(100% x 800)	(800)
Gross (or full) goodwill at acquisition		500

Remember that when the NCI is determined at the year-end it will now have to include the goodwill attributable to the NCI i.e. the $80 above will now be added to the NCI% in the year-end net assets.

(ii) W4 NCI

		$
NCI% in the year-end net assets	(40% x 950)	380
Plus the goodwill attributable to the NCI	w3	80
		460

However the NCI at the year-end can be calculated by reference to the increase that will have taken place from when it was first measured at fair value at the date of acquisition. We already know that the fair value of the NCI at acquisition is $400.

What increases the fair value of the NCI acquisition is its share of the subsidiary's post acquisition profits. You will remember that the parent's share of the subsidiary's post acquisition profits increase the accumulated profits at w5. So all that we are doing is taking the NCI's share of the subsidiary's post acquisition profits to increase the fair value of the NCI at acquisition.

Since acquisition the net assets of the subsidiary have risen from $800 to $950 thus the post acquisition profits are $150.

Accordingly the NCI at the year-end of $460 can be calculated as follows;

		$
Fair value of NCI at acquisition		400
Plus the NCI% of the post acquisition profits w2	(40% x 150)	60
		460

I think this little working is very important.

» Double entry

The introduction of the extra goodwill attributable to the NCI can be thought of in double entry terms.

To increase the goodwill attributable by the parent by the goodwill attributable to the NCI is to increase an asset. When an asset is increased this is a DR.

To increase the NCI in the net assets of the subsidiary by the goodwill attributable to the NCI is to increase equity (as NCI is part of equity). When equity is increased this is a CR.

		$	$
DR	Goodwill (w3)	40	
CR	NCI (w4)		40

Mind Map

A matter of accounting policy

The fair value of the NCI at acquisition is the value of the subsidiary's shares not acquired by parent

NCI at fair value at acquisition

Results in goodwill being gross i.e. in full

Means that goodwill and NCI are both increased compared to the proportionate method of calculating goodwill

⚙ Technical corner

Comments on the significance of measuring NCI at fair value at acquisition

IFRS3 *Business Combinations* and IAS 27 *Consolidated and Separate Financial Statements* were revised in January 2008 and it was at this time that the concept of the fair value of the NCI at acquisition and gross goodwill were introduced into IAS GAAP.

Personally I find the recording of the subsidiary's goodwill gross a conceptually sound idea and a development that I welcome.

When we are consolidating all the other assets of the subsidiary they are always fully consolidated i.e. cross cast and then the NCI in them is reported. This reflects the fact that the group has full control over those assets and it is necessary for stewardship and accountability to show all the resources under the control of the group. As such I would argue that to show the gross goodwill of the subsidiary is simply being consistent with the accounting treatment for all the other assets of the subsidiary.

The origins of recording the NCI at acquisition at fair value and hence goodwill gross comes from the IASB talking with the regulators in the USA. The revised US standard dealing with this issue, SFAS 141 Business Combinations requires the use of the fair value of NCI at acquisition. The introduction of this idea means that the IASB has taken another practical step on the way of converging US GAAP and IAS GAAP. In my view this can only be a good thing, particularly for users wanting to make comparisons between companies. It also helps pave the way for the US regulators at some stage in the future to migrate to using IAS GAAP in place of US GAAP.[1]

What I find less palatable is that groups have an accounting policy choice on an acquisition by acquisition basis as to whether to measure the NCI at acquisition at fair value or not, and thus to calculate goodwill gross or on a proportionate basis. In my view having this choice will lead to inconsistency not only between groups but also within the same group.

---

1   In November 2008 the SEC (Securities and Exchange Committee) released a road map for the transition by U.S. public companies to the use of International Financial Reporting Standards. Under the proposal, the SEC would decide in 2011 whether to proceed with rulemaking to require that U.S. companies use IFRS beginning in 2014 but with early adoption being allowed for certain companies.

Proportions of goodwill attributable to the parent and the NCI

Finally, can I clear up an issue that you may not have even spotted!

You may have noticed that the gross goodwill of $360 was not attributable to the parent and the NCI in the normal proportions of the group, which in the example in this chapter was 80/20. In other words the goodwill attributable to the parent was $320 and they have acquired 80% of the subsidiary so how come the goodwill attributable to the NCI of 20% was only $40?

Well maybe this is unimportant if you are head down in a number crunching question – but it is the case that the goodwill attributable to parent should normally be in a greater proportion than the goodwill attributable to the NCI. The reason for this is because the parent will have paid a higher price for the shares that give it control i.e. the parent has paid a control premium. The shares not acquired are a minority and as such not very valuable as they do not confer any influence over the subsidiary.

When we come to look at impairment of goodwill in Chapter 7 *Impairment review of goodwill* we shall look at this issue again to explain some surprising figures when the impairment losses are allocated in the normal proportion that the group share profits and losses between the parent and the NCI.

Subsequent measurement of the NCI

Where the NCI is measured at fair value at acquisition it will not subsequently be remeasured at fair value again. However the carrying value of the NCI's interest in the subsidiary will subsequently change over time by the NCI's interest in the accumulated profits that are attributable to it. This leads to an alternative calculation of the NCI in the subsidiary's net assets at the year-end using the following proforma.

Alternative W4 NCI

		$
Fair value of the NCI at acquisition		XX
Plus the NCI% of the post acquisition profits w2	(XX% x XX)	XX
		XX

In the event that the subsidiary incurs post acquisition losses it is possible that the NCI is reduced to a negative figure representing an interest in the net liabilities of the subsidiary rather than the net assets.

The calculation of goodwill gross and the year-end NCI are very important techniques to master so please have a look at three questions.

Question Thames

Thames acquired 75% of River's share capital several years ago.

Cost of investment	Fair value of the NCI at acquisition	Net assets at acquisition	Net assets at year end
$	$	$	$
1,000	300	800	3,000

Required

(i)   Calculate the gross goodwill arising at acquisition (w3).

(ii) Calculate the NCI at the year-end (w4).

Question Yangtze

Yangtze acquired 60% of River's share capital several years ago.

Cost of investment	Fair value of the NCI at acquisition	Net assets at acquisition	Net assets at year-end
$	$	$	$
500	200	400	600

Required

(i)   Calculate the gross goodwill arising at acquisition. (w3).

(ii) Calculate the NCI at the year-end (w4).

Question Ganges

Ganges acquired 80% of River's share capital several years ago.

Cost of investment	Fair value of the NCI at acquisition	Net assets at acquisition	Net assets at year end
$	$	$	$
300	86	400	620

Required

(i) Calculate the gross goodwill arising at acquisition (w3).

(ii) Calculate the NCI at the year-end (w4).

chapter 6

Net assets of the subsidiary at fair value

" Morality, like art, means drawing a line someplace. "

What's new?

Well, we have just been seeing that the parent's cost of investment has to be at fair value at the date of acquisition, and that the NCI at acquisition is also at fair value to calculate gross goodwill, so it is no real surprise that the other ingredient in the calculation of goodwill, the subsidiary's net assets at the date of acquisition, will also have to be at fair value as well.[1]

In all the examples we have done so far the net assets of the subsidiary at the date of acquisition have not been adjusted for fair values and so have been represented at w2 column 1 as the share capital plus the reserves at acquisition. Strictly however, when a subsidiary is acquired it is necessary to do a fair value review of the assets and liabilities that are acquired by the group and thus fair value adjustments at the date of acquisition of the subsidiary's assets and liabilities can be necessary.

The simplest fair value adjustment on a subsidiary's net assets at acquisition is an upward adjustment on land. The fair value adjustment will increase the net assets at acquisition (w2 column 1) and assuming that the asset remains with the subsidiary at the year-end it will also increase the net assets at the year-end (w2 column 2).

The amount of the fair value adjustment to be applied to the subsidiary's net assets at the date of acquisition will normally be given in the exercise, so that the total of the fair value of the net assets at acquisition is determined by adding up the column. However it can be the case that the total of the fair value of the net assets at the date of acquisition is given, but not the fair value adjustment. In this case the balancing figure in w2 column becomes the fair value adjustment itself.

If the asset subject to the fair value adjustment is in turn subject to depreciation e.g. plant, then in addition to increasing both the net assets at acquisition and at the year-end by the fair value adjustment then the additional depreciation required will be deducted from the net assets at the year end (w2 column 2)

Of course by adjusting both columns in w2 the fair value adjustment automatically will ensure the calculations for goodwill w3, NCI w4 and the post acquisition profits in w5 will be correct.

When preparing the group statement of financial position the assets and liabilities that have been subject to fair value adjustments will also have to be updated and this working can be done on the face of the statement of financial position.

---

[1] Exceptions do exist to the principle of remeasuring all the assets and liabilities of the subsidiary at acquisition date to fair value e.g. defined benefit pension funds (IAS19 *Employee Benefits*), deferred tax (IAS12 *Income Taxes*) and share based payments awards (IFRS2 *Share Based Payments*)

Example

One year ago Malta made an acquisition of 90% of the shares in Clarke. The following information relates to Clarke at the date of acquisition.

Retained profits at acquisition	Fair value adjustment on plant at acquisition	Cost of the investment	Fair value of the NCI at acquisition
$m	$m	$m	$m
200	50	900	50

The plant subject to the fair value adjustment had a remaining life of five years at the date of acquisition. Goodwill is to be calculated gross.

	Malta	Clarke
	$m	$m
Investment in Clarke	900	
Assets	600	650
	1,500	650
Ordinary shares ($1)	800	200
Accumulated profits	400	350
Equity	1,200	550
Liabilities	300	100
	1,500	650

Required

Prepare the consolidated statement of financial position for the Malta group.

In the group structure it is now highly relevant to note that the subsidiary was acquired one year ago as this will mean that there will be one year of extra depreciation required on the plant.

W1 Group structure

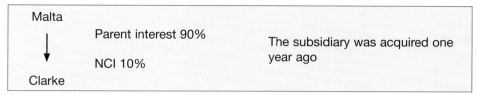

Malta

Parent interest 90%

NCI 10%

The subsidiary was acquired one year ago

Clarke

The fair value adjustment of $50m on the plant increases the net assets both at acquisition as well as at the year-end on the reasonable assumption that the asset remains held by the subsidiary. Because the plant is being increased in value there will be an increase in depreciation in the post acquisition period. The plant has a remaining five year life and has been held by the group for one year.

The additional depreciation is $50m x $^{1}/_{5}$ x 1 year = $10m.

This additional depreciation decreases the net assets at the year-end.

W2 Net assets of the subsidiary

	At acquisition $m	At year end $m
Share capital	200	200
Accumulated profits	200	350
Fair value adjustment	50	50
Additional depreciation	Nil	(10)
	450	590
	Used to calculate goodwill in w3	Used to calculate the NCI in w4

The increase in the net assets since acquisition is $140m ($590m - $450m) and this represents the profits the subsidiary has made since acquisition. The parent's share of this will be taken to the group accumulated profits in w5. The post acquisition profits of $140m include the additional depreciation that has been charged.

As a proof the $140m can be thought of as the rise in the unadjusted profits of the subsidiary since acquisition ($350m - $200m) = $150 less the additional depreciation of $10m arising from the fair value adjustment.

The net assets at the year-end of $590m, on which the NCI is based, reflects both the fair value adjustment and the additional depreciation.

The goodwill, NCI and group accumulated profits can now be processed in the normal way.

W3 Goodwill

		$m	$m
Cost of the parent's investment (at fair value)		900	
Less the parent's % of the net assets at acquisition w2	(90% x 450)	(405)	
Goodwill (attributable to the parent)			495
Fair value of the NCI at acquisition		50	
Less the NCI % of the net assets at acquisition	(10% x 450)	(45)	
Goodwill (attributable to the NCI)			5
Gross (or full) goodwill at acquisition			500

Proof of W3 Goodwill

		$m
Cost of the parent's investment (at fair value)		900
Fair value of the NCI at acquisition		50
Less 100% of the net assets at acquisition w2	(100% x 450)	(450)
Gross (or full) goodwill		500

W4 NCI

		$m
NCI % of the net assets at year end w2	(10% x 590)	59
Plus the goodwill attributable to the NCI w3		5
		64
OR		
Fair value of the NCI at acquisition		50
Plus the NCI% of the post acquisition profits w2	(10% x 140)	14
		64

You will note how gross goodwill and the year-end NCI have both been calculated in two different ways. Clearly this is not good exam technique, but is excellent for your understanding.

W5 Group accumulated profits

		$m
Parent's accumulated profits		400
Plus the parent % of the post acquisition profits w2	(90% x 140)	126
		526

Malta Group statement of financial position

		$m
Goodwill	w3	500
Assets	((600 + 650) plus the fair value adjustment 50 less the additional depreciation 10))	1,290
		1,790
Ordinary shares ($1)		800
Accumulated profits	w5	526
NCI	w4	64
Equity		1,390
Liabilities	(300 + 100)	400
		1,790

» Double entry bookkeeping

The initial fair value adjustment increasing the plant can be thought of in double entry terms.

One effect of the fair value adjustment is to increase the assets of the subsidiary as consolidated in the group statement of financial position. When assets go up this is a DR.

The fair value adjustment also creates an increase in the pre acquisition reserves so increasing net assets at w2. When equity goes up this is a CR.

		$m	$m
DR	Plant	50	
CR	Pre acquisition reserves		50

Any subsequent additional depreciation required following the fair value adjustment is also a double entry.

One effect of the additional depreciation is to record an extra expense in the post acquisition profits thus reducing profit. When equity goes down this is a DR.

The additional depreciation also writes down the asset. When assets go down this is a CR.

		$m	$m
DR	Post acquisition reserves	10	
CR	Plant		10

The DR for the additional depreciation to the post acquisition reserves of the subsidiary will decrease the net assets of the subsidiary at the year-end in w2.

The additional depreciation is an extra expense for the subsidiary arising in the post acquisition period and as such the effect of this loss will be shared between the parent and the NCI in the normal proportions that they share profits and losses. By deducting the whole of the subsidiary's additional depreciation from the net assets at the year-end this is automatically achieved. However the DR of additional depreciation to the post acquisition profits of the subsidiary can also be thought of as the parent's share (90%) DR $9m to group accumulated profits and the NCI's share (10%) DR $1m to NCI.

Mind Map

Fair value adjustments can be given in which case the fair value of the net assets is then determined as the balancing figure

or

Fair value adjustments can be balancing figures, in which case the fair value of the net assets is given

Net assets of the subsidiary at acquisition must be at fair value

With investment at fair value and NCI at fair value this means all the ingredients for gross goodwill are at fair value

A fair value adjustment increasing plant means more depreciation

✿ Technical corner

Accounting for intangible assets at acquisition

On acquisition the group should recognise separately from goodwill, the fair value of identifiable intangible assets of the subsidiary even if they have not been accounted for as an asset in the subsidiary's individual accounts. An intangible asset will be identifiable in this context if it is either separable or contractual and has a reliable measure. As result it is possible for customer lists and brand names of the subsidiary to be recognised as intangible assets in the group accounts.

The intangible assets are recognised by making a fair value adjustment, which increases the net assets at acquisition and thus reduces the goodwill arising at acquisition. However, whilst the goodwill has been diminished by the separate recognition of such intangibles, the overall intangible assets otherwise recognised does not.

Consider a 100% subsidiary that is acquired for $100m when the fair value of its net assets are $60m. This will result in the goodwill arising of $40m. Goodwill is recognised as an intangible asset in the group accounts i.e. the group has intangible assets of $40m.

However if the subsidiary has a brand name that it has not purchased and so it is not recognised in its own statement of financial position but nevertheless the parent can ascribe a reliable value to it of $10m, then on acquisition this can be recognised in the group accounts by making a fair value adjustment at acquisition of $10m. The net assets now being acquired will be $70m ($60m plus $10m) and the goodwill arising will only be $30m. The group will still have intangible assets of $40m comprising the goodwill of $30m and the brand name of $10m. In the group accounts the brand will then be systematically amortised (written off through the income statement) over its estimated useful life, or be regarded as having an infinite life and so be subject to annual impairment review.

Revising fair values

When a subsidiary is acquired shortly before the group's reporting date, then it may be that the subsidiary's net assets are assigned only provisional fair values, as a comprehensive valuation process may not have been completed.

If within 12 months of the acquisition further information comes to light to revise those provisional fair values then this will change the measurement of the fair value of the net assets acquired and hence the goodwill arising.

Consider, if the parent has paid $200m to acquire 100% of the net assets of a subsidiary that are initially assessed as having a fair value of $150m, then the goodwill arising will be initially measured at $50m. If, however, within 12 months of the acquisition further information comes to light such that the fair value of the net assets at acquisition are now regarded as having a fair value of $140m, then the goodwill arising will be remeasured to $60m.

However, if that information had come to light more than 12 months after the date of acquisition, whilst that still means the assets are remeasured, goodwill remains unchanged and a post acquisition loss of $10m has to be recognised in the income statement.

Fair value adjustments on assets

Most fair value adjustments to the subsidiary's net assets at the date of acquisition come in the form of upward adjustments to tangible assets.

Fair value adjustments are consolidation adjustments that arise as a consequence of preparing the group accounts and the need for the parent to ascertain the cost of the assets and liabilities acquired rather than rely on the existing book values of the subsidiary. The individual subsidiary company does not record the fair value adjustment in its own accounting records. Such a fair value consolidation adjustment creates a pre acquisition reserve increasing the net assets of the subsidiary at the date of acquisition.

When the upwards fair value adjustment is to a depreciable asset e.g. plant and equipment, then in the group accounts a further consolidation adjustment of additional depreciation will arise.

Because the original fair value adjustment was not recorded by the subsidiary, the depreciation it charges will be based on the lower original cost to the subsidiary and not the fair value at the date of acquisition.

In the group accounts, however the depreciation should be based on the fair value at the date of acquisition. Therefore as a consolidation adjustment subsequent additional depreciation will be required that reduces the post acquisition profits and the net assets at the year-end.

Once the asset is sold then whilst the original fair value adjustment at the date of acquisition permanently remains in the net assets at acquisition, the net assets at the year-end and the statement of financial position will no longer reflect either the asset or the adjustments.

Fair value adjustments on liabilities

However, not all fair value adjustments relate to tangible assets, as they can relate to liabilities and monetary assets (e.g. receivables). The fair value of monetary assets and liabilities is the present value of the amounts expected to be paid or received.

Fair value adjustments will arise in respect of long term fixed interest liabilities, which are accounted for at amortised cost when the effective rate of interest at the date of acquisition is different from when the liability was incurred.

Example of a fair value adjustment on a loan

At the date of acquisition the subsidiary has a three year zero coupon rate loan that was issued one year ago at its nominal value of $10,000, when the effective rate of interest was 5% and it is redeemable in two year's time at £11,576. At the date of acquisition the loan has a carrying value of $10,500 inclusive of the accrued interest. At the date of acquisition the current effective rate of interest is 4%.

As the fair value of such a long term liability is the present value of the future cash flow for consolidation purposes the loan should be measured by discounting the obligation to pay $11,576 in two year's time at the now current effective rate of interest of 4%:

$$\$11,576 \quad \times \quad \frac{1}{1.04^2} \quad = \quad \$10,703$$

Accordingly, at the date of acquisition there will be a fair value adjustment increasing the liability from $10,500 to $10,703 i.e. a loss decreasing the net assets at acquisition in w2 by $203.

But following the same principle as the additional depreciation adjustment following the fair value adjustment, there will need to be a further fair value adjustment in respect of the finance cost because of the fair value adjustment on the loan.

In the subsidiary individual accounts over the next two years the loan of $10,500 will continue to be accounted for using its historic effective rate of interest of 5% as follows.

	Opening balance	Income statement finance cost at the effective rate of 5%	Cash paid	Carrying value of the loan on the statement of financial position of the subsidiary
Second year	$10,500	$525	(Nil)	$11,025
Third year	$11,025	$551	($11,576)	Nil

But in the group accounts the loan has been adjusted to its fair value of $10,703 and so will be accounted for using an effective rate of interest of 4%.

	Opening balance	Income statement finance cost at the effective rate of 4%	Cash paid	Carrying value of the loan on the statement of financial position of the group
Second year	$10,703	$428	(Nil)	$11,131
Third year	$11,131	$445	($11,576)	Nil

So if we were faced with having to prepare the group accounts one year after the acquisition, in the group income statement the finance cost in respect of the subsidiary's loan would have to be adjusted from $525 to $428 i.e. down by $97.

One year after acquisition in the group statement of financial position the loan would have to be increased from $11,025 to $11,131 i.e. up by $106. This consolidation adjustment is made up of the original fair value loss $203, less the $97 gain adjusting the finance cost. In w2 the net assets at the year-end will therefore be reduced by the figure of $106.

Once the loan is repaid then whilst the original fair value adjustment at the date of acquisition permanently remains in the net assets at acquisition, the net assets at the year-end and the statement of financial position will no longer reflect either the loan or the adjustments.

Question Barbados

The statement of financial position of two companies are as follows.

	Barbados	Bridgetown
	$m	$m
Investment in Bridgetown	1,000	
Assets	600	800
	1,600	800
Ordinary shares ($1)	650	100
Accumulated profits	250	500
Equity	900	600
Liabilities	700	200
	1,600	800

Additional information

1   Two years ago Barbados made an acquisition of 90% of the shares in Bridgetown.

NCI will be 10%.

2   At the date of acquisition the plant of Bridgetown had a fair value in excess of its carrying value of $100m. This plant had a remaining life of four years.

Excess depreciation will be required from the date of acquisition.

3   At the date of acquisition the accumulated profits of Bridgetown were $250m.

4   Goodwill is calculated using the proportionate approach.

Proportionate approach means no gross goodwill and no fair value of the NCI at acquisition.

Required

Prepare the consolidated statement of financial position for the Barbados group.

Question Mauritius

The following is an extract from the statement of financial position of Port Louis showing its equity at the year-end.

	$m
Share capital	200
Share premium	500
Accumulated profits	1,000
	1,700

Mauritius acquired 90% of Port Louis's shares one year ago for $3,000m when the fair value of the NCI was $260m. The subsidiary's retained profits for the year were $250m.

The fair value of the net assets at the date of acquisition were $2,000m, with any fair value adjustment relating to plant with a remaining useful life of 5 years at the date of acquisition.

The fair value of the net assets of the subsidiary at the date of acquisition is given as $2,000m. This is the total of column 1 in w2. The fair value adjustment on the plant therefore becomes the balancing figure in column 1 w2.

Required

Calculate the gross goodwill arising at acquisition, and the NCI at the year-end.

Question Bangladesh

The following is an extract from the statement of financial position of Dhaka showing its equity at the year-end.

	$m
Ordinary share capital	400
Share premium	800
Accumulated profits	600
	1,800

Bangladesh acquired 80% of the shares in Dhaka three years ago for $2,000m when the accumulated profits were $250m and the fair value of the NCI was $400m.

At the date of acquisition there were two assets subject to a fair value adjustment. Inventory was subject to an upwards fair value adjustment of $10m. This inventory was subsequently sold before the year end. Plant with a useful life of 10 years was also subject to a fair value adjustment of $110m.

Required

Calculate the gross goodwill arising at acquisition, and the NCI at the year-end.

chapter 7
Impairment review of goodwill

> " It is always a silly thing to give advice, but to give good advice is fatal. "

What's new?

In the examples we have looked at to date the goodwill that has arisen at acquisition has remained intact at the year-end. Strictly goodwill is subject to an annual impairment review and so at the reporting date it may be necessary to write off some or all of the goodwill that arose at acquisition.

Impairment of an asset

An asset is impaired when its carrying value exceeds its recoverable amount. The impairment loss is therefore calculated using the following proforma:

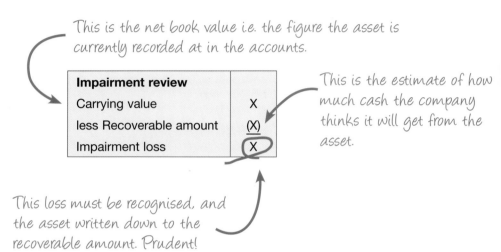

This is the net book value i.e. the figure the asset is currently recorded at in the accounts.

Impairment review	
Carrying value	X
less Recoverable amount	(X)
Impairment loss	X

This is the estimate of how much cash the company thinks it will get from the asset.

This loss must be recognised, and the asset written down to the recoverable amount. Prudent!

For example if the carrying amount of an asset was $100, but only $80 could be recovered from the asset then the impairment loss is $20.

Impairment review	$
Carrying value	100
less Recoverable amount	(80)
Impairment loss	20

Please bear in mind that if the recoverable amount exceeds the carrying value then the impairment review results in no impairment loss. We do not record impairment gains!

There are no accounting choices or accounting policy decisions to be made in respect of impairment. The impairment loss must be recorded and the asset written down to its recoverable amount.

Impairment of gross goodwill

When goodwill is subject to an impairment review it is necessary to do this at the level of a cash generating unit. A cash generating unit is a collection of assets and liabilities that generate an independent stream of cash. This is because goodwill is inseparable from the net assets of the subsidiary. That it is to say the subsidiary is the cash generating unit so the net assets and the goodwill together are considered as the carrying value to be compared to the recoverable amount

Where there is an impairment loss in respect of a cash generating unit the impairment loss will be applied to write down the goodwill and also be charged against profits. Where the NCI has been calculated at fair value i.e. goodwill is gross, the impairment loss relates to the subsidiary's profits so will be split between the parent and the NCI in the proportion that they normally share profits and losses.

In the context of a group statement of financial position this will mean the parent's share of the impairment loss will reduce the group accumulated profits in w5 and the impairment loss attributable to the NCI will reduce the NCI in w4.

In all our examples the impairment loss arising from the impairment review will be used to write down the goodwill. Strictly though, if the cash generating unit has another asset that is specifically damaged or otherwise impaired then the impairment loss would first be allocated to that asset. If the impairment loss exceeded the goodwill then the remaining balance of the loss will be allocated against the other assets on a pro-rata basis.

Example

The following information relates to Oman and Muscat, an 80% subsidiary acquired four years ago.

	Oman $m	Muscat $m
Non current assets		
Tangible	100	100
Investment in Muscat	175	
Current assets		
Inventory	140	200
Receivables	160	100
Cash at bank	125	200
	700	600
Ordinary shares ($1)	160	50
Accumulated profits	240	100
Equity	400	150
Non current liabilities	100	250
Current liabilities	200	200
	700	600

Additional information

Fair value of the NCI at acquisition $m	Parent's cost of investment $m	Net assets at acquisition $m	Net assets at year-end $m	Recoverable amount at year-end $m
25	175	100	150	230

Goodwill is calculated with the NCI at acquisition at fair value, and is subject to an impairment review at the year-end. No goodwill has previously been impaired.

Required

Prepare the consolidated statement of financial position of the Oman group.

The first three workings are all fairly routine.

W1 Group structure

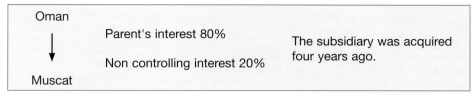

Oman

Muscat

Parent's interest 80%

Non controlling interest 20%

The subsidiary was acquired four years ago.

W2 Net assets of the subsidiary

	At acquisition $m	At year-end $m
Share capital	50	50
Accumulated profits	50	100
	100	150

The post acquisition profits of the subsidiary are $50m ($150m - $100m).

W3 Goodwill

		$m	$m
Cost of the parent's investment (at fair value)		175	
Less the parent's % of the net assets at acquisition w2	(80% x 100)	(80)	
Goodwill (attributable to the parent)			95
Fair value of the NCI at acquisition		25	
Less the NCI % of the net assets at acquisition w2	(20% x 100)	(20)	
Goodwill (attributable to the NCI)			5
Gross (or full) goodwill at acquisition			100

Proof of W3 Goodwill

		$m
Cost of the parent's investment (at fair value)		175
Fair value of the NCI at acquisition		25
Less 100% of the net assets at acquisition w2	(100% x 100)	(100)
Gross (or full) goodwill at acquisition		100

Now we can proceed to consider the year-end impairment review.

The impairment review of goodwill is conducted by aggregating the net assets at the year-end with the goodwill arising, to form the cash generating unit that we can then compare with the recoverable amount.

Impairment review of Muscat

	$m	$m
Carrying value		
Net assets of the subsidiary at year end	150	
Goodwill	100	
		250
Recoverable amount		(230)
Impairment loss		20

To the extent that the carrying value of $250m exceeds the recoverable amount of $230m this reveals an impairment loss of $20m.

This means that the goodwill that will appear as an asset in the group accounts will be $80m ($100m less the impairment loss of $20m).

	$m
Gross (or full) goodwill at acquisition	100
Less the impairment loss	(20)
Goodwill at year end	80

The reduction in the asset of goodwill will be matched by the loss being written off against equity. The impairment loss will be split and the parent's share of $16m (80% x $20) will reduce the accumulated profits in w5 and the NCI's share of the impairment loss $4m (20% x $20) will reduce the NCI in w4 (however it is calculated).

W4 NCI

		$m
NCI% in the net assets at year end w2	(20% x 150)	30
Plus the goodwill attributable to the NCI		5
Less the NCI% of the impairment loss w3	(20% x 20)	(4)
		31
OR		
Fair value of the NCI at acquisition.		25
Plus the NCI% of the post acquisition profits w2	(20% x 50)	10
Less the NCI% of the impairment loss w3	(20% x 20)	(4)
		31

W5 Group accumulated profits

		$m
Parent's profits		240
Less the parent's % of the goodwill impairment loss w3	(80% x 20)	(16)
Plus the parent's % of the post acquisition profits w2	(80% x 50)	40
		264

Oman group statement of financial position

		$m
Non current assets		
Goodwill	w3 post impairment	80
Tangible assets	(100 + 100)	200
Current assets		
Inventory	(140 + 200)	340
Receivables	(160 + 100)	260
Cash at bank	(125 + 200)	325
		1,205
Ordinary shares ($1)	parent only	160
Accumulated profits	w5	264
Non controlling interest	w4	31
Equity		455
Non current liabilities	(100 + 250)	350
Current liabilities	(200 + 200)	400
		1,205

Impairment of goodwill when calculated on a proportionate basis

When goodwill has been calculated on a proportionate basis, for the purposes of conducting the impairment review it is necessary to crudely gross up goodwill proportionally so that in the impairment review goodwill will include an unrecognised notional goodwill attributable to the NCI.

This is because the recoverable amount will relate to the whole cash-generating unit, so it is argued some of this must relate to the unrecognised notional goodwill attributable to the NCI.

Any impairment loss that arises is first allocated against the total of recognised and unrecognised goodwill in the normal proportions that the parent and NCI share profits and losses.

Any amounts written off against the notional goodwill will not affect the consolidated financial statements. Any amounts written off against the recognised goodwill will be attributable to the parent only, without affecting the NCI.

If the total amount of impairment loss exceeds the amount allocated against recognised and notional goodwill, the excess will be allocated against the other assets on a pro-rata basis. This further loss will be shared between the parent and the NCI in the normal proportion that they share profits and losses.

Example

At the year-end an impairment review is being conducted on the 80% owned subsidiary David Leigh. At the date of the impairment review the carrying value of the subsidiary's net assets were $600 and the goodwill calculated on a proportionate basis $80 and the recoverable amount of the subsidiary $510.

Required

Determine the outcome of the impairment review.

In conducting the impairment review of proportionate goodwill it is first necessary to gross it up.

Proportionate goodwill	Grossed up	Goodwill including the notional unrecognised NCI of $20
$80 x	100/80 =	$100

Now for the purposes of the impairment review, the goodwill will be $100 and together with the net assets of $600 forms the carrying value of the cash-generating unit - the subsidiary.

Impairment review

Carrying value	$	$
Net assets of subsidiary at year end	600	
Goodwill	100	
		700
Recoverable amount		(510)
Impairment loss		190

The impairment loss of $190 exceeds the total of the recognised and notional goodwill of $100 so it is not only the goodwill that has been impaired, the net assets have also been impaired.

The impairment loss is first allocated $100 against the recognised and notional goodwill. The parent's share of $80 (80% x $100 = $80) is recognised and therefore the goodwill that was recognised is now written down to nil. This impairment loss of $80 is wholly attributable to the parent as the proportionate goodwill is only attributable to the parent. The notional NCI's share of $20 (20% x $100 = $20) cancels out the notional goodwill but this does not affect the consolidated financial statements.

As the total impairment loss exceeds the amount allocated against the recognised and notional goodwill, the remainder of the impairment loss of $90 ($190 - $100) is then allocated to other assets on a pro-rata basis. The year-end net assets will therefore now be $510 ($600 - $90). This impairment loss will be shared between the parent and the NCI in the normal proportion that they share profits and losses which in this example is 80/20.

To recap

In the group statement of financial position the recognised proportionate goodwill of $80 will be written off, so that there will not be an intangible asset of goodwill appearing. Other assets in the group statement of financial position will be written down by $90.

In total, assets are reduced by $170 ($80 + $90).

In the group statement of financial position the accumulated profits will be reduced $152 ($80 + (80% x $90)). There is no impact on the NCI in respect of the write off of goodwill, but the NCI will be reduced by $18 (20% x $90).

In total, equity has been reduced by $170 ($152 + $18).

In the group income statement the impairment loss of $170 will be charged as an extra operating expense. The NCI in the subsidiary's profits will be reduced by $18 (20% x $90).

» Double entry

The recording of impairment losses on gross goodwill can be thought of in double entry terms.

Let us consider the recording of the impairment loss of $20m on the gross goodwill of Muscat, the 80% subsidiary.

The impairment loss reduces the asset of gross goodwill in the top half of the group statement of financial position and it also reduces the equity (split between the accumulated profits and the NCI).

To record the impairment loss is to recognise an expense that will decrease equity, i.e. the accumulated profits and also the NCI. To reduce equity is a DR.

To record the impairment loss is to write down an asset. To reduce an asset is a CR.

		$m	$m
DR	Accumulated profits (w5)	16	
DR	NCI (w4)	4	
CR	Goodwill (w3)		20

The recording of impairment losses on proportionate goodwill can be thought of in double entry terms.

Let us consider the recording of the impairment loss of $190 on the proportionate goodwill of David Leigh. Whilst the proportionate goodwill is notionally grossed up by $20 this notional goodwill is unrecognised and unrecorded.

The actual impairment loss of $170 wrote off all the asset of goodwill as well as writing down some other assets and the loss also reduces the equity (split between the accumulated profits and the NCI).

To record the impairment loss is to recognise an expense that will decrease equity, i.e. the accumulated profits and in this case the NCI. To make equity down is a DR.

To record the impairment loss is to write off the asset of goodwill as well as reducing other assets on a pro-rata basis. To reduce an asset is a CR.

		$	$
DR	Accumulated profits (w5)	152	
DR	NCI (w4)	18	
CR	Goodwill (w3)		80
CR	Assets		90

Mind Map

Goodwill is part of a cash generating unit

Impairment losses arise when the carrying value exceeds the recoverable amount

Annual impairment review of goodwill is required

Impairment losses on gross goodwill are charged against profit and NCI

Impairment losses on proportionate goodwill reduces accumulated profits

⚙ Technical corner

Allocation of the impairment loss on gross goodwill

In the Muscat example it can be noted that the proportions in which the gross goodwill of $100m is attributable to the parent and the NCI is 95/5. This is different from the proportions in which the other net assets and the profits and losses are shared (80/20). Thus the parent takes a disproportionately larger share of the goodwill.

This actually reflects a normal situation where the parent company will have paid a buyer's premium to acquire control of the subsidiary. In other words the parent will have paid more for the shares it has purchased than the value of the shares that it has not purchased! Those of you who love your financial management and stock market theory and have studied share valuations can identify that the majority holding can be valued using an earnings basis, where as the minority holding can be valued using a dividend yield basis.

It is possible however that the goodwill attributable to the NCI can be in greater proportion than the goodwill to the parent, implying that the parent has acquired the shares cheaper than the fair value ascribed to the minority shares.

However the impairment loss to be shared between the parent and the NCI will be in the ratio that profits and losses are shared. Thus of the impairment loss of $20m, the accumulated profits attributable to the parent suffered 80% i.e. $16m whilst the NCI were charged 20% i.e. $4m

This means that whilst the poor old NCI are generally given a small interest in the goodwill the impairment loss they bear is proportionately larger.

Determining the recoverable amount

There are two ways of recovering cash from an asset or group of assets.

One way of recovering cash from an asset is to sell it. The measurement of the recoverable amount can therefore be the fair value less costs to sell i.e. sale proceeds less any costs necessary to achieve the sale.

The other way of recovering cash from an asset is to keep and use the asset so that it generates a cash flow in the future. This second way is termed the "value in use". When measuring the future cash flows it will be necessary to discount the figures to a present value.

The recoverable amount is the higher of the net sale proceeds and the value in use. It is the higher because that is what the standard[1] says – but actually also to reflect the common sense that losses will always try to be minimised.

For example if an asset could be sold for $230m net of selling costs, but has a value in use of $150m, the recoverable amount will be $230m (the higher) as the sensible decision will be to sell the asset. But if the asset could be sold for $125m net of selling costs and has a value in use of $200m, then the asset will be kept, making the recoverable amount $200m. The recoverable amount will always be the higher of the two figures on offer.

The measurement of the recoverable amount is of course subjective since the sale proceeds are an estimate as indeed are the future cash flows in the value in use calculation.

---

1   IAS36 Impairment of Assets

Question Singapore

The following information relates to Singapore a 60% subsidiary.

Net assets at acquisition	Net assets at year-end	Fair value of the NCI at acquisition	Cost of the investment at acquisition	Recoverable amount at year-end
$m	$m	$m	$m	$m
500	600	250	800	1,000

Required

Determine the outcome of the impairment review of Singapore, to show the amount of gross goodwill that would appear on the group statement of financial position.

All the ingredients are given to calculate goodwill and then to do the impairment review, providing you know the proforma!

Question Hong Kong

At the year-end an impairment review is being conducted on the 60% owned subsidiary Hong Kong. At the date of the impairment review the carrying value of the subsidiary's net assets were $250 and the goodwill $300 (calculated on a proportionate basis) and the recoverable amount of the subsidiary $700.

Required

Determine the outcome of the impairment review, of Hong Kong, to show the amount of goodwill that would appear on the group statement of financial position.

As goodwill has been calculated on a proportionate basis, so it will be necessary to notionally gross up for the purpose of the impairment review.

recap

on the fair value section

What's new?

Absolutely nothing!

Let's take this opportunity to recap on the key messages that we have learnt in the last four chapters.

♀ Key messages

- Fair value is the amount for which an asset or liability can be exchanged between informed and willing parties in an arm's length transaction.

- The parent has to record the investment at the fair value of the consideration given.

- The fair value of the parent's shares issued (or to be issued) for the investment in the subsidiary will be measured at their market value.

- The fair value of deferred consideration given for the investment in the subsidiary that will create a liability is initially measured at the present value of the future cash flow.

- Liabilities initially measured at present value will subsequently require a finance cost to be charged to unwind the discounting.

- The fair value of deferred consideration given for the investment in the subsidiary that will be shares is initially recorded as in equity reserves at the market value of the shares at acquisition.

- Consideration given for the investment that is dependant on a contingency is included at fair value and creates a provision for a liability (if to be settled in cash) or an equity reserve (if to be settled in shares).

- In the event that the provision for the liability for the contingent consideration does not have to be paid it is derecognised and a gain recognised in income.

- Goodwill at acquisition can be measured on a proportionate basis i.e. as the difference between the parent's investment and the parent's share of the subsidiary's net assets.

- Alternatively the NCI at acquisition can be measured at fair value with the consequence that goodwill is calculated gross and NCI also increases.

- The fair value of the NCI at acquisition is the value of the shares in the subsidiary not acquired by the parent company.

- At the date of acquisition the net assets of the subsidiary have to be adjusted to their fair value.

- Where at the year-end net assets that were subject to a fair value adjustment at the date of acquisition remain held, then the fair value adjustment will also affect the net assets at the year-end. If these assets are depreciable non current assets then there will also be additional depreciation that decreases the year-end net assets of the subsidiary.

- An asset is impaired when the carrying value exceeds the recoverable amount.

- Goodwill, together with the net assets of the subsidiary form a cash-generating unit and will be subject to an annual impairment review.

- Where goodwill is calculated gross with the NCI at fair value then the impairment loss will be shared between the parent and the NCI in the proportion that they share profits and losses.

section 3

Introducing further adjustments

chapter 8

Inter-company
current accounts

> It is a very sad thing that
> nowadays there is so little
> useless information.

What's new?

It is fairly common for group companies to trade with each other on credit terms and so at the year-end each company may owe each other money, which will be represented in current accounts with the other. These balances are referred to as current account balances since they will be part of current assets and current liabilities. It is also possible in these circumstances that at the year-end there will be either goods or cash that have been accounted for by the sending company but not yet accounted for by the intended recipient because they have not yet received them. These are known as goods or cash in transit.

Current accounts

Let us consider the situation where the parent has been selling goods to the subsidiary and at the year-end $100 is still owed. The parent will have the asset (of a current account) receivable of $100 and the subsidiary will have the liability (of a current account) payable of $100.

In a group context both these two current balances have to be eliminated, as neither represent an external asset or liability. They are equal and opposite and simply cancel out against each other. This adjustment can be picked up in the cross casting process when preparing the group statement of financial position and requires no special working as such. It will not affect any of the workings w1 to w5

> Less Payables $100 when cross casting
>
> Less Receivables $100 when cross casting

Cash in transit

However the two current accounts at the year-end are not always exactly equal and opposite, and this will be because of either goods or cash in transit.

For example where the parent has been selling goods to the subsidiary and the parent has recorded the asset of current account receivable as being owed $300, the subsidiary may have the liability of current account payable recorded as $250 because just prior to the year-end a $50 cheque was sent by the subsidiary that the parent company at the year-end had not received.

In a group context these two current balances still have to be eliminated. In addition the cash that is in transit has to be included in the group accounts despite not being included in either company's accounts. This adjustment can be picked up in the cross casting process and requires no special working as such. It will not affect any of the workings w1 to w5.

> Less Payables $250 when cross casting
>
> Plus Cash at bank $50 when cross casting
>
> Less Receivables $300 when cross casting

The group's cash at bank will be increased on the assumption that there is cash at bank! The convention is to think that the transaction is being accelerated so if the recipient company has in fact an overdraft then the cash in transit will reduce the current liabilities.

Goods in transit

On the same basis, goods that are in transit at the year-end will also cause the current accounts to be out of kilter and the goods in transit will also have to be included in the group accounts.

For example where the parent has been selling goods to the subsidiary and the parent has recorded the asset of current account receivable as owed $500, the subsidiary may have the current account payable recorded as $400 because just prior to the year-end goods of $100 were sent by the parent to the subsidiary but at the year-end those goods had not yet been received by the subsidiary.

In a group context these two current balances still have to be eliminated, but in addition the goods that are in transit have to be included in the group accounts. This adjustment can be picked up in the cross casting process and requires no special working as such. It will not affect any of the workings w1 to w5.

Less Payables $400 when cross casting

Plus Inventory $100 when cross casting

Less Receivables $500 when cross casting

Other inter-company balances

The principle of cancelling out inter-company current accounts because neither represent an external asset or liability is equally applicable should the parent and subsidiary have non current balances (e.g. one has given the other a long term loan).

Example

The following are the extracts from the statements of financial position of Vietnam and its subsidiary Hanoi.

	Vietnam	Hanoi
	$m	**$m**
Current assets		
Inventory	250	150
Receivables	400	300
Cash at bank	150	120
	800	570
Current liabilities	340	260

Additional information

1   Vietnam's trade receivables at the year-end include $100m due from Hanoi. This included goods of $15m that had been despatched by Vietnam on the last day prior to the year-end but had not arrived at Hanoi by the year-end.

2   Hanoi's trade payables at the year-end include $60m due to Vietnam. This was after the deduction of $25m in respect of cash sent by Hanoi on the last day prior to the year-end but had not arrived at Vietnam by the year-end.

Required

Prepare the current asset and current liabilities extracts from the Vietnam group statement of financial position.

The current accounts must be eliminated on consolidation as neither the current account receivable of $100m in the parent's accounts or the current account payable of $60m in the subsidiary accounts actually represents external group items.

Further the goods in transit of $15m and the cash in transit of $25m both need to be included in group inventory and cash respectively.

			$m
Less	Receivable in current assets	by the current account balance of	100
Less	Payables in current liabilities	by the current account balance of	60
Plus	Inventory in current assets	by the goods in transit	15
Plus	Cash in current assets	by the cash in transit	25

Extract of Vietnam's group statement of financial position.

		$m
Current assets		
Inventory	(250 + 150 plus the goods in transit 15)	415
Receivables	(400 + 300 less the current account 100)	600
Cash at bank	(150 + 120 plus the cash in transit 25)	295
		1,310
Current liabilities	(340 + 260 less the current account 60)	540

The rules are quite simple. With a parent and subsidiary always **exclude** any inter company **current account** balance and always **include** any **goods** and **cash in transit**.

» Double entry

The elimination of the above current accounts can be thought of in double entry terms. Let us reconsider the Vietnam example.

To cancel the current account liability will decrease the liability of payables. When liabilities go down it is DR.

To cancel the current account asset will decrease asset of receivables. When assets go down it is CR.

To bring in the cash in transit will increase the asset of cash. When assets go up it is DR.

To bring in the goods in transit will increase the asset of inventory. When assets go up it is DR.

		$m	$m
DR	Payables in current liabilities	60	
CR	Receivable in current assets		100
DR	Cash in current assets	25	
DR	Inventory in current assets	15	

Mind Map

Current accounts are not group assets

Cash in transit is a group asset

Current accounts are not group liabilities

Goods in transit are a group asset

✿ Technical corner

What is a subsidiary?

At minimum a group of companies will comprise two companies, one a parent company and the other its subsidiary company. We can summarise the relationship that exists between the parent and the subsidiary as one of control.

Control is presumed when the parent acquires more than half of the voting rights of the subsidiary. So where all shares have equal voting rights this means control will be established when the parent owns a majority of the shares. The proportion of shares not owned by the parent is termed the non controlling interest.

Even when a majority of the voting rights is not acquired, control may be evidenced by the power

1   to control more than one half of the voting rights by virtue of an agreement with other investors; or

2   to govern the financial and operating policies of the subsidiary under a statute or an agreement; or

3   to appoint or remove the majority of the members of the board of directors; or

4   to cast the majority of votes at a meeting of the board of directors.

Lets consider the following situation

Sami has recently acquired 4,000 shares in Connie, which has a share capital of 10,000 shares. It is noted that Connie has an unusual share structure. It has two classes of equity shares – class A and class B. There are 5,000 of each class of share in issue. The two classes share profits and losses equally, but Class B shares have no voting rights. Each class A share carries one vote. Sami's investment in Connie's shares comprises 3,000 class A shares and 1,000 class B shares.

The first thing that strikes me is that Sami only owns 40% (4,000 / 10,000) of the total share capital of Connie, so that it does not own a majority of the shares. But as the share capital of Connie is unusual and carries different voting rights it is necessary to consider whether Sami has a majority of Connie's voting rights, as it is the voting rights that give control.

The only shares that really matter when it comes to determining control over Connie are the class A shares as the class B shares have no votes. Sami has 3,000 of the 5,000 class A shares i.e. a 60% majority of the class A shares and therefore a majority of the voting rights. On this basis we can see that Sami does control Connie. As Sami controls Connie, Connie will therefore be treated as a subsidiary of Sami in the group accounts.

In this unusual situation when preparing the group accounts it will be necessary to note that whilst Connie is indeed a subsidiary, Sami does not enjoy the same interest in Connie's profits and net assets as it does the voting rights.

The class A and class B shares share profits and losses equally and only differ in respect of the voting rights. Sami's group interest in the overall share capital (and therefore in the profits and net assets) is only 40%. The logical conclusion of this is that is the NCI will be 60%! This is correct, although at first it may seem a bizarre situation. Having an NCI in excess of 50% is something we shall see again when we consider complex group structures in Chapter 17 *Vertical group structures*.

There is a further discussion of control in the Technical Corner of Chapter 10 *Questions*, which also addresses the impact of potential voting rights.

Question Turkey

The following are the extracts from the statements of financial position of Turkey and its subsidiary Ankara.

	Turkey	Ankara
	$m	$m
Current assets		
Inventory	200	250
Receivables	100	140
Cash at bank	50	160
	350	550
Current liabilities	100	160

Additional information

1 Turkey's trade receivables at the year-end include $25m due from Ankara. This included goods of $5m that had been despatched by Turkey on the last day prior to the year-end but had not arrived at Ankara by the year-end.

2 Ankara's trade payables at the year-end include $12m due to Turkey. This was after the deduction of $8m in respect of cash sent by Ankara prior to the year-end but had not arrived at Turkey by the year-end.

Required

Prepare the current asset and current liabilities extracts from the Turkey group statement of financial position.

chapter 9

Provision for unrealised profits (purps)

What's new?

I don't think you can make a profit from selling to yourself!

So on that basis, as the group is in substance a single entity there can be no profits from the sale and purchase of goods between the parent and the subsidiary!

Where there is trading between the parent and the subsidiary the sale of goods may be sold at a transfer price rather than at cost. For example the parent may have sold goods that it purchased for $80 to the subsidiary for $100 and the goods remain in inventory at the year-end. The parent company therefore has recognised a profit of $20 on the sale and the subsidiary has inventory in its accounts at a cost of $100.

However if we consider the group context, the parent and subsidiary as if they were a single economic entity, then there has been no profit to the group from the inter-company sale and the cost to the group of the inventory remains at $80. We cannot make a profit by simply selling goods to ourselves.

Therefore a consolidation adjustment is required to both eliminate the unrealised profit of $20 and to reduce the asset of inventory by $20 to bring it back to the original cost when it was first purchased by a group company.

This consolidation adjustment is known as making a "provision for unrealised profit" (purp).

When the amount of the purp is known it is adjusted for by reducing the amount of the inventory on the statement of financial position when cross casting and also by reducing equity.

Where the parent is the selling company then the whole purp is deducted from the accumulated profits of the group in w5.

Where the subsidiary is the seller, because the parent and the NCI share post acquisition profits and losses of the subsidiary in proportions, only the parent's % of the purp should be deducted from accumulated profits w5 and the NCI % of the purp deducted from the NCI working at w4.

When calculating the purp remember that it only applies to the unsold inventory at the year-end subject to inter-company sales.

The information provided may be expressed in terms of being a gross profit margin or a gross profit mark-up.

Calculation of the purp with a margin

If the question gives a gross profit margin, this is a % based on the sales price, and as the unsold inventory is at the internal selling price this % can be multiplied with the unsold inventory to determine the purp.

To illustrate, the example could be expressed in a question as "The parent has sold inventory for $100 to the subsidiary at a margin of 20% and at the year-end all remain in inventory at the year-end."

The unsold inventory at the year-end		The gross profit margin		The purp
$100	x	20%	=	$20

Calculation of the purp with a mark-up

If the question gives a gross profit mark-up this is a % based on the cost of sales, so this % needs to be adapted before being multiplied by the unsold inventory to determine the purp.

To illustrate, the example could be expressed in a question as "During the year the parent has sold inventory for $100 to the subsidiary at a mark-up of 25%. At the year-end it all remains in inventory."

The unsold inventory at the year-end		The gross profit mark-up		The purp
$100	x	25/125	=	$20

Example

There were inter-company sales of $900 at a mark-up on cost of 50%. At the year-end the buying group company had sold on $150 of these goods. The parent has an 80% interest in the subsidiary.

Required

(i)   Calculate the purp.

(ii) Show the accounting treatment of the purp if the parent company is the seller.

(iii) Show the accounting treatment of the purp if the subsidiary company is the seller.

(i)   First we determine the amount of the unsold inventory, and then apply the gross profit mark-up % to ascertain the amount of the purp.

Unsold inventory		Mark-up		purp
($900 – $150) = $750	x	50/150	=	$250

(ii) Where the parent is the seller the parent will bear all the loss.

The consolidation adjustment for this parent purp is

less $250 from the accumulated profits (w5) (the parent is the seller)

less $250 from inventory in cross casting current assets.

(iii) However where the subsidiary is the seller, then the reduction in profits would relate to the subsidiary and as such is shared between the parent and the NCI in the proportion that profits and losses are shared. Only 80% of the $250 ie. $200 is taken against accumulated profits and 20% of the $250 ie. $50 is charged to the NCI.

The consolidation adjustment for this subsidiary purp is

less $200 from the accumulated profits (w5)

less $50 from the NCI (w4)

less $250 from inventory in cross casting current assets.

NB As we shall see later when we consider the preparation of the group income statement in addition to making an adjustment for the purp it will also be necessary to eliminate both the inter-company sale and purchase.

» Double entry

Like all consolidation adjustments the purp adjustment can be thought of as a double entry. The nature of a purp adjustment is to eliminate a profit that is unrealised in a group context and to ensure that assets are not overstated from internal transfer pricing.

Let's first consider the example we have just been looking at assuming that the parent is the seller.

The whole purp is charged against the accumulated profits as all the parent's profits are consolidated. Accumulated profits are part of equity. To decrease equity this is a DR.

The purp also means that the asset of inventory goes down to ensure that the asset is stated at the cost to the group. To decrease an asset is a CR.

Thus a $250 purp on inventory where the parent is the seller is recorded by:

DR	Accumulated profits w5	$250	
CR	Inventory		$250

However if the seller is the subsidiary then only the parent's % is charged to the accumulated profits and the NCI are charged with their share.

Accumulated profits and NCI are both part of equity. To decrease equity this is a DR.

The purp also means that the asset of inventory goes down. To decrease an asset is a CR.

Thus a $250 purp on inventory where a 80% subsidiary is the seller is recorded by:

DR	Accumulated profits w5	(80% x 250)	$200	
DR	NCI w4	(20% x 250)	$50	
CR	Inventory			$250

Mind Map

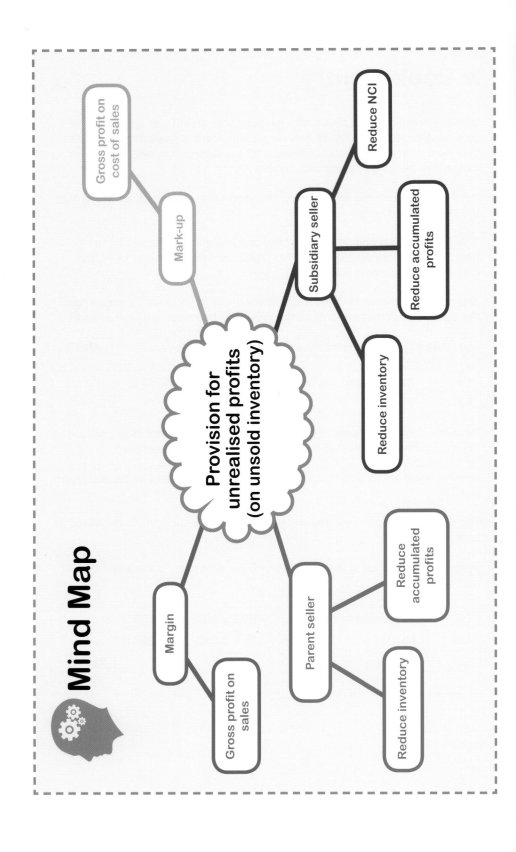

✿ Technical corner

Provision for unrealised profits on inter-company sales of non current assets

It is possible that group companies sell non current assets to each other rather than just inventory. Following on from the principles that we have seen above it will be necessary to reverse out the effects of the inter-company transaction thus eliminating any unrealised profit.

With non current assets there will be the further complication of having to make a further consolidation adjustment for depreciation because the buying company will have recognised the plant at the transfer price and thus be charging more depreciation than necessary. The group will only want depreciation based on the cost to the group.

The reversal of the additional depreciation will cause the purp to become realised. As such it is necessary to consider making a net purp consolidation adjustment from the perspective of the selling company.

If the parent is the selling company there will be no effect on the NCI as a result of the purp.

If the subsidiary is the selling company then the accumulated profits and the NCI will both be reduced in the normal proportion that profits and losses are shared.

Lets consider the following situation

Houillon the parent company had an item of plant with a carrying value of $800. On the first day of the current accounting period this asset was sold to Houillon's subsidiary company for $1,000 and accordingly Houillon reported a profit of $200. The subsidiary has charged depreciation of $250 in the current financial year on the basis that the asset had a remaining useful life of four years when it was transferred.

As a consolidation adjustment in the group accounts it is first appropriate to make a provision for unrealised profit of $200 as Houillon made the sale to its subsidiary company. The initial provision for unrealised profit reduces the parent's profits and reduces the plant in non current assets. There is no impact on the NCI as the parent is the seller.

There is however a further consolidation adjustment, as the initial recording of depreciation will have been overstated by the buying company.

The further consolidation adjustment can be thought of as the difference in the depreciation charged (¼ x $1,000 = $250) and the depreciation that would have been charged if the asset had not been transferred within the group (¼ x $800 = $200). This difference is $50 ($250 - $200).

However a better way to think of the further consolidation adjustment is to consider that the parent's purp of $200 needs reversing back over the remaining four year life of the asset, of which one year has lapsed. This $50 is therefore expressed as ($200 x ¼ x 1 year).

In this latter way I think of the further consolidation adjustment not so much in terms of adjusting depreciation rather as a reversal, as a realisation if you like, of the seller's (and therefore parent company's) purp of $200.

As a consolidation adjustment the reversal of the purp will increase the parent's profit and increase the asset, again with no effect on the NCI, as the parent was the original seller.

To conclude the net adjustment that is required is a purp of $150 (being the original $200 less the reversal of the $50) which reduces the accumulated profits and the plant in the non current assets.

		$	$
Reduce	Accumulated profits w5	150	
Reduce	Plant, non current assets		150

If the subsidiary had been the seller, then after one year we would still have a net adjustment to make of $150, with the reduction in equity being shared between the accumulated profits and the NCI in the proportion that they share profits and losses as well as the non current asset of plant being decreased.

If it had been an 80% subsidiary, and the subsidiary is the seller then this adjustment would be:

			$	$
Reduce	Accumulated profits w5	(80% x 150)	120	
Reduce	NCI w4	(20% x 150)	30	
Reduce	Plant, non current assets			150

Question Thomas

In the Thomas group there were inter-company sales of $500 at a mark-up on cost of 25%. At the year-end the buying group company had sold on $300 of these goods. The parent has an 80% interest in the subsidiary Sweeney.

Required

(i) Calculate the purp.

(ii) Show the accounting treatment of the purp if the parent company is the seller.

(iii) Show the accounting treatment of the purp if the subsidiary company is the seller.

Question Felix

In the Felix group there were inter-company sales of $500 at a margin of 10%. At the year-end the buying group company had sold on one quarter of these goods. The parent has a 60% interest in the subsidiary Barr.

Required

(i) Calculate the purp.

(ii) Show the accounting treatment of the purp if the parent company is the seller.

(iii) Show the accounting treatment of the purp if the subsidiary company is the seller.

Question Alice

The Alice group had inter-company sales of $500 during the year with a margin of 50%. At the year-end the buying group company had two thirds of the goods remaining in inventory. The parent has a 75% interest in the subsidiary O'Reilly.

Required

(i) Calculate the purp.

(ii) Show the accounting treatment of the purp if the parent company is the seller.

(iii) Show the accounting treatment of the purp if the subsidiary company is the seller.

chapter 10
Questions

" Whenever people agree with me I always feel I must be wrong. "

What's new?

Not a lot! As we have done a lot on preparing group statements of financial position, we need to practise what we have learnt by putting it all together in proper questions rather than just sample exercises. So here are two questions. Enjoy!!

Question England

The statements of financial position of two companies are as follows.

	England $m	London $m
Non current assets		
Tangible	500	300
Investment in London	350	
Current assets		
Inventory	30	110
Receivables	20	105
Cash at bank	50	35
	950	550
Ordinary shares ($1)	200	60
Share premium	50	140
Accumulated profits	350	100
Equity	600	300
Non current liabilities	230	140
Current liabilities	120	110
	950	550

Additional information.

1 England acquired 36m shares in London one year ago when the accumulated profits of London were $38m.

The pre acquisition profits will be part of the net assets at acquisition.

2 The fair values of London's net assets at acquisition were equal to their book value with the exception of an item of plant, which had a fair value of $12m in excess of its book value. This plant had a remaining useful life of four years at the date of acquisition and is still held by London.

Fair value adjustments on plant means more depreciation.

3 The fair value of the non controlling interest at the date of acquisition is $150m. The recoverable amount of London at the year-end is $499m.

This means that good will has to be calculated gross and is subject to an impairment review.

4 England sells goods to London during the year at a margin of 10%. At the year-end London has goods purchased form its parent company at a cost of $20m.

The parent is the seller so there is no charge to the NCI in respect of the purp.

5 At the year-end England's trade receivables at the year-end include $10m due from London. London's trade payables at the year-end include $6m due to England, which did not agree with England's corresponding receivable. This was due to cash in transit.

Current accounts will have to be eliminated and items in transit included.

Required

Prepare the consolidated statement of financial position for the England group.

⚙ Technical Corner

Potential voting rights and how that affects control

The definition of a subsidiary is, "An entity, including an unincorporated entity such as a partnership, that is controlled by another entity (known as the parent)".

The key aspect to this definition of a subsidiary revolves around the concept of control rather than legal ownership or the precise legal nature of the entity. To have control will mean that the parent is able to exercise a dominant influence over the subsidiary's operating and financial policies. This means that the subsidiary has to carry out the wishes of the parent.

There are instruments that an investor can hold that give rise to potential voting rights e.g. convertible loan stock, share call options and share warrants, and therefore potentially contribute to being able to control the entity.

Where potential voting rights are currently exercisable or convertible, they are considered when assessing whether the investor has the power to govern another entity's financial and operating policies.

However where the potential voting rights are not exercisable or convertible until a future date or until the occurrence of a future event, they are not considered in making that assessment.

In assessing whether potential voting rights do contribute to control, all of the facts and circumstances that affect those rights should be considered except the intention of management and the financial ability to exercise or convert such rights.

The effect of these requirements is that where the threat of exercise or conversion of these instruments is such that the holder does actually direct the company concerned then a parent subsidiary relationship exists, though the proportions of profit between the parent and the NCI will not reflect the potential voting rights.

Consider

Sally, Caroline and Judith own 40%, 30% and 30% respectively of the ordinary shares where each share carries equal voting rights of the company Elizabeth.

Sally also owns call options that are exercisable at any time and if exercised would give it an additional 20% of the voting rights in Elizabeth and reduce Caroline's and Judith's interests to 20% each.

Since if the options are exercised Sally will have control over a majority i.e. 60% of the voting power, then it is the case that Sally controls Elizabeth. When consolidating Elizabeth as a subsidiary Sally's interest in Elizabeth will be 40% and the NCI 60%.

What is a business combination?

Whilst in all the examples in the book it is a parent company that is acquiring a subsidiary company, IFRS3 *Business Combinations* actually applies to all business combinations whether or not the assets of the business being acquired are held by a legally formed limited liability company with shareholders and directors.

This is yet another example of substance over form, i.e. IFRS3 *Business Combinations* is applicable whenever there is a business combination whatever the legal form. For example the parent company may be acquiring a partnership, a going concern from a sole trader or even just a portfolio of assets.

So what exactly is meant by a business combination? Well IFRS3 *Business Combinations* now defines a business combination as "a transaction or event in which an acquirer obtains control of one or more businesses". It then goes on to define a business as "an integrated set of activities and assets that is capable of being conducted and managed for the purpose of providing a return directly to investors or other owners, members or participants". IFRS3 *Business Combinations* elaborates that "in the absence of evidence to the contrary, a set of assets and activities in which goodwill is present shall be presumed to be a business. However, a business need not have goodwill". Further guidance is given in the appendix to the standard describing a business as having inputs, process and outputs.

The revision to this definition when IFRS3 *Business Combinations* was revised in January 2008 has resulted in some commentators picking up on the significance of the new phrase "capable of being conducted and managed" to suggest that this revised definition widens the scope of business combinations. Business combinations can now include assets that are acquired that have not already been operated as a business, but simply have the capability of being operated as a business.

The distinction between what is a business combination and what is a straight forward purchase of assets could potentially be important as the two are accounted for in subtly different ways as set out below.

	Business combination	**Asset acquisition**
Goodwill	On a business combination the asset of goodwill can arise.	When buying an asset no goodwill can arise.
Acquisition costs	On a business combination the directly attributable acquisition related costs e.g. legal fees must be written off and not capitalised.	When buying an asset the directly attributable acquisition related costs e.g. legal fees are capitalised as part of the cost of the asset.
Deferred tax	On a business combination deferred tax assets and liabilities arising on initial recognition may have to be recognised.	The purchase of an asset has no immediate deferred tax implications.

Identifying the acquirer

For each business combination an acquirer and an acquiree must be identified.

The distinction between the acquirer and acquiree is important as fair value adjustments are made to the acquiree's net assets at acquisition. It is only the acquiree's post acquisition profits that are consolidated and goodwill arises in respect of the acquiree and not the acquirer.

In all of the examples in the book it is straightforward to identify the parent company as the acquirer, as it is listed first, has purchased shares in the subsidiary company (the acquiree) and is generally named after a country!

Prior to 2004 it was possible not to make the distinction and to have a business combination where neither party was identified as either the acquirer or acquiree. These types of business combinations were relatively unusual and were known as a merger or a pooling of interests. Acquisition accounting was not used for these types of business combinations. There were practical problems in distinguishing when a business combination was a merger of two equals, and when there was an acquisition with an acquirer and acquiree. Since 2004 all business combinations have had to identify an acquirer and an acquiree and only acquisition accounting used.

Where however it is not immediately clear which of the combining entities is the acquirer the following factors can be considered.

Relative size	The entity that has significantly greater assets, revenue or profit is usually the acquirer.
Consideration in the form of cash or deferred consideration	The entity that has paid out cash or incurs liabilities is usually the acquirer.
Consideration in the form of shares issued	The entity that has issued the shares is usually the acquirer. However, an exception to this is when there is a reverse acquisition.
Composition of the board of directors of the combined entity	The entity whose owners appoint the majority of the board is usually the acquirer

Reverse acquisitions

A reverse acquisition occurs when the company in the business combination that has issued the shares and has the investment in the subsidiary, i.e. the legal parent company, is in substance and for accounting purposes actually the acquiree (the subsidiary!).

This is a mind-blowing concept! Rest assured that reverse acquisitions are very rare.

Reverse acquisitions have occurred when the shareholders of a large private company wish to obtain a listing on a stock exchange and this liquidity of share price is achieved in a business combination via a share for share exchange with a small quoted company. Instead of the large private company issuing shares and becoming the parent of the smaller company, the business combination is structured such that the small quoted company issues a large number of shares and becomes the legal parent company of the group. The large private company is said to have reversed into the smaller quoted company.

With a reverse acquisition the group accounts will be a continuation of the results of the legal subsidiary and it is the legal parent's financial statements that will have fair value adjustments, goodwill and only the results consolidated from the date of the combination.

The actual accounting for reverse acquisitions is quite complicated but the clear aim of the requirements of IFRS3 *Business Combinations* is to apply substance over form such that the group accounts account for the combination as if the legal subsidiary was the acquirer and the legal parent the acquiree!

Question Wales

The statements of financial position of two companies are as follows.

	Wales $m	Cardiff $m
Tangible non current assets	10,000	5,000
Investment in Cardiff	4,000	
Current assets	3,000	4,000
	17,000	9,000
Ordinary shares ($1)	5,000	3,000
Accumulated profits	6,000	3,500
Equity	11,000	6,500
Non current liabilities	4,000	2,000
Current liabilities	2,000	500
	17,000	9,000

Additional information.

1 Wales acquired 1,800m shares in Cardiff six months ago. During the last year Cardiff has reported profits of $2,500m. You may assume that profits accrue evenly.

Having acquired the subsidiary six months ago will mean that the accumulated profits of the subsidiary at acquisition i.e. at the mid year point will need to be determined.

2 Wales paid an immediate $4,000m in cash and issued 500m shares with a market value of $3 each. In addition Wales agreed to pay a further $2,000 three years after the date of acquisition. Wales has yet to record either the issue of the shares or the deferred consideration. The annual discount rate is 10%.

Not only will the deferred consideration need discounting, but there will also be an extra expense and liability is respect of the unwinding of the discount.

3   Goodwill is to be calculated in full. The fair value of the non controlling interest at the date of acquisition is $3,000m. The impairment review on goodwill revealed that goodwill has to be written down by $300m

The impairment loss on the gross goodwill has to split between the parent and the NCI.

4   Cardiff had established a line of products under the brand name of "Bay". Acting on behalf of Wales a firm of specialists had valued the brand at a value of $500m with an estimated useful life of 10 years as at the date of acquisition. The brand is not recognised in Cardiff's statement of financial position.

The brand will be recognised in the group accounts as a fair value adjustment, and then amortised.

5   During the year Cardiff has sold goods to Wales for $20m at a margin of 25%. All of these goods remain unsold by Cardiff at the year-end. There are no current account balances at the year-end.

The subsidiary is the seller, so the NCI will be charged.

Required

Prepare the consolidated statement of financial position for the Wales group.

recap

on further adjustments

66 Most modern calendars mar the sweet simplicity of our lives by reminding us that each day that passes is the anniversary of some perfectly uninteresting event. 99

What's new?

Absolutely nothing!

Let's take this opportunity to recap on the key messages from this section.

🔑 Key messages

- When cross casting the parent and subsidiary's receivables in preparing the group accounts always deduct any inter-company current account balance.

- When cross casting the parent and subsidiary's liabilities in preparing the group accounts always deduct any inter-company current account balance.

- When cross casting the parent and subsidiary's inventory in preparing the group accounts always look to add any goods in transit

- When cross casting the parent and subsidiary's cash at bank in preparing the group accounts always look to add any cash in transit.

- Where a group company has at the year-end unsold inventory that it has purchased from another group company at a mark-up or margin it will be necessary to make a provision for unrealised profit (purp).

- The purp will be deducted from inventory and also used to reduce equity. If the parent is the seller the whole of the purp is charged against accumulated profits. But if the subsidiary is the seller then it is only the parent's share charged against accumulated profits and the NCI are then charged with their share.

We have so far looked at the consolidation adjustments that can be necessary when preparing the group statement of financial position. What is not included in the summary overleaf is those situations where the accounts of one group member are initially incorrect e.g. the receivables are a bad debt and need writing off. Such an adjustment is an accounting correction rather than anything to do with the process of consolidation.

Statement of financial position

Non Current Assets

Intangibles	Parent plus subsidiary.	Plus the goodwill arising on the consolidation of the subsidiary less any impairment losses.	Plus intangible assets of the subsidiary recognised as a fair value adjustment less any amortisation
Tangibles	Parent plus subsidiary.	Plus the fair value adjustments at acquisition on subsidiary assets that remain held less any cumulative depreciation.	Less the provision for unrealised profit (net of reversal of depreciation) on inter-company transfers of non current assets between group companies.
Investments	Parent plus subsidiary.	Less inter-company long term loans.	Less the investment that the parent has made on acquiring the subsidiary.

Current assets

Inventory	Parent plus subsidiary.	Plus goods in transit.	Less provision for unrealised profit.
Receivables	Parent plus subsidiary.	Less inter-company current accounts.	
Cash at bank	Parent plus subsidiary.	Plus cash in transit.	

Equity			
Ordinary share capital	Parent only.	Plus any previously unrecorded shares issued on the acquisition.	
Share premium	Parent only.	Plus any previously unrecorded premium on shares issued on the acquisition less issue costs.	
Other reserves	Parent plus the parent's share of the subsidiary's post acquisition increases.		
Accumulated profits	w5		
Non controlling interest	w4		
Liabilities			
Non current liabilities	Parent plus subsidiary.	Less inter-company long term loans.	Plus any previously unrecorded deferred or contingent consideration on the acquisition, including the finance costs to date.
Current liabilities	Parent plus subsidiary.	Less inter-company current accounts.	

section 4

Introducing the group statement of comprehensive income

The group income statement

One should always play fairly when one has the winning cards.

What's new?

To date we have looked at preparing the group statement of financial position by consolidating the statements of financial position of the parent company and the subsidiary.

Well now the time has come for us to consider the preparation of the group of income statement. This will of course be achieved by consolidating the income statement of the parent company and the subsidiary as they are presented to you in the question.

Whilst a statement of financial position is drawn up as at a particular date to show the assets, liabilities and equity, an income statement is prepared to show the income and expenses for the reporting period (usually one year) and thus measure profit. For the avoidance of doubt here is what a typical income statement of an individual company looks like.

Income statement

	$
Revenue	X
Cost of sales	(X)
Gross profit	X
Distribution costs	(X)
Administration expenses	(X)
Operating profit	X
Exceptional gain	X
Investment income	X
Finance costs	(X)
Profit before tax	X
Tax	(X)
Profit for the year	X

The principles that we have used to prepare the group statement of financial position are equally applicable when preparing group income statements. Have a look at this table – as you remember and understand what it says about the statement of financial position you will able to relate it to what we are about to do in the context of the preparing the group income statement.

	Group statement of financial position	Group income statement	Comment
Cross casting	The basic rule is that the assets and the liabilities of the parent and subsidiary are fully cross cast.	The basic rule is that the income and expenses of the parent and subsidiary are fully cross cast.	The results of the subsidiary will need to be time apportioned if it has only been a subsidiary for part of the year i.e. has been acquired during the reporting period.
Inter-company items	Current account balances between the parent and the subsidiary have to be excluded from the group statement of financial position because they represent inter-company items i.e. are not external assets or liabilities.	Inter-company sales and purchases between the parent and the subsidiary have to be excluded from the group income statement because they represent inter-company items i.e. are not external income or expenses.	If the question says that the parent has sold goods to the subsidiary then by definition the subsidiary has purchased goods from the parent, so both the sales and the cost of sales must be reduced.
	The same principle applies with long term inter-company loans.	The same principle applies with inter-company interest.	
	Eliminating these inter-company balances does not affect the NCI.	Eliminating these inter-company transactions does not affect the NCI.	

	Group statement of financial position	Group income statement	Comment
Provision for unrealised profit	When a purp is required (because there is unsold inventory at the year end at a transfer price between group companies) the consolidation adjustment causes a reduction in both the inventory and equity. If the subsidiary is the seller the NCI is charged.	The purp consolidation adjustment reduces the profits and will manifest itself as an additional expense. If the subsidiary is the seller the NCI is charged.	The extra expense in respect of the provision for unrealised profit is included in the cost of sales.
Fair value adjustments and additional depreciation	When at the date of acquisition of the subsidiary there is an upwards fair value adjustment on plant, the asset increases by the fair value adjustment and then decreases by the subsequent additional depreciation. The NCI reflects the fair value adjustments.	The additional depreciation following a fair value adjustment the year will be an additional expense. The NCI are charged with the depreciation adjustment.	The extra depreciation expense for the year on the fair value adjustment is included in cost of sales.

	Group statement of financial position	Group income statement	Comment
Goodwill and the impairment loss	The goodwill arising on the acquisition of the subsidiary is an additional group asset and is subject to an annual impairment review. Where the impairment loss is on gross goodwill the NCI will be charged.	Any impairment loss arising in the accounting period will be an additional expense. Where the impairment loss is on gross goodwill the NCI will be charged.	The extra expense in respect of the impairment loss arising in the year is included in cost of sales.
NCI	The NCI in the subsidiary's net assets will reflect adjustments made in respect of fair value adjustments on assets and additional depreciation, purps (where the subsidiary is the seller) and the impairment loss on gross goodwill.	The NCI in the subsidiary's profit will reflect adjustments made in respect of additional depreciation on fair value adjustments, purps (where the subsidiary is the seller) and the impairment loss on gross goodwill.	By showing the profit of the subsidiary that is attributable to the NCI, the group income statement can show as a balancing figure the total group profits that are attributable to the parent company's shareholders.

Let's now go straight into a group income statement question and put that theory into practice.

Example

Cairo is an 80% subsidiary of Egypt that was acquired one year ago.

The following information relates to Cairo at the date of acquisition.

Ordinary share capital	Reserves	Fair value of the net assets	Fair value of the NCI	Cost of the investment
m	$m	$m	$m	$m
300	500	1,000	250	2,000

Income statements

	Egypt $m	Cairo $m
Revenue	9,000	4,000
Cost of sales	(5,000)	(2,000)
Gross profit	4,000	2,000
Operating costs	(2,000)	(1,698)
Finance costs	(500)	(2)
Profit before tax	1,500	300
Tax	(700)	(100)
Profit for the year	800	200

Additional Information

1 During the year Egypt has sold goods to Cairo for $100 million. These goods were sold at a margin of 40% and one half remains in inventory at the year-end.

2 At the date of acquisition the fair values of Cairo's net assets were equal to their book value with the exception of an item of plant that had a remaining useful life of five years.

3 Goodwill is to be calculated using the fair value of the non controlling interest at the date of acquisition. An impairment review at the year-end reveals that one tenth of the goodwill that arose on acquisition was impaired during the year.

Required

Prepare the consolidated income statement for the Egypt Group.

Well the first thing to do is to make sure that we are happy with the group structure.

W1 Group structure

Egypt

↓ Parent's interest 80%
NCI 20%

Cairo

The acquisition was one year ago so there will be no need to time apportion the results of Cairo.

Now there are some consolidation adjustments in respect of the inter-company sale and purp that it is worthwhile clearing up at this stage. The question informs us that there has been an inter-company sale (and therefore automatically an inter-company purchase) and that a purp will arise in respect of the unsold inventory.

To eliminate the effects of the inter-company sale both revenue and cost of sales will be reduced. The elimination of the inter-company transaction has no impact on the NCI.

Reduce revenue	$100m	
Reduce cost of sales		$100m

There is a provision for unrealised profit in this question that arises from the unsold goods following the inter-company sale at a transfer price.

Unsold inventory at the year end		Gross profit margin			
(½ x $100m)	X	40%		=	$20m

This $20m is an extra expense.

Increase cost of sales	$20m	
Reduce inventory (in current assets)		$20m

As the parent is the seller in the inter-company transaction there will be no impact on the NCI as the adjustment to profit relates to the parent.

W2 Net assets

In this question there is no need to do a net asset calculation at the year-end because the result of the impairment review has been given and there is no requirement to do the statement of financial position, so no need for NCI in the net assets.

However it is necessary to do the net assets working at the date of acquisition in order to determine goodwill – of which one tenth is impaired giving rise to an additional loss in the group income statement. It is also necessary to discover the fair value adjustment on the plant which is derived as a balancing figure and is then used to calculate the additional depreciation expense.

	At acquisition $m
Share capital	300
Accumulated profits	500
Fair value adjustment (bal fig)	200
Total	1,000

The fair value adjustment is derived as a balancing figure.

The fair value adjustment relates to plant with a five year life so there will be additional depreciation to be charged in the current year.

$200m x 1/5 x 1 year = $40m

This $40m extra depreciation is an extra expense.

Increase cost of sales	$40m	
Reduce non current assets		$40m

This additional depreciation charge specifically relates to the subsidiary's plant and therefore to the subsidiary's profits. As such it will be taken into account in determining the NCI in the subsidiary's profit for the year.

W3 Goodwill

		$m	$m
Cost of the parent's investment		2,000	
Less the parent's % of the net assets at acquisition	(80% x 1,000)	800	
Goodwill (attributable to the parent)			1,200
Fair value of the NCI at acquisition		250	
Less the NCI % of the net assets at acquisition	(20% x 1,000)	200	
Goodwill (attributable to the NCI)			50
Gross goodwill at acquisition			1,250

Proof of W3 Goodwill

		$m
Cost of parent's investment		2,000
Fair value of the NCI at acquisition		250
Less 100% of the net assets at acquisition	(100% x 1,000)	(1,000)
Gross goodwill at acquisition		1, 250

Goodwill has been calculated gross, which by now I hope you consider being the normal way. The impairment loss was stated as being an arbitrary one tenth of the goodwill.

$1,250m x 1/10 = $125m

This $125m impairment loss represents an extra expense

Increase cost of sales	$125m	
Reduce goodwill (intangible asset)		$125m

As goodwill has been calculated gross (with the NCI having a share) and then has been impaired so the NCI will have a share of the impairment loss which will be reflected when determining the NCI in the subsidiary's profit for the year.

W4 Cost of sales

Because of the number of adjustments to expenses it is often necessary to do a working for the cost of sales – it certainly is in this example!

The basic premise of cost of sales is that it is cross cast, but there is an intercompany transaction to eliminate and the additional expenses of the provision for unrealised profit, additional depreciation and impairment loss on the goodwill to pick up.

Cost of sales		$m
Parent		5,000
Subsidiary		2,000
Less the inter-company purchase		(100)
Plus the purp		20
Plus the additional depreciation		40
Plus the impairment loss	w3	125
		7,085

W5 NCI

Finally in a group income statement we need to calculate the NCI in the subsidiary's profit. As with the calculation of the NCI for the statement of financial position we have to adjust the raw data for the consolidation adjustments affecting the NCI e.g. for depreciation adjustments, purps (where the subsidiary is the seller) and the impairment loss on gross goodwill.

			$m
NCI in the subsidiary's profits as given		(20% x 200)	40
Less the NCI % of depreciation on the FVA		(20% x 40)	(8)
Less the NCI % of the (gross goodwill) impairment loss	w3	(20% x 125)	(25)
			7

We can now proceed to prepare the group income statement. The income and expenses of the subsidiary are cross cast in full.

Egypt group income statement

		$m
Revenue	(9,000 + 4,000 less inter company sale 100)	12,900
Cost of sales	w4	(7,085)
Gross profit		5,815
Operating costs	(2,000 + 1,698)	(3,698)
Finance costs	(500 + 2)	(502)
Profit before tax		1,615
Tax	(700 + 100)	(800)
Profit for the year		815
Attributable to the parent	Balancing figure	808
Attributable to the NCI	w5	7
Profit for the year		815

Having ascertained the group profit for the year of $815m it necessary to acknowledge on the face of the group income statement how much of that profit is attributable to the shareholders of the parent and how much is attributable to the NCI shareholders in the subsidiary.

The NCI in the subsidiary's profit has been calculated in w5 and so (by working backwards) the profit attributable to the parent's shareholders is the balancing figure.

» Double entry

As with the preparation of the group statement of financial of position the basic rule in consolidating the group income statement is to cross cast the parent and the subsidiary together. In the statement of financial position the basic rule is to cross cast the assets and liabilities and to consider the adjustments, whilst in the income statement the basic rule is to cross cast the income and expenses and to consider the adjustments.

However the adjustments that are made can be thought of in double entry terms. Let's take the adjustments made in the preparation of Egypt's group income statement.

Intercompany sale

When eliminating the intercompany sale this means that we have to eliminate both the sale and the purchase.

To eliminate an inter company sale is to reduce revenue. To reduce revenue is a DR.

To eliminate an inter company purchase is to reduce expenses (cost of sales). To reduce expenses is a CR.

DR	Reduce revenue	$100m	
CR	Reduce cost of sales		$100m

Purp

When making a purp, the asset needs to be reduced and so reinstated to the true cost to the group and the unrealised profit on the sale eliminated by increasing expenses.

The purp increases expenses (cost of sales) to prevent profits being overstated. To increase expenses is a DR

The purp decreases the asset of inventory. To reduce assets is a CR.

DR	Increase cost of sales	$20m	
CR	Reduce inventory (in current assets)		$20m

Depreciation on the fair value adjustment

When adjusting for the additional depreciation on the fair value adjustment there is an additional expense and a write down of an asset.

To record the additional expense of depreciation on the fair value adjustment is to increase expenses (cost of sales). To increase expenses is a DR.

To record the write down of the non current asset due to the additional expense of depreciation is to reduce an asset. To decrease an asset is a CR.

DR	Increase cost of sales	$40m	
CR	Reduce non current assets		$40m

Impairment loss on goodwill

When recording impairment losses there is an additional expense and a write down of the asset

To record the additional expense of the impairment loss is to increase expenses (cost of sales). To increase expenses is a DR.

To record the write down of the intangible asset of goodwill is to reduce an asset. To decrease an asset is a CR.

DR	Increase cost of sales	$125m	
CR	Reduce goodwill (intangible asset)		$125m

Mind Map

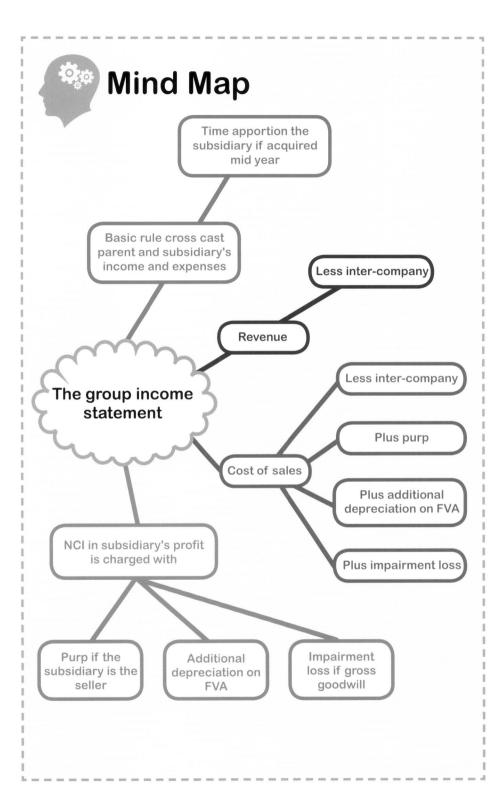

The group income statement

Time apportion the subsidiary if acquired mid year

Basic rule cross cast parent and subsidiary's income and expenses

Revenue
- Less inter-company

Cost of sales
- Less inter-company
- Plus purp
- Plus additional depreciation on FVA
- Plus impairment loss

NCI in subsidiary's profit is charged with
- Purp if the subsidiary is the seller
- Additional depreciation on FVA
- Impairment loss if gross goodwill

⚙ Technical corner

Dividends are distributions and not expenses

When I was a student (a long time ago) the dividends paid by a company would be deducted in the profit and loss account as the income statement was then called. This potentially confused some users as it implied that the dividends distributed by a company to the shareholders were an expense, a loss, which they are not.

The dividends paid by a company are an appropriation of profit, a distribution of profit and not a charge on profit. As such they have no place whatsoever in the income statement, the purpose if which is to recognise income and expenses in order to measure the profit that has been made.

These days the dividends made by companies are accounted for as a movement in accumulated profits i.e. are reported as part of the statement of changes in equity.

A group statement of changes in equity reconciles the opening to closing balances within equity.

Group statement of changes in equity

	Share capital	Share premium	Revaluation reserve	Accumulated profits	NCI	Total Equity
Opening balance	X	X	X	X	X	X
New shares	X	X				X
Revaluation gain			X		X	X
Profits for the year				X	X	X
Less dividends	—	—	—	(X)	(X)	(X)
Closing balance	X	X	X	X	X	X

When the parent company issues new ordinary shares equity is increased. The share capital will increase by the nominal value of shares and the share premium by any excess consideration received over and above the nominal value.

When the parent company records a revaluation surplus in equity e.g. in respect of a financial asset classified as "Available For Sale", or in respect of land, then the revaluation reserve is increased.

When the subsidiary is in the same situation and has a post acquisition revaluation surplus to record in equity then the parent's share also increases the revaluation reserve, and the NCI's share will increase the NCI.

The profit for the year attributable to the parent shareholders will increase the group accumulated profits, and the profit attributable to the NCI will increase the NCI.

The dividend deducted from the accumulated profits will be that of the parent company only. The dividend deducted from the NCI will be the NCI% of the subsidiary's dividend.

Question Bahamas

This income statement question also has with it a statement of financial position. It also requires the preparation of the group's statement of changes in equity.

Nassau is a 90% subsidiary of Bahamas that was acquired one year ago for $4,000m when the accumulated profits of Nassau were $800m.

Luckily no need to time apportion in income statement.

Income statements

	Bahamas $m	Nassau $m
Revenue	20,000	4,000
Cost of sales	(12,000)	(2,000)
Gross profit	8,000	2,000
Distribution costs	(2,100)	(300)
Administration expenses	(1,400)	(500)
Operating profit	4,500	1,200
Exceptional gain	Nil	580
Investment income	90	Nil
Finance costs	(600)	(150)
Profit before tax	3,990	1,630
Tax	(700)	(130)
Profit for the year	3,290	1,500

Statements of financial position

	Bahamas $m	Nassau $m
Investment in Nassau	4,000	
Assets	20,000	5,000
	24,000	5,000
Share capital ($1)	5,000	1,000
Accumulated profits	15,690	2,200
Equity	20,690	3,200
Liabilities	3,310	1,800
	24,000	5,000

Bahamas Statement of changes in equity

	Share capital $m	Accumulated profits $m	Total Equity $m
Opening balance	5,000	12,600	17,600
Profits for the year		3,290	3,290
Less dividends		(200)	(200)
Closing balance	5,000	15,690	20,690

Nassau Statement of changes in equity

	Share capital $m	Accumulated profits $m	Total Equity $m
Opening balance	1,000	800	1,800
Profits for the year		1,500	1,500
Less dividends		(100)	(100)
Closing balance	1,000	2,200	3,200

Additional information

4 During the year Bahamas has sold goods to Nassau for $100m. These goods were sold at a margin of 20% and one quarter remain in inventory at the year-end.

Inter company sales must be eliminated, and a purp made. The sales are made by the parent so the NCI will not be charged with the purp.

5 During the year Nassau has sold goods to Bahamas for $180m. These goods were sold at a mark–up of 50% and one half remain in inventory at the year-end.

These sales are made by the subsidiary so the NCI will be charged with the purp.

6 At the year-end there were no outstanding inter company current account balances.

7 At the date of acquisition the fair values of Nassau's net assets were equal to their book value with the exception of an item of plant that had a fair value of $200m in excess of its carrying value and a remaining useful life of four years.

8 Goodwill is to be calculated using the proportionate basis. An impairment review at the year-end reveals that no impairment loss arose.

So no gross goodwill or fair value of the NCI.

9 Both companies have paid a dividend during the year. The dividend distributed by Bahamas was $200m and that of Nassau $100m. The investment income that Bahamas has recognised is the dividend received from Nassau shortly before the year-end.

The dividend received by the parent from the subsidiary is not external group income and so must be eliminated.

Required

Prepare the consolidated statement of financial position, consolidated income statement and the consolidated statement of changes in equity for the Bahamas Group.

chapter 12

The group statement of comprehensive income

"I am not young enough to know everything."

What's new?

There is a shortcoming in the income statements that we have looked at to date as they have not been comprehensive in that they have only included those gains and losses that have been recognised directly in the income statement!

Not all gains and losses recognised by companies are recognised directly in the income statement because some gains are losses are specifically required to be recognised directly in equity (i.e. in reserves).

The simplest example of a gain recognised in reserves, and therefore outside of the income statement, is when a company in accordance with IAS16 *Property Plant and Equipment* has a policy of revaluing its land and buildings. For example if land had a historical cost two years ago of $40,000 but now has a value of $50,000 then the gain of $10,000 to be recorded will be recognised in Revaluation Reserve and will not be included as part of the profit for the year in the income statement.

IAS1 *Presentation of Financial Statements* was revised with effect for accounting periods from 1 January 2009 so there is now a requirement to present "other comprehensive income" items (such as revaluation gains), as well as the usual income statement items, on the face of the primary financial statements. IAS1 *Presentation of Financial Statements* allows this information to be presented in one "statement of comprehensive income" or in two separate statements; an "income statement" and a "statement of comprehensive income". For the avoidance of doubt whenever a "statement of comprehensive income" is referred to, this always relates to the single statement format. If "income statements" are referred to, this relates to the statement from "revenue" to "profit for the year".

The statement of comprehensive income includes the profit for the year but goes on to report all the other gains and losses recognised directly in reserves in an other comprehensive income section and thus reports the total comprehensive income of the period. This helps users appreciate that the income statement does not include all the gains and losses that the company recognised in the period.

This is what a typical group statement of comprehensive income looks like.

Group statement of comprehensive income

	$
Income statement	
Revenue	X
Cost of sales	(X)
Gross profit	X
Distribution costs	(X)
Administration expenses	(X)
Operating profit	X
Exceptional gain	X
Investment income	X
Finance costs	(X)
Profit before tax	X
Tax	(X)
Profit for the year	X
Other comprehensive income	
Revaluation gains	X
Total comprehensive income for the year	X
Attributable to the parent	X
Attributable to the NCI	X
Profit for the year	X
Attributable to the parent	X
Attributable to the NCI	X
Total comprehensive income for the year	X

The NCI in the group profit and the group comprehensive income must be shown, which leaves the 'attributable to the parent' as balancing figures.

For the record all the components of other comprehensive income[1] are

- gains or losses on the revaluation of non current assets recognised in accordance with IAS16 *Property Plant and Equipment* (as illustrated above)

- the group exchange gains and losses arising from translating the financial statements of a foreign operation in accordance with IAS21 *The Effects of Changes in Foreign Exchange Rates* (see Chapter 20 *Overseas subsidiaries*)

- the actuarial gains and losses on defined benefit pension plans recognised in accordance with IAS19 *Employee Benefits*

- gains and losses on remeasuring Available For Sale financial assets in accordance with IAS39 *Financial Instruments: Recognition and Measurement*

- the effective portion of gains and losses on hedging instruments in a cash flow hedge in accordance with IAS39 *Financial Instruments: Recognition and Measurement.*

The objective of this book is to concentrate on the preparation of group accounts and not to explain the finer points of accounting for financial instruments or defined benefit pensions plans!

For further details on why these gains and losses are treated in this way and information on all other international financial reporting standards please see *A student's guide to International Financial Reporting Standards* by Clare Finch (Kaplan publishing 2008).

---

1   Strictly the tax on these items should also be recognised in other comprehensive income.

Example

Tokyo is an 80% subsidiary of Japan that was acquired two years ago.

Statements of comprehensive income

	Japan	Tokyo
Income statement	**$m**	**$m**
Revenue	5,000	1,000
Cost of sales	(2,000)	(200)
Gross Profit	3,000	800
Operating costs	(1,500)	(450)
Operating profits	1,500	350
Investment income	1,500	350
Finance costs	(300)	(50)
Profit before tax	2,700	650
Tax	(400)	(100)
Profit for the year	2,300	550
Other comprehensive income		
Revaluation gains	100	50
Total comprehensive income for the year	2,400	600

1 During the year Tokyo has sold goods to Japan for $750m. These goods were sold at a mark-up of 50%. At the year-end one fifth of these goods remain unsold by Japan.

2 An impairment review was conducted at the year-end. This reveals that no goodwill was impaired during the year.

3 On the acquisition of Tokyo a fair value adjustment of $50m was made to the plant of Tokyo. The plant had a remaining useful life of five years and is depreciated on a straight-line basis down to a nil residual value. The fair value adjustment had not been incorporated into the accounting records of the subsidiary.

4 At acquisition Japan advanced Tokyo a loan of $500m and charged its subsidiary an effective rate of interest of 10%. Both companies have correctly accounted for the transaction.

Required

Prepare the consolidated statement of comprehensive income for the Japan Group

It is not necessary to calculate goodwill (w3), as the impairment review is not required. There is no need to do net assets (w2) at all, but let's start with the group structure, after all it only takes a moment to do.

W1 Group structure

Japan		
↓	Parent's interest 80%	The acquisition was two years ago so there will no need for time apportionment.
	NCI 20%	
Tokyo		

W2

The question tells us there has been an inter-company sale and there is a purp to calculate.

To eliminate the effects of the inter-company sale both revenue and cost of sales will be reduced. The elimination of the inter-company transaction has no impact on the NCI in the subsidiary's profits.

Reduce revenue	$750m	
Reduce cost of sales		$750m

As the subsidiary is the seller so the purp will have an impact on the NCI in the subsidiary's profits.

Unsold inventory at year end	Gross profit mark-up	Provision for unrealised profit to increase cost of sales
($750m x $1/5$) x	50/150 =	$50m

W3

The question also points to there being an additional depreciation expense following the fair value adjustment to the subsidiary's plant at the date of acquisition. Again this will have an impact on the NCI in the subsidiary's profits. Only this year's additional depreciation is relevant to this year's profit.

Fair value adjustment	Remaining useful life of the asset	Extra depreciation to increase cost of sales
$50m x	$1/5$ =	$10m

W4

The question also informs us that Tokyo has a finance cost of 10% x $500m = $50m that will be paid over to Japan its parent company as a result of the inter-company loan. This interest is inter-company so will need to be eliminated by reducing the group investment income and finance cost. The elimination of the inter-company transaction has no impact of the NCI on the subsidiary's profits.

Reduce investment income	$50m	
Reduce finance cost		$50m

There are two other workings that can now be done before we have all the pieces to put together in the income statement. Next we can calculate the cost of sales.

W5 Cost of sales

	$m
Parent	2,000
Subsidiary	200
Less the inter company	(750)
Plus the purp w2	50
Plus the depreciation on the FVA w3	10
	1,510

Now we can calculate NCI in the profit and the comprehensive income.

W6 NCI in the subsidiary's profits

		$m
NCI in the subsidiary's profit for the year as given	(20% x 550)	110
Less the NCI % of depreciation on the FVA w3	(20% x 10)	(2)
Less the NCI % of the purp (subsidiary is the seller) w2	(20% x 50)	(10)
		98

The NCI in the total comprehensive income will be the NCI in the subsidiary's profit plus the NCI in the subsidiary's other comprehensive income.

W7 NCI in the subsidiary's total comprehensive income

		$m
NCI % of the subsidiary's profit (as above)		98
NCI % of the subsidiary's other comprehensive income	(20% x 50)	10
		108

Japan group statement of comprehensive income

Income statement		$m
Revenue	(5,000 + 1,000 less inter-company sale 750 (w2))	5,250
Cost of sales	w5	(1,510)
Gross profit		3,740
Operating costs	(1,500 + 450)	(1,950)
Operating profit		1,790
Investment income	(1,500 + 350 less inter company interest 50 (w4))	1,800
Finance costs	(300 + 50 less inter company interest 50 (w4))	(300)
Profit before tax		3,290
Tax	(400 + 100)	(500)
Profit for the year		2,790
Other comprehensive income		
Revaluation gains	(100 + 50)	150
Total comprehensive income for the year		2,940
Attributable to the parent	Balancing figure	2,692
Attributable to the NCI	w6	98
Profit for the year		2,790
Attributable to the parent	Balancing figure	2,832
Attributable to the NCI	w7	108
Total comprehensive income for the year		2,940

During the year the parent has recognised a revaluation gain of $100m and the subsidiary has recognised a revaluation gain of $50m. In the group statement of comprehensive income this is reported gross i.e. the share of the NCI in the subsidiary's post acquisition gain of $10m (20% x $50m) is reported within the total comprehensive income for the year attributable to the NCI (w6).

In the group statement of financial position the group revaluation reserve will be reported net i.e. will be that of the parent plus the parent's share of the subsidiary's post acquisition gain of $140m ($100m + (80% x $50m)). NCI will be increased by its share i.e. $10m (20% x $50m).

» Double entry bookkeeping

The revaluations by the group companies can be thought of in double entry terms.

Japan, the parent had recorded a revaluation gain of $100m that it had recognised directly in equity and therefore also presented in the other comprehensive income section of the statement of comprehensive income.

The revaluation surplus of $100m reflects an increase in the value of the asset and the recognition of an unrealised gain directly in reserves.

When an asset is revalued upwards this increases the asset. When an asset is increased this is a DR.

When an asset is revalued upwards this increases the revaluation reserve (within equity). When reserves are increased this a CR.

| DR | Asset | $100m | |
| CR | Revaluation reserve | | $100m |

In the group accounts the parent's gain of $100m is reported in the other comprehensive income.

Tokyo, the 80% subsidiary had recorded a revaluation gain of $50m that it had recognised directly in reserves and therefore also presented in its individual accounts in the other comprehensive income section of the statement of comprehensive income.

The revaluation surplus of $50m reflects an increase in the value of the asset and from a group perspective the recognition of a post acquisition gain directly in reserves that the parent and the NCI will share in the normal proportions.

When an asset is revalued upwards this increases the asset. When an asset is increased this is a DR.

When the subsidiary's assets are revalued in the post acquisition period the parent's share will increase the group's revaluation reserve and the NCI element will increase the NCI (both within equity). When reserves and NCI are increased these are CRs.

DR	Asset	$50m	
CR	Revaluation reserve		$40m
CR	NCI		$10m

In the group statement of comprehensive income the subsidiary's gain of $50m is reported in the other comprehensive income together with NCI in it of $10m.

Mind Map

Statement of comprehensive income

Income statement

Measures profit

From revenue to profit for the year

Other comprehensive income

Measures comprehensive income

Shows gains and losses recognised in equity (i.e. reserves)

e.g. Revaluation gains

⚙ Technical corner

Consolidating all subsidiaries

IAS27 *Consolidated and Separate Financial Statements* is quite explicit in requiring that the consolidated accounts should include all of the parent's subsidiaries.

For the avoidance of doubt there is specifically no exemption from consolidating a subsidiary on the grounds that

- it's an overseas subsidiary

- the subsidiary conducts a business of a different nature from the parent's

- or even that the subsidiary operates under severe long-term restrictions impairing the subsidiary's ability to transfer funds to the parent. Control must be lost for exclusion to occur.

Held for sale exemption

There is however one situation where a subsidiary is not consolidated in the normal way. That is where control over the subsidiary is intended to be temporary because the subsidiary was acquired and is held exclusively with a view to its subsequent disposal in the near future. For such a subsidiary, if it is highly probable that the sale will be completed within 12 months then the parent should account for its investment in the subsidiary as an asset that is held for sale in accordance with IFRS5 *Non-current Assets Held for Sale and Discontinued Operations*. In other words the subsidiary is treated as a current asset investment and held at the lower of cost and the fair value less costs to sell.

Creative accounting and off balance sheet finance

All this regulation is designed to prevent creative accounting i.e. the manipulation of the group accounts by the deliberate non consolidation of an entity that is nevertheless controlled by the group. The hope of the creative accountant is that, by the non consolidation of a particular subsidiary, in some way the users of the group accounts will have a more favourable impression of the group's performance and position.

For example if a subsidiary has been making losses then creative accountants may try to find excuses for the non aggregation of the subsidiary's losses.

Another situation where groups try to avoid consolidating subsidiaries is where the subsidiary is highly geared i.e. has a relatively large amount of liabilities compared to its equity. If a group has a high debt to equity ratio it is perceived to be highly geared and then investors and other users may regard the group as being a high risk. In these circumstances the group can find it harder to refinance debt and borrow new funds or be charged a higher rate of interest to compensate for the lender's increase in risk.

Being perceived as highly geared can also potentially have a negative impact on the share price as one method of a highly geared group raising funds is from the shareholders in the form of a rights issue of shares. The shares issued in a rights issue are issued at a discount on the current market price with the result that normally after the rights issue the share price of the company will fall due to the increased shares in circulation. Now it can be argued that if there is a perception that the company is highly geared and so may make a rights issue the share price may fall as shareholders sell in anticipation of the fall in the share price. Fear of a fall in the share price can therefore become a self-fulfilling prophecy.

Special purpose entities (SPE)

To back up the accounting standards in this area the International Accounting Standards Board (the IASB) through its Standards Interpretation Committee issued SIC12 Consolidation – Special Purpose Entities (SPE). SPE can be set up by groups to conduct specialist transactions. Under SIC12, the group must consolidate a SPE when, in substance, the group controls the SPE. The control of an SPE by the group may be indicated if the group has the right to the majority of the SPE's benefits, the group is exposed to the SPE's business risks, or the SPE conducts its activities to meet the group's specific needs.

Let us consider an example of a group that has a SPE

Charlie is the parent of a group of companies that trades in precious metals and minerals thoughout the world and has a large number of companies. Last year the group finance director, set up a company called Henry through which Charlie will conduct derivative trading in the hope of making large profits from short term fluctuations in gold and silver prices. The share capital of Henry only comprises one hundred equity shares, which were all subscribed for by a Mr Alex at the nominal value of $1. Mr Alex is the sole director of Henry and a former employee of Charlie. Charlie has lent Henry $100 million. An agreement drawn up by Charlie with Mr Alex sets out the operating guidelines for Henry and prohibits Mr Alex from obtaining access to the investments for his benefit. Further, 95% of the profits and 100% of the losses of Henry are to be transferred to Charlie on an annual basis. At the year-end Henry has incurred losses of $40 million and has borrowed $800 million from third parties. The finance director of Charlie wishes to account for its financing of Henry as a simple investment.

Well in considering this situation, it is noted that Henry was set up by a director of Charlie in order to enable Charlie to conduct speculative derivative trading. Further, Charlie does not own Henry as Mr Alex holds all the share capital. As such we can identify this as a SPE as it is not a normal subsidiary. However in preparing the group accounts and identifying what is to be consolidated legal ownership is not the decisive factor. Whilst not technically the legal owner of Henry, Charlie does enjoy the risks and rewards of ownership of the company as it will bear 100% of the losses and reap 95% of the profits.

Further, under an agreement with the sole director of Henry, Charlie sets out the operating guidelines for Henry and in this unorthodox way achieves control over Henry.

In conclusion therefore Henry is to be consolidated into the Charlie group accounts. The losses of $40 million are to be recognised and the liabilities of $800 million recognised on the group statement of financial position.

One can momentarily sympathise with Charlie not wanting to consolidate the losses and liabilities of Henry as by doing so the Charlie group accounts will only show a worse performance and weaker financial position. Nevertheless as accountants we need to be independent and produce accounts that are true and fair by ensuring completeness, transparency and the faithful representation of events and transactions.

I have a problem with the finance director of Charlie. I would argue that the setting up of Henry and the suggestion of its non consolidation looks like an attempt at off balance sheet finance, an attempt to hoodwink and deceive the users of the group accounts. If this is the case such behaviour is surely unethical as it shows a lack of integrity. If the finance director genuinely thought that the appropriate accounting treatment of Henry was as a simple investment then this shows an ignorance of international accounting standards and incompetence. Either way it is unethical, as ethical behaviour by accountants assumes integrity and competence.

Question Kenya

Nairobi is a 75% subsidiary of Kenya that was acquired six months ago.

Where the subsidiary is acquired during the year only the post acquisition profits can be consolidated so time apportionment is necessary.

Statements of comprehensive income

	Kenya	Nairobi
Income statement	**$m**	**$m**
Revenue	10,000	1,000
Cost of sales	(2,000)	(200)
Gross profit	8,000	800
Operating costs	(1,500)	(450)
Profit before tax	6,500	350
Tax	(2,500)	(150)
Profit for the year	4,000	200
Other comprehensive income		
Revaluation gain	1,000	100
Total comprehensive income	5,000	200

Share capital of Nairobi ($1)	Fair value of the net assets at acquisition	Fair value of the NCI at acquisition	Cost of the investment in Nairobi
$m	**$m**	**$m**	**$m**
100	600	250	1,000

1 Nairobi was acquired on the basis that Kenya would pay the shareholders of Nairobi $1,000m two years after the date of the acquisition. In preparing its accounts Kenya has recorded the investment and the liability at $1,000m. The relevant discount rate per six months is 4%.

The recording of the investment has to be corrected – i.e. the deferred consideration discounted, which will also create an extra finance cost.

2   One month prior to the year-end Nairobi sold goods to Kenya for $100m.

The inter-company transaction must be eliminated from both sales and cost of sales. There appears to be no need for a purp.

3   On the acquisition of Nairobi a fair value adjustment arose on the plant of Nairobi. The plant had a remaining useful life of five years and is depreciated on a straight-line basis down to a nil residual value. The fair value adjustment had not been incorporated into the accounting records of the subsidiary.

More depreciation – more cost of sales.

4   Nairobi has not issued any shares since the date of acquisition and had no reserves other than accumulated profits at acquisition. Goodwill is to be calculated gross. Nairobi is a separate cash generating unit and at the year end has a recoverable amount of $900m. The trading profits of Nairobi are deemed to accrue evenly through out the year. At the start of the accounting period i.e. one year ago the accumulated profits of Nairobi were $300m.

Impairment review required and the loss will impact on NCI.

5   The revaluation gain of $100m Nairobi has included in other comprehensive income arose from the revaluation of land at the year-end i.e. the gain has arisen since the date of acquisition.

As the gain arose in the post acquisition period this can be cross cast without time apportionment.

Required

Prepare the consolidated statement of comprehensive income for the Kenya Group.

recap

on the group statement of comprehensive income

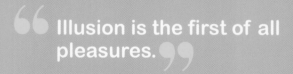

Illusion is the first of all pleasures.

What's new?

Absolutely nothing!

Let's take this opportunity to recap on the key messages when preparing group statements of comprehensive income and to look at some new useful proformas.

🔑 Key messages

- The income and expenses of the parent and subsidiary are basically cross cast.

- If the subsidiary has been acquired during the year then on consolidation its results will require time apportionment on a line by line basis.

- Group revenue and group cost of sales will be reduced to the extent of inter-company trading.

- Group cost of sales will be increased by the purp on unsold inventory that has been subject to an inter-company sale.

- Group cost of sales will be increased by any additional depreciation on fair value adjustments on the subsidiary's assets at acquisition.

- Group cost of sales will be increased by any impairment losses arising at the year-end.

- Group investment income and finance costs will be reduced to the extent of interest on inter-company loans.

- The finance costs should reflect any unwinding of the discount on deferred consideration.

- Group investment income should not include any inter-company dividend income that the parent has accounted as receivable from the subsidiary.

- The NCI in the subsidiary's profits will be adjusted to reflect the purp (if the subsidiary is the seller) the additional depreciation charge and the impairment loss (if goodwill has been calculated gross).

- The other comprehensive income of the parent and the subsidiary are cross cast, subject to possible time apportionment.

- The NCI in the subsidiary's total comprehensive income is the aggregate of the NCI in the subsidiary's profit and the NCI in the subsidiary's other comprehensive income.

Statement of comprehensive income

Where the subsidiary has been acquired during the year only its post acquisition results will be consolidated on a line by line basis.

Revenue	Parent plus subsidiary.	Less the inter-company sale	
Cost of sales	Parent plus subsidiary.	Less the inter-company sale	Plus the purp. Plus the depreciation on the FVA. Plus the impairment loss.
Distribution costs	Parent plus subsidiary.		
Administration expenses	Parent plus subsidiary.		
Exceptional gain	Parent plus subsidiary.		
Investment income	Parent plus subsidiary.	Less the inter-company interest receivable.	Less the parent's dividend income from the subsidiary.
Finance costs	Parent plus subsidiary.	Less the inter-company interest payable.	Plus any unwinding of the discount on deferred consideration.
Tax	Parent plus subsidiary.		
Other comprehensive income			
Revaluation gains	Parent plus subsidiary.		

The profit for the year is split between the parent and the NCI (see working below).

The total comprehensive income is split between the parent and NCI (see working below).

Extra standard workings applicable for the group statement of comprehensive income.

Group cost of sales

	$
Parent	X
Subsidiary (time apportion if necessary)	X
Less the inter-company purchase	(X)
Plus the purp (who ever is the seller)	X
Plus the additional depreciation on FVA (time apportion if necessary)	X
Plus the impairment loss	X
	X

NCI in the subsidiary's profits

	$
NCI % of the subsidiary's profits as given	X
Less the NCI % of depreciation on the FVA	X
Less the NCI % of the purp (subsidiary is seller)	X
Less the NCI % of the impairment loss (gross goodwill)	X
	X

NCI in the subsidiary's total comprehensive income

	$
NCI % of the subsidiary's profit (as above)	X
NCI % of the subsidiary's other comprehensive income	X
	X

section 5

Introducing associates, investments and joint ventures

chapter 13
Associates

What's new?

So far we have considered consolidating subsidiary companies into the group accounts. Subsidiaries are those companies that are controlled by the parent, that is to say the parent owns a majority of the shares, so it is assumed that the parent has a dominant influence over the subsidiary.

Where instead of dominant influence, the parent company has significant influence over another then that company is said to be an associate undertaking.

Significant influence means that the parent (investing company) is able to affect the operating and financial policies of the associate, e.g. the associate's dividend policy. The investing company having one director appointed to a board of say three directors would be good evidence of significant influence. However in questions and exam situations, unless it is very clearly indicated otherwise, it is assumed that associate status exists where there is a holding of 20% or more of the shares (or voting rights) and it is not a subsidiary.

Associates are consolidated into the group accounts using equity accounting. This method means that the associate will be represented by only one line in the group income statement and one line in the group statement of financial position.

Associates in the group statement of financial position

In the group statement of financial position the parent's share in the associate appears in the one line, investment in associate, within non current assets.

The carrying value of the associate is determined as:

Investment in associate		
Cost of investment	X	
Plus the parent's % of the post acquisition profits	X	Per w2 and w5
Less any impairment loss	(X)	
	X	

This shows that the original cost of the associate will rise with the share of the post acquisition profits that are recognised and that is a very useful principle to understand.

We have already seen this principle being applied in the calculation of the NCI in the net assets of a subsidiary.

The accumulated profits in w5 will include the parent's share of the post acquisition profits of the associate just like a subsidiary.

Associates in the group income statement

In the group income statement the parent's share of the profit of the associate will be presented in one line, income from the associate, immediately before group profit before tax. This is calculated as follows.

Income from associate	
Parent's % of the associate's profit for the year	X
Less any impairment loss in the current year	(X)
Less the parent's % of additional depreciation on fair value adjustments	(X)
	X

If the associate has any other comprehensive income the parent's % of that will appear in the other comprehensive income section of the statement of comprehensive income.

When consolidating associates into the group accounts:

- fair value adjustments on the associate's net assets are be accounted for
- current account balances between the associate and group companies remain as they cannot be eliminated
- sales and purchases between the associate and group companies remain as they cannot be eliminated
- the parent's dividend income from the associate will not be reported as group income
- there will be adjustments for the parent's share of the purps. The explanations for associate purps will be dealt with in detail below.

Well let's have a look at a question.

Example

The following are the summarised accounts of India, New and Delhi for the year ended 30 June 20X8.

Statements of financial position	India	New	Delhi
Non current assets	$	$	$
Tangible	90,000	80,000	60,000
Investment in New	92,000		
Investment in Delhi	30,000		
Current assets	88,000	50,000	10,000
	300,000	130,000	70,000
Share capital ($1 shares)	175,000	75,000	40,000
Accumulated profits	114,000	51,000	29,000
Equity	289,000	126,000	69,000
Liabilities	11,000	4,000	1,000
	300,000	130,000	70,000
Income statements			
Revenue	500,000	200,000	100,000
Operating costs	(400,000)	(140,000)	(60,000)
Profit before tax	100,000	60,000	40,000
Tax	(25,000)	(20,000)	(14,000)
Profit for the year	75,000	40,000	26,000

Additional information

1   India acquired 60,000 shares in New three years ago when the accumulated profits were $15,000.

2   At the date of acquisition the fair value of New's non current assets, which at that time had a remaining useful life of ten years, exceeded their book value by $5,000.

3   The group policy is to calculate the goodwill arising on the consolidation of a subsidiary gross with the NCI at fair value. At acquisition the fair value of the NCI of New was $24,000.

4   The impairment review reveals that no impairment losses have arisen.

5 India acquired 12,000 shares in Delhi three years ago when the accumulated profits were $5,000.

6 At the date of acquisition the fair value of Delhi's non-current assets, which at that time had a remaining useful life of four years, exceeded the book value by $20,000.

7 The impairment review reveals the recoverable amount of Delhi at their year-end to be $103,333.

Required:

Prepare the consolidated income statement and the consolidated statement of financial position for the India group.

As always the first thing to do is to sort out the group structure. Note that as India owns more than 20% but less than 50% of the shares of Delhi then Delhi can be assumed to be an associate and therefore equity accounted.

W1 Group structure

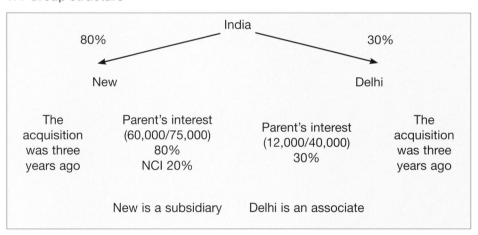

Let's set about doing the workings for the group statement of financial position.

In preparing w2 for net assets we shall calculate the net assets at acquisition and at the year-end for both the subsidiary New and the associate Delhi.

W2 Net assets

	New		Delhi	
	At acquisition $m	At year-end $m	At acquisition $m	At year-end $m
Share capital	75,000	75,000	40,000	40,000
Accumulated profits	15,000	51,000	5,000	29,000
Fair value adjustment	5,000	5,000	20,000	20,000
Less additional depreciation	———	(1,500)	———	(15,000)
	95,000	129,500	65,000	74,000

The parent's % of the post acquisition profits of New, the subsidiary are represented by the increase in the net assets and will be taken to w5 (80% x (129,500 – 95,000)) = $27,600.

The parent's % of the post acquisition profits of Delhi, the associate are represented by the increase in the net assets and will be taken to increase the carrying value of the investment in the associate and to accumulated profits in w5 (30% x (74,000 – 65,000)) = $2,700.

New was acquired three years ago. The fair value adjustment of $5,000 at acquisition relates to an asset with a ten year life. The additional depreciation by the year-end is therefore $5,000 x 1/10 x 3 years = $1,500.

Delhi was acquired three years ago. The fair value adjustment of $20,000 at acquisition relates to asset with a four year life. The additional depreciation is therefore $20,000 x 1/4 x 3 years = $15,000.

There is an impairment review to be conducted on the associate. First however let's ascertain separately what the carrying amount of the associate is before the impairment review.

Investment in associate

		$
Cost of investment		30,000
Plus the parent's % of the post acquisition profits w2	(30% x 9,000)	2,700
		32,700

If there is no impairment loss then $32,700 will be the carrying value of the associate on the group statement of financial position. However following the impairment review it will be necessary to write it down to the recoverable amount.

Impairment review

		$
Carrying value of the associate		32,700
Recoverable amount	(30% x 103,333)	(31,000)
Impairment loss		1,700

The carrying value of the associate on the group statement of financial position will be $31,000 and there will be an impairment loss of $1,700 to be charged against group accumulated profits in w5. This impairment loss has arisen in the current year so it will also be taken into account when arriving at the income from the associate in the group income statement.

Investment in associate

		$
Cost of investment		30,000
Plus the parent's % of the post acquisition profits w2	(30% x 9,000)	2,700
Less the impairment loss		(1,700)
		31,000

W3 Goodwill

		$	$
Cost of the New investment		92,000	
Less the parent's % of the net assets at acquisition	(80% x 95,000)	(76,000)	
Goodwill (attributable to the parent)			16,000
Fair value of the NCI at acquisition		24,000	
Less the NCI % of the net assets at acquisition	(20% x 95,000)	(19,000)	
Goodwill (attributable to the NCI)			5,000
Gross goodwill at acquisition			21,000

Or

		$
Cost of the New investment		92,000
Fair value of the NCI at acquisition		24,000
Less 100% of the net assets at acquisition	(100% x 95,000)	(95,000)
Gross goodwill at acquisition		21,000

There is no impairment loss on the subsidiary's goodwill so it appears on the statement of financial position as an intangible asset.

W4 NCI

		$
NCI % of the net assets at year-end	(20% x 129,500)	25,900
Plus the goodwill attributable to the NCI		5,000
		30,900
Or		
Fair value of the NCI at acquisition		24,000
Plus the NCI % of the post acquisition profits w2	(20% x 34,500)	6,900
		30,900

W5 Accumulated profits

		$
Parent's accumulated profits		114,000
Less impairment loss on the associate Delhi		(1,700)
Plus the parent's % of the post acquisition profits of the subsidiary New w2	(80% x 34,500)	27,600
Plus the parent's % of the post acquisition profits of the associate Delhi w2	(30% x 9,000)	2,700
		142,600

Now we can prepare the group statement of financial position, remembering that the assets and liabilities that are cross cast are those of the parent and the subsidiary only, and the interest in the associate is represented in a single line as a non current asset investment.

India group statement of financial position

		$
Non current assets		
Goodwill	w3	21,000
Tangible	(90,000 + 80,000 plus the FVA 5,000 less the depreciation of 1,500	173,500
Investment in associate	w2	31,000
Current assets	(88,000 + 50,000)	138,000
		363,500
Ordinary shares ($1)		175,000
Accumulated profits	w5	142,600
Non controlling interest	w4	30,900
Equity		348,500
Liabilities	(11,000 + 4,000)	15,000
		363,500

Now we can prepare the group income statement for the year remembering that the income and expenses that are cross cast are those of the parent and the subsidiary only. The income from the associate will be dealt with in a single line – to be included immediately before the group profit before tax.

It will be necessary to bring into the group income statement the additional depreciation on the subsidiary's fair value adjustment. The additional depreciation and the impairment loss relating to the associate will be dealt with in the single line.

As the associate has been an associate for the entire year there is no need to time apportion its results.

W6 Income from associate

		$
Parent's % of the associate's profit for the year	(30% x 26,000)	7,800
Less the parent's % of the additional depreciation arising for the year	(30% x 5,000)	(1,500)
Less the impairment loss arising in the year		(1,700)
		4,600

W7 NCI in the subsidiary's profit for the year

		$
NCI % of the subsidiary's profits as given	(20% x 40,000)	8,000
Less the NCI % of the depreciation on FVA	(20% x 500)	(100)
		7,900

India group income statement

		$
Revenue	(500,000 + 200,000)	700,000
Operating costs	(400,000 + 140,000 + 500 being the additional depreciation for the year on the subsidiary's fair value adjustment (5,000 x $^1/_{10}$))	(540,500)
Operating profit		159,500
Income from associate	w6	4,600
Profit before tax		164,100
Tax	(25,000 + 20,000)	(45,000)
Profit for the year		119,100
Attributable to the parent	Balancing figure	111,200
Attributable to the NCI	w7	7,900
Profit for the year		119,100

» Double entry

In the India example we saw that using equity accounting means that in the group accounts the share of the post acquisition profits of the associate Delhi is recognised. Recognising profit increases assets. The carrying value of the associate in the group accounts will therefore be its original cost plus the share of the post acquisition retained profits.

In other words using equity accounting means that the carrying value of the associate every year will increase by the share of the associate's retained profits recognised in the period.

As every year the carrying value of the associate will increase in respect of the retained profits of the associate recognised in the group accounts, so will the group accumulated profits increase by the same amount.

This lends itself to being confirmed using double entry.

		$
Cost of investment		30,000
Plus the parent's % of the post acquisition profits w2	(30% x 9,000)	2,700
Less the impairment loss		(1,700)
		31,000

The parent's % of the post acquisition profits of the associate will represent both an increase in the profits and a rise in the asset of investment in associate.

The recognition of an increase in the investment is to increase an asset. When assets increase this is a DR.

The recognition of accumulated profits since acquiring the investment will increase accumulated profits. To increase profits is to record a CR.

DR	Investment in Associate	$2,700	
CR	Group accumulated profits		$2,700

The impairment loss of the associate will represent both a loss and a decrease in the carrying value of the associate.

The recognition of an impairment loss on the carrying value of the associate is to decrease profits (and therefore equity). When profits decrease this is a DR.

The recognition of an impairment loss on the carrying value of the associate is to decrease the asset. When assets decrease this is a CR.

DR	Group accumulated profits	$1,700	
CR	Investment in Associate		$1,700

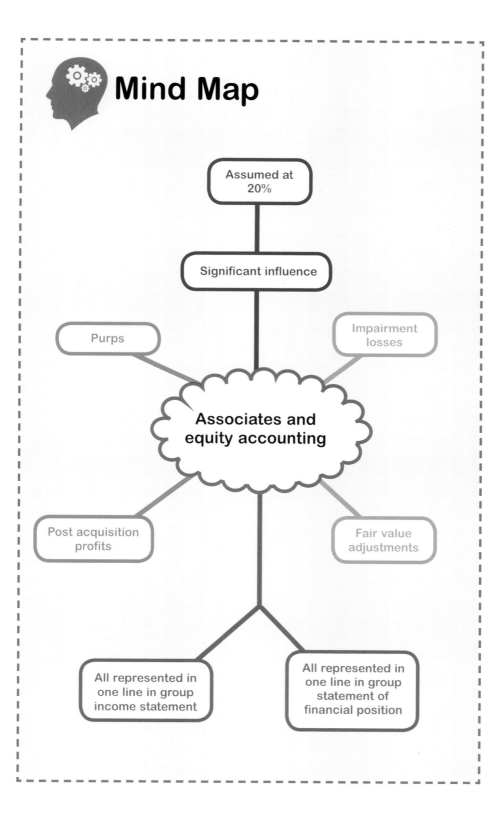

Mind Map

Assumed at 20%

Significant influence

Purps

Impairment losses

Associates and equity accounting

Post acquisition profits

Fair value adjustments

All represented in one line in group income statement

All represented in one line in group statement of financial position

✿ Technical corner

Defining an associate

IAS28 *Investments in Associates* defines an associate as " An enterprise in which an investor has significant influence but not control or joint control."

The key aspect to this definition of an associate revolves around the concept of significant influence. This is in turn defined as the "power to participate in the financial and operating policy decisions but not control them."

As we have seen a holding of 20% or more of the shares will presume that significant influence, and therefore associate status exists. If the holding is less than 20%, the investor will be presumed not to have significant influence unless such influence can be clearly demonstrated.

The existence of significant influence by an investor is usually evidenced in one or more of the following ways:

- representation on the board of directors
- participation in the policy-making process
- material transactions between the investor and the investee
- interchange of managerial personnel or
- provision of essential technical information
- potential voting rights.

Consider the status of the following investments

The River group of companies has recently acquired a number of investments and wishes to confirm how they should be accounted for in the group accounts.

(i)   Nile is a company with a share capital of ordinary shares that all carry equal voting rights. River has acquired 15% of the share capital and therefore voting rights. The board of directors of Nile comprises three executive directors and following the investment the River group has secured a seat on the board of directors. Nile is a local manufacturer and as the River group is an international group it will be able to assist Nile develop its export markets.

With Nile, whilst the assumption is that River's holding of 15% is not enough to give significant influence there is an opportunity to actually examine the circumstances of the investment to see if significant influence can be clearly demonstrated. It is noted that not only does River have board representation but also it is active in the provision of technical information that will help Nile expand its business. In conclusion River's investment Nile is to be accounted for as an associate and equity accounting applied.

(ii) Zambezi is a company with ordinary shares that all carry equal voting rights. River has acquired 25% of the ordinary share capital and therefore 25% of the voting rights. The board of directors of Zambezi comprises three executive directors but River has been unsuccessful in securing a seat on the board. The single largest shareholder in Zambezi who owns 60% of the shares appoints all three directors.

With Zambezi there is a holding of 25% and so an assumption that it is able to exercise significant influence. However a closer examination of the circumstance reveal that River has no board representation and that Zambezi has a majority shareholder. In these circumstances the 60% shareholder is in control of Zambezi and River has no influence. In conclusion River's investment in Zambezi is not an associate but a mere investment, so equity accounting is not applied.

Losses and equity accounting

On the group statement of financial position the carrying value of the investment in the associate is a positive figure amongst assets. It represents the investment plus the parent's share of the post acquisition profits and will year on year increase by the parent's share of the associate's retained profits.

If the associate reports a loss for the accounting period then the carrying value of the associate will be written down by the parent's share of those losses.

If the associate incurs substantial losses, such that the investment is written down to nil, thereafter additional losses would not continue to be recognised. The investment in the associate can only be an asset and not a liability.

However if the parent does have a legal or constructive obligation in respect of the associate's cumulative losses then the parent's share of losses continue to be recognised in group income and a provision for losses (a liability) is established.

Accounting for associate purps

Let me try and once for all nail the tricky issue of what adjustments are made when there is trading with associate companies and there is a need to account for a provision for unrealised profits. It is one of the most commonly asked questions by diligent students.

All the examples are based on a sale of $500 with a margin of 20% and so an original cost of $400 with all inventory being unsold i.e. the unrealised profit is $100. The group structure is as follows.

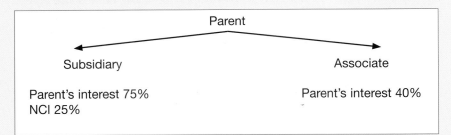

First let us remind ourselves how inter company trading and purp are dealt with between the parent and a 75% subsidiary and vice versa. All this should be familiar to you from Chapter 9 *Provision for unrealised profits.*

In the group income statement

Parent sells to subsidiary	$
Less revenue	500
Less cost of sales	500
Plus cost of sales	100

Subsidiary sells to parent	$
Less revenue	500
Less cost of sales	500
Plus cost of sales	100
Less NCI in the profit for the year (25% x 100)	25

In the group statement of financial position

Parent sells to subsidiary	$
Less inventory	100
Less accumulated profits	100

Subsidiary sells to parent	$
Less inventory	100
Less accumulated profits (75% x 100)	75
Less NCI in the net assets (25% x 100)	25

Now let's move on to consider what happens when one of the parties to the transaction is the associate. IAS28 *Investments in Associates* requires that the parent's share of the provision for unrealised profit has to be accounted for. In our example therefore a purp of 40% x $100 = $40 comes into play in both the group statement of financial position and the group income statement. What IAS28 *Investments in Associates* doesn't do is to precisely inform us how to account for the adjustment and over the years I have seen a variety of approaches used.

In my view it is only necessary to account for the purp arising from the transactions with the associate, and not the transactions themselves, and the approach I recommend is set out below.

In the group income statement where the associate is the seller then the purp of $40 should be deducted from the income from the associate to reduce profit, but if the parent or the subsidiary sells to the associate then increasing the cost of sales reduces profits.

In the group statement of financial position where the associate sells to the parent or the subsidiary the purp of $40 is deducted from the inventory as that is where the unsold inventory is, but if the parent or the subsidiary is the seller to the associate then the purp of $40 is deducted from the investment in the associate as that is where the inventory is.

Where the subsidiary is the seller then there will be an adjustment to the NCI.

This can all be resummarised as follows.

In the group income statement

Parent sells to associate		Subsidiary sells to the associate		Associate sells to parent		Associate sells to subsidiary	
Plus the cost of sales	40	Plus the cost of sales	40	Less income from associate	40	Less income from associate	40
		Less the NCI (25% x 40)	10				

In the group statement of financial position

Parent sells to associate		Subsidiary sells to associate		Associate sells to parent		Associate sells to subsidiary	
Less investment in associate	40	Less investment in associate	40	Less inventory	40	Less inventory	40
Less accumulated profits	40	Less accumulated profits (75% x 40)	30	Less accumulated profits	40	Less accumulated profits	40
		Less the NCI (25% x 40)	10				

However I have seen a number of alternative presentations being used, which in the absence of clear guidance in the standard are also acceptable.

For example one lecturer I know instructs his students always to deduct the purp away from the income from the associate and the investment in the associate regardless of whether the associate is the seller or the buyer. In this way cost of sales and inventory are never adjusted. This has the advantage of simplicity!

Another variation I have seen is always to deduct the purp away from the investment in the associate and never from inventory, perhaps on the grounds that a deduction from inventory of a share of a purp does not leave inventory at either the lower of cost or net realisable value.

Yet another way of adjusting is to reduce the group revenue by the parent's % of the sales (i.e. by 40% x $500 = $200) and the group cost of sales by the parent's % of the cost of sales (i.e. by 40% x $400 = $160) and in this way the group profit is automatically reduced by the purp of $40. Personally I do not favour this approach as it means that the group revenue is not actually reporting the sales of the group.

Question Sierra

Sierra acquired shares in Leone and Freetown exactly one year ago.

	Accumulated profits at acquisition	The total fair value of net assets at acquisition	Cost of investment	Number of ordinary shares acquired
	$	$	$	
Leone	30,000	150,000	100,000	45,000
Freetown	25,000	70,000	30,000	10,500

At the date of acquisition neither company had a revaluation reserve.

At the date of acquisition the fair value of the NCI of Leone was $63,000.

The summarised accounts of the three companies are as follows.

Statements of financial position

Non current assets	Sierra $	Leone $	Freetown $
Tangible	100,000	80,000	60,000
Investments in group companies	130,000		
Current assets			
Inventory	22,000	30,000	15,000
Receivables	58,000	10,000	2,000
Cash at bank	40,000	20,000	3,000
	350,000	140,000	80,000
Share capital ($1 shares)	100,000	75,000	35,000
Revaluation reserve	50,000	1,000	2,000
Accumulated profits	150,000	49,000	38,000
Equity	300,000	125,000	75,000
Liabilities	50,000	15,000	5,000
	350,000	140,000	80,000

Statements of comprehensive income

	Sierra	Leone	Freetown
Income statement	$	$	$
Revenue	500,000	200,000	150,000
Cost of sales	(300,000)	(140,000)	(110,000)
Gross profit	200,000	60,000	40,000
Administration costs	(50,000)	(10,000)	(10,000)
Operating profit	150,000	50,000	30,000
Interest receivable	10,000	Nil	4,000
Finance cost	Nil	(10,000)	Nil
Profit before tax	160,000	40,000	34,000
Tax	(60,000)	(20,000)	(19,000)
Profit for the year	100,000	20,000	15,000
Other comprehensive income			
Revaluation gains	10,000	1,000	2,000
Total comprehensive income for the year	110,000	21,000	17,000

1   The fair value adjustment in respect of Leone relates to tangible assets with a five year life. It is group policy to calculate goodwill valuing the non controlling interest at fair value at acquisition. Leone has been subject to an impairment review and no loss arises.

Having been given the fair value of the net assets at acquisition, the fair value adjustment will be the balancing figure in the net asset working.

2   The fair value adjustment in respect of Freetown relates to land. Freetown has been subject to an impairment review and no loss arises.

3   During the year Leone sold goods to Sierra for $10,000 at a margin of 40%. At the year end 80% of these goods had been sold on.

Leone looks like the subsidiary so the inter-company sale has to be eliminated and the purp will effect the NCI.

4   During the year Freetown sold goods to Sierra for $15,000 at a margin of 50%. At the year-end 20% of these goods remain unsold.

Freetown looks like the associate so the sale will stand and only the parent's % of the purp accounted for.

5   During the year Sierra advanced Leone substantial loans – most of which was repaid shortly before the year-end, but there remained a final balance of $5,000 outstanding at the year-end that is included in current assets and current liabilities. The interest charged in Leone's income statement and the interest receivable in Sierra's income statement represents interest on this loan.

The elimination of such inter-company transactions and balances has no impact on the NCI or the accumulated profits.

Required

Prepare the consolidated statement of comprehensive income and consolidated statement of financial position for Sierra group.

chapter 14
Investments and joint ventures

> " I always like to know everything about my new friends, and nothing about my old ones. "

What's new?

Investments

In addition to a parent company having in its group subsidiaries (which it controls) and associates (over which it has significant influence) there can be investments over which the parent has no influence.

These mere investments are assumed where the holding is less than 20% and will be accounted for in accordance with IAS39 *Financial Instruments: Recognition and Measurement*.[1] This standard requires that these investments are accounted for in the statement of financial position at fair value.

The gains and losses arising from changes in the fair value are normally recognised directly in equity and so also reported in other comprehensive income (when the investment is classified as "Available For Sale") but in certain circumstances can be recognised directly in the income statement (when the investment is classified as "Fair Value through Profit or Loss").

Joint Ventures

Yet another type of investment that can exist in a group context is that of the joint venture. A joint venture is a "contractual arrangement whereby two or more parties undertake an economic activity that is subject to joint control". In this situation the parent company becomes a venturer i.e. is a party to a joint venture and has joint control over that joint venture.

Having joint control means that no individual venturer has control. All venturers holding equal shares in the joint venture company is normally evidence of this in exam situations. For example, where there are two venturers then each will hold 50% of the shares in the joint venture company.

When a joint venture company is incorporated each venturer will contribute cash or other resources to the jointly controlled company in return for shares being issued. The contributions made are recognised in the venturer's individual accounts as the original cost in the investment of a joint venture. Where the assets transferred to the joint venture company are valued in excess of the carrying value then in substance the venturer has sold the asset to the joint venture company and in the group accounts a provision for unrealised profit is required.

So far so good, but IAS31 *Interests in Joint Ventures* unfortunately then allows two different accounting treatments for joint ventures in the group accounts.

- One acceptable accounting treatment is equity accounting (as we have seen used for associates). In this way the venturer's interest in the joint venture will be accounted for in the group statement of financial position and the group income statement in a single line.

1 For further information on IAS39 *Financial Instruments Recognition and Measurement* go to www.accaglobal.com/students/acca/exams/p2/technical_articles

- The other acceptable accounting treatment is proportionate consolidation. Under proportionate consolidation, the group statement of financial position will include the venturer's share of the assets that it controls jointly and its share of the liabilities for which it is jointly responsible. The group income statement will include its share of the income and expenses of the jointly controlled company.

Even more unfortunately IAS31 *Interests in Joint Ventures* then allows for the use of two different reporting formats for presenting proportionate consolidation.

- the venturer may combine its share of each of the assets, liabilities, income and expenses of the jointly controlled entity with the similar items, line by line, in its financial statements; or

- the venturer may include separate line items for its share of the assets, liabilities, income and expenses of the jointly controlled company in its financial statements.

Let's look at an example to see how proportionate consolidation works.

Example

The group accounts of Botswana have already been prepared with the exception of consolidating the parent's interest in the new joint venture company of Gaborone. Gaborone was incorporated three months ago by Botswana and another company each of whom contributed cash of $500 in return for being issued with 50% of the share capital of Gaborone.

Botswana wishes to consolidate the financial statements of Gaborone using proportionate consolidation on a line by line basis.

The financial statements of the Botswana group and Gaborone are as follows.

Statements of financial position	Botswana	Gaborone
	$	$
Non current assets		
Goodwill	8,000	Nil
Tangible	12,000	800
Investment in Gaborone	500	Nil
Current assets		
Inventory	6,000	250
Receivable	8,400	110
Cash at bank	12,500	130
	47,400	1,290
Share capital ($1 shares)	5,000	1,000
Share premium	5,000	Nil
Accumulated profits	19,400	190
Non controlling interest	8,000	Nil
Equity	37,400	1,190
Non current liabilities	4,000	60
Current liabilities	6,000	40
	47,400	1,290

	$	$
Income statements		
Revenue	100,000	900
Cost of sales	(55,000)	(250)
Gross profit	45,000	650
Operating costs	(20,000)	(300)
Profit before tax	25,000	350
Tax	(12,000)	(160)
Profit for the year	13,000	190
Attributable to the parent	10,500	
Attributable to the NCI	2,500	
Profit for the year	13,000	

Required

Prepare the group statement of financial position and the group income statement of the Botswana group.

In accounting for the joint venture the cost of the parent company's original investment in the joint venture and the share of the net assets acquired at acquisition as represented by the share capital and the pre acquisition reserves will be cancelled against each other to reveal any goodwill arising. I hope that this sounds familiar, and also a bit unnecessarily complicated, as because the joint venture was incorporated by Botswana there will be no pre acquisition profits and no goodwill arising in the first place. This is because no business was actually acquired so there is no existing reputation or customer relations!

Yes I can do w1 and show the group structure, but it will show Gaborone being a 50% joint venture and I can note that it has been a joint venture for three months and that these three months are the whole of its existence.

Yes I can do w2 to show the net assets of Gaborone at acquisition, but it will only comprise the share capital of $1,000 at the date of acquisition and net assets at the year-end of $1,190, having increased due to the profit made of $190 by Gaborone in the period.

Yes I can do w3 the goodwill calculation but the cost of investment of $500 is exactly going to cancel out against the parent's 50% of the share capital revealing no goodwill.

No I cannot do w4, as there is no NCI to calculate

And as for w5 the group's profits accumulated will simply increase by 50% of the post acquisition profit of $190 i.e. by $95.

But I am not inclined to do these workings at all. Instead I am going to move straight into the answer – aggregating 50% of each line of Gaborone's figures as I go, remembering to remove the investment in and the share capital of Gaborone.

Botswana group statement of financial position

Non current assets		$
Goodwill	as given	8,000
Tangible	(12,000 + (800 x 50%))	12,400
Current assets		
Inventory	(6,000 + (250 x 50%))	6,125
Receivable	(8,400 + (110 x 50%))	8,455
Cash at bank	(12,500 + (130 x 50%))	12,565
		47,545
Share capital ($1 shares)	Parent only	5,000
Share premium	Parent only	5,000
Accumulated profits	(19,400 + (190 x 50%))	19,495
Non controlling interest	as given	8,000
Equity		37,495
Non current liabilities	(4,000 + (60 x 50%))	4,030
Current liabilities	(6,000 + (40 x 50%))	6,020
		47,545

There are no barriers to moving straight on to the preparation of the group income statement. Note that although the joint venture Gaborone was only formed three months ago, all of its income is post acquisition, so there is no need for any time apportionment.

Botswana group income statement

		$
Revenue	(100,000 + (900 x 50%))	100,450
Cost of sales	(55,000 + (250 x 50%))	(55,125)
Gross profit		45,325
Operating costs	(20,000 + (300 x 50%))	(20,150)
Profit before tax		25,175
Tax	(12,000 + (160 x 50%))	(12,080)
Profit for the year		13,095
Attributable to the parent	Balancing figure	10,595
Attributable to the NCI	as given	2,500
Profit for the year		13,095

Accounting for joint ventures is straightforward enough not to warrant a question or a double entry example.

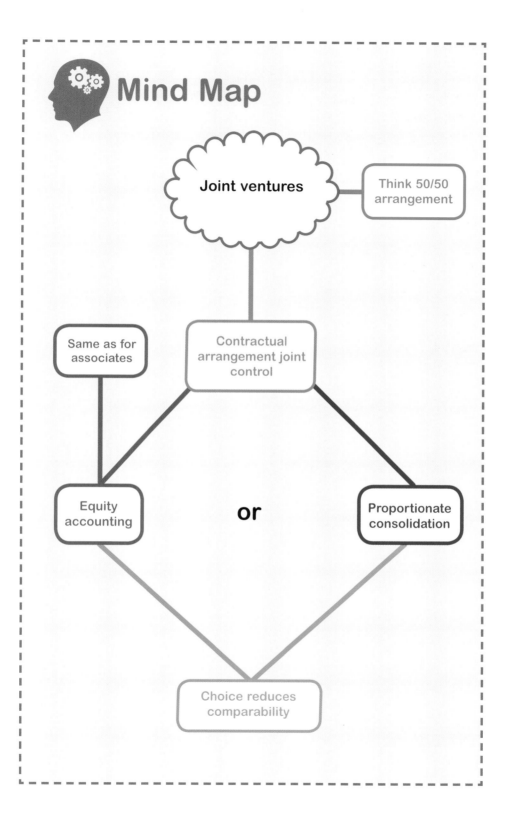

⚙ Technical corner

Critcisims of IAS31 *Interests in Joint Ventures*

IAS31 *Interests in Joint Ventures* has recently been the subject of some debate centred on the following areas.

- In defining a joint venture as "a contractual arrangement whereby two or more parties undertake an economic activity that is subject to joint control", IAS31 uses the legal form of the arrangement as the primary determinant of the accounting. But it should be the case that the accounting treatment should depend on the substance and not on the legal form.

- IAS31 gives a choice of accounting treatment of equity accounting or proportionate consolidation for interests in joint ventures. But it is a basic characteristic of useful information that information should be comparable. Having a choice of accounting treatments will naturally lead to inconsistency between companies and thus reduce the comparability of financial reports to the detriment of users.

- Proportionate consolidation leads to a conceptual problem as it is inconsistent with the IASB's own principles as laid out in its framework[2]. It is simply inappropriate to recognise assets, liabilities, income and expenses when the venturer is merely entitled to a share of the outcome of the underlying activities but not the assets and liabilities themselves. Therefore, it is argued, if the company has a share in the joint venture's output it should apply the equity method and consequently proportionate consolidation should be prohibited.

- However the elimination of proportionate consolidation will result in a loss of information for users as proportionate consolidation better enables users to project future cash flows whereas applying the equity method collapses all the information into one number.

- Further if proportionate consolidation is prohibited, the equity method will be applied for two very different types of investments: associates (in which the investor has only significant influence) and joint ventures (in which the investor has joint control).

---

2 The IASB's Framework for the Preparation and Presentation of Financial Statements describes the basic concepts by which financial statements are prepared. The Framework serves as a guide to the IASB in developing accounting standards. The Framework defines an asset as "a resource controlled by the enterprise as a result of past events and from which future economic benefits are expected to flow to the enterprise". A venturer in a joint venture does not have sole control over the assets in the joint venture and so should not be reporting them in the statement of financial position.

Exposure Draft 9 Joint Arrangements.[3]

In September 2007, the IASB published Exposure Draft 9 proposing to replace IAS31 *Interests In Joint Ventures* with a new standard to be titled Joint Arrangements.

The ED proposes a substance over form approach to joint arrangements rather than the legalistic approach taken by IAS31 and to prohibit proportionate consolidation.

It was originally planned that the new accounting standard would be issued in the second quarter of 2009, however the feedback on ED9 was that a majority of respondents were not supportive of the proposed changes. Accordingly in May 2009 the IASB delayed the issue of a new standard in order to have more time to consider the issues.

In ED9 the proposal was to define a joint arrangement as "a contractual arrangement whereby two or more parties undertake an economic activity together and share decision-making relating to that activity". Joint arrangements is an umbrella term including joint ventures and joint operations.

The following table summarises the accounting treatment proposed for joint ventures and joint arrangements under ED9.

	Characteristics	Ownership of assets	Summary of accounting required
Joint Venture	Joint arrangement that is jointly controlled by the venturers. Each venturer is entitled to a share of the outcome of the activities of the joint venture.	Venturers do not have rights to individual assets or responsibility for obligations of the venture.	Recognise the interest in the joint venture using equity accounting. Proportionate consolidation would not be permitted.
Joint Operation	Involves the use of the assets and other resources of the parties, often to manufacture and sell a product.	Each party generally owns its own assets that it uses to create the joint product.	Recognise controlled assets and incurred liabilities, expenses incurred and share of revenues and expenses from the sale of goods or services by the joint arrangement.

---

3   Exposure drafts are proposed accounting standards that are issued by the IASB for public comment.

recap

associates, investments and joint ventures

> 66 The only thing to do with good advice is pass it on. It is never any use to oneself. 99

What's new?

Absolutely nothing!

Let's take this opportunity to recap on the key messages when preparing group accounts and to look at some new useful proformas.

🔑 Key messages

- An associate is an entity over which the parent has significant influence.

- Significant influence is assumed when the parent has a holding of 20% or more of the shares but it is not a subsidiary or joint venture.

- Associates are consolidated using equity accounting.

- Equity accounting represents the parent's interest in the associate in a single line in the group income statement and the group statement of financial position.

- With equity accounting consolidation adjustments are made for fair value adjustments, impairment losses and purps, but inter-company sales and current accounts are not eliminated.

- Joint ventures are entities that the parent controls jointly by a contractual agreement with another party.

- Joint control is assumed when the parent has 50% of the shares and another party holds the other 50%.

- Joint ventures are consolidated in the group accounts using either equity accounting or proportionate consolidation.

Extra standard workings applicable with equity accounting

Group statement of financial position	
Investment in associate	
Cost of investment	X
Plus the parent's % of the post acquisition profits w2	X
Less the impairment loss	(X)
Less parent's % of the associate's purp (parent or subsidiary is seller)	(X)
	X

Group income statement	
Income from associate	
Parent's % of the associate's profit for the year	X
Less current year's impairment loss	(X)
Less the parent's % of additional depreciation on fair value adjustments	(X)
Less the parent's % of the associate purp (associate is seller)	(X)
	X

Recap on the relationships that a parent company can have, and the accounting treatment in the group accounts

0-20%	No influence assumed	Investment	Held at fair value
20-50%	Significant influence assumed	Associate	Equity accounting
50%	Joint control assumed	Joint venture	Proportionate consolidation or equity accounting
50-100%	Dominant influence assumed	Subsidiary	Acquisition accounting

The following group structure shows the range of relationships

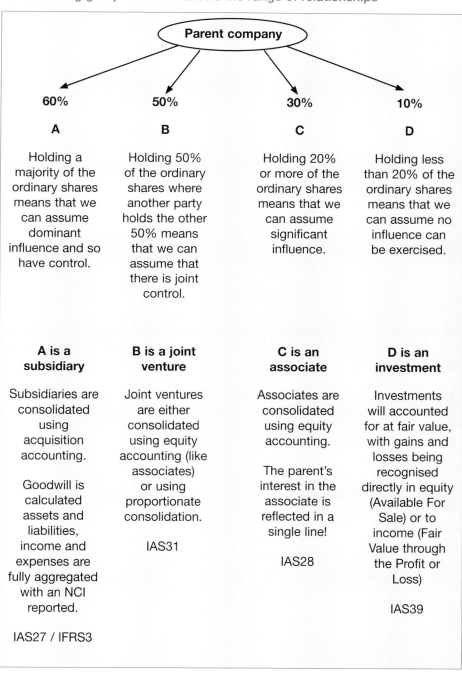

60%	**50%**	**30%**	**10%**
A	**B**	**C**	**D**
Holding a majority of the ordinary shares means that we can assume dominant influence and so have control.	Holding 50% of the ordinary shares where another party holds the other 50% means that we can assume that there is joint control.	Holding 20% or more of the ordinary shares means that we can assume significant influence.	Holding less than 20% of the ordinary shares means that we can assume no influence can be exercised.
A is a subsidiary	**B is a joint venture**	**C is an associate**	**D is an investment**
Subsidiaries are consolidated using acquisition accounting. Goodwill is calculated assets and liabilities, income and expenses are fully aggregated with an NCI reported. IAS27 / IFRS3	Joint ventures are either consolidated using equity accounting (like associates) or using proportionate consolidation. IAS31	Associates are consolidated using equity accounting. The parent's interest in the associate is reflected in a single line! IAS28	Investments will accounted for at fair value, with gains and losses being recognised directly in equity (Available For Sale) or to income (Fair Value through the Profit or Loss) IAS39

section 6

Advanced issues: changes in the group structure

chapter 15

Changes in the group structure due to buying more shares

66 There are only two things in life that are certain, death and taxes. 99

What's new?

In the examples we have looked at to date the parent company has achieved control by purchasing a single block of shares that immediately gives the parent a majority of the subsidiary's shares and therefore we have assumed control.

Of course it is possible (when accounting for subsidiaries) that the parent has purchased shares on different dates. At the time of the subsequent purchase of shares we need to examine the effect very carefully.

Parent achieves control – crossing the line of control - a step acquisition

Where the subsequent purchase of shares achieves control then the group has a new subsidiary. This represents a radical change in the group structure! A mere investment or perhaps an associate has now become a subsidiary. This is a significant economic event.

With this new status of subsidiary it is necessary to calculate the goodwill at that date and to consolidate the profits and net assets. Achieving control will be evidenced by the subsequent purchase of shares taking the cumulative holding to above 50%.

For example where the first investment in shares in the company is 15% and then later there is a 40% investment, the subsequent investment achieves control and makes the investment a new subsidiary as it takes the cumulative interest from 15% to 55%.

Parent acquires NCI - decrease in the NCI

Where the subsequent purchase is of shares in an existing subsidiary, then the impact on the group accounts is minimal. All that is really happening is that the parent is buying out the NCI i.e. there is a decrease in the NCI.

Before the purchase there was a subsidiary and afterwards it remains a subsidiary. This means the additional purchase of shares is not really a significant economic event.

For example where the first investment in shares in the company is 60%, and then later there is a 40% investment, the subsequent investment does not achieve control, as it was already a subsidiary. The NCI of 40% is reduced to nil, as the 60% subsidiary now becomes 100% owned.

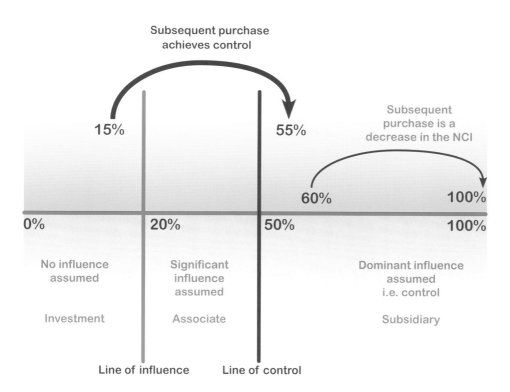

The distinction is very important to make, as the accounting for the subsequent purchase will vary depending on whether it achieves control, and thus a new subsidiary is formed, or simply, is an acquisition of the NCI.

Parent's subsequent investment achieves control (step acquisition)

When the parent achieves control with a subsequent investment it has a new subsidiary, and that is when the goodwill of the subsidiary is calculated. This is a significant economic event. The previous holding is revalued to fair value, with the gain (or possibly loss) being recognised in the income statement. This now means that all the consideration paid by the parent is recorded at fair value at the date control is achieved. In substance it is as if the parent has sold the original holding, recorded the gain or loss arising and then reacquired it!

Like with any acquisition if this occurred mid year then in the group income statement it would be necessary to time apportion the results of the subsidiary from the date of acquisition.

To summarise in order to calculate goodwill with a step acquisition, it will be necessary to:

- revalue the first investment
- take the gain on the revaluation to income statement
- both investments are now at fair value at acquisition ie. the date control is achieved.

Example: Step acquisition

Several years ago Ryland acquired a 15% investment in Susan for $10,000 and that remains carried at cost in Ryland accounts. This investment now has a fair value of $30,000. Ryland has just made a further acquisition of 40% of the shares in Susan for $100,000. The net assets of Susan have now been determined at $60,000 and the fair value of the non controlling interest at $80,000.

Required

Calculate the gross goodwill arising on the acquisition of Susan.

As a result of the subsequent purchase of shares Ryland has obtained control of Susan as its shareholding has moved from 15% to 55%. The addition of the newly acquired 40% means the cumulative holding crosses the line of control and thus Susan becomes a 55% subsidiary with an NCI of 45%.

The group structure in working 1 will look like this

Susan is now a subsidiary and goodwill must be calculated by reference to the investments being at the fair value at the date of the acquisition (date control is achieved). The original investment is revalued.

	$
Fair value of the original investment	30,000
Less the cost of the original investment	(10,000)
Gain to the income statement	20,000

Now we can add the fair values of the investments together to get the total cost of the investments to calculate goodwill at the date of control was achieved over the subsidiary. In this example there is no need to do w2 net assets, as the figure is given, so we can proceed straight to w3 goodwill

w3 Goodwill

		$	$
Fair value of the original investment		30,000	
Fair value of the consideration given for the second investment		100,000	
Cost of investment			130,000
Less the parent's % of the net assets at acquisition	(55% x 60,000)		(33,000)
Goodwill (attributable to the parent)			97,000
Fair value of the NCI at acquisition		80,000	
Less the NCI % of the net assets at acquisition	(45% x 60,000)	(27,000)	
Goodwill (attributable to the NCI)			53,000
Gross goodwill at acquisition			150,000

Alternatively the gross goodwill can be calculated as follows

		$
Fair value of the original investment		30,000
Fair value of the consideration given for the second investment		100,000
Fair value of the NCI at acquisition		80,000
Less 100% of the net assets at acquisition	(100% x 60,000)	(60,000)
Gross goodwill at acquisition		150,000

Subsequent investment decreases the NCI

From the perspective of the group accounts where there is a purchase of more shares in a subsidiary then it is not an acquisition of a new subsidiary but rather a purchase of the NCI.

As such it is a transaction within equity as the NCI is now regarded as part of equity. A difference arises where the cost (cash outflow) of the subsequent investment is different from the reduction in the NCI.

- There is no change in the goodwill asset.
- No gain or loss arises.
- A difference will arise that will be taken to an equity reserve.

	$
Cash paid out for the subsequent investment	X
Transfer from NCI of a proportion of the NCI (to decrease the NCI)	X
Difference to an equity reserve	X

Where the cost of the subsequent investment exceeds the decrease in the NCI then the difference taken to reserves will be a decrease in reserves and equity.

Where the cost of the subsequent investment is less than the decrease in the NCI then the difference taken to equity will be an increase in reserves and equity.

Example: reduction in the NCI

Truran, the parent has owned 80% of the subsidiary for many years. The NCI in the subsidiary is currently measured at $100,000.

(i) Truran, the parent has just acquired all the remaining shares paying $90,000.

(ii) Truran, the parent has acquired 5% of the shares reducing the NCI to 15% paying $80,000.

Required

Calculate the difference arising that will be taken to equity in both situations

(i) First let us consider what happens when all the NCI is purchased.

		$
Cash paid out		90,000
Transfer from NCI decreasing the NCI	(20/20 x 100,000)	100,000
Difference to equity (increase)		10,000

The NCI was 20% but the purchase of the remaining shares has reduced the NCI to nil ie. the cash paid out has purchased 20/20 of the NCI.

The cash paid out reduces the assets in the top half of the statement of financial position. Where this is less than the reduction in the NCI (bottom half of the statement of financial position) then the difference will be taken to reserves as an increase to the reserves (equity).

Another way of thinking about this is to consider the NCI as a liability (though that is rather dangerous as NCI is not a liability). Then we have paid out only $90,000 to settle a liability of $100,000 and so have a gain of $10,000 and gains will increase equity. Of course NCI is not a liability, it is part of equity and no gain or loss arises on a decrease in the NCI as it is transaction within equity – but all that might help explain why the $10,000 is an increase to equity!

(ii) Secondly let us consider what happens when only part of the NCI is bought out.

		$
Cash paid out		80,000
Transfer from NCI decreasing the NCI	(5/20 x 100,000)	25,000
Difference to equity (decrease)		55,000

The NCI was 20% but the purchase of the remaining of shares has reduced the NCI by 5% to 15%. The cash paid out has purchased some of the NCI – in this case 5/20. The NCI after the acquisition will be $75,000.

The difference of $55,000 taken to equity will reduce reserves. The cash paid out has reduced assets by more than the reduction in equity and therefore to make the statement of financial position balance equity needs to be further reduced.

» Double entry

In the example where Ryland's subsequent investment in Susan achieved control the revaluing of the original investment can be thought of in double entry terms.

The original investment is being revalued upwards by $20,000. This has the effect of increasing the asset of investment. To increase an asset is a DR.

By increasing the asset this also has the effect of recognising a gain. This gain is recorded in the income statement. Recording a gain is a CR.

DR	Investment	$20,000	
CR	Income statement		$20,000

In the first example of Truran's decrease in the NCI the difference arising on the decreases in the NCI can be thought of in double entry terms.

By reducing NCI equity is decreased. To record a decrease in equity is a DR.

By paying out cash this is a reduction in assets. To record a decrease in an asset is a CR.

The difference is then a balancing figure – which in this case happens to be a CR so will increase the reserves.

DR	NCI	$100,000	
CR	Cash		$90,000
CR	Equity reserve (balancing figure)		$10,000

In the Truran example, in the second situation, the decreases in the NCI can also be thought of in double entry terms.

By reducing NCI equity is decreased. To record a decrease in equity is a DR.

By paying out cash this is a reduction in assets. To record a decrease in an asset is a CR.

The difference is then a balancing figure – which in this case happens to be a DR so will decrease the reserves.

DR	NCI	$25,000	
CR	Cash		$80,000
DR	Equity reserve (balancing figure)	$55,000	

Mind Map

Buying more shares

Crossing the line of control / step acquisition

Creates a new subsidiary

Significant economic event

Revalue prior investment with gain to income

Start acquisition accounting

In an existing subsidiary

Reduces the NCI

No gain or loss arises

Difference to reserves

Goodwill asset remains the same

Technical corner

Revaluation of investments

IAS27 *Consolidated and Separate Financial Statements* requires that in the parent's / investor's individual financial statements, investments in subsidiaries, associates, and jointly controlled entities are accounted for either at cost; or at fair value in accordance with IAS39 *Financial Instruments: Recognition and Measurement*. If the investment does not confer any influence then it should be carried at fair value.

Where investments are measured at fair value they can be classified as "Available For Sale" so that revaluation gains are recognised by the parent in equity (revaluation reserve), but technically it is possible for the investment to have been classified as "Financial Assets at Fair Value through Profit or Loss" in which case the revaluation gains are recognised in income by the parent.

This means that where the parent company in its individual accounts has opted to revalue its investment in the subsidiary a consolidation adjustment will be necessary to reverse out the revaluation in order to have the investment at its original cost at acquisition in order to determine goodwill.

This also means that on step acquisitions the revaluation of the prior investment raises issues to do with the realisation of previously recognised gains and differences between the gain recognised by the group and the gain recognised by the parent.

Step acquisition, when an investment becomes a subsidiary, accounting for the revaluation of the prior investment

This is what we saw in the example of Ryland and Susan, only in that example the original investment in Susan was still carried at the cost of $10,000 by both the parent individual company and the group, so when it was revalued to $30,000 there was a straight forward gain to be recognised in both incomes of $20,000.

Now as a simple investment, Ryland really should have carried the investment in Susan at fair value and if it had been classified as "Available For Sale" the gain of $20,000 would have already have been recognised in a revaluation reserve. In such circumstances on the step acquisition the revaluation reserve is deemed to become realised and is recycled to both income statements where it is reported, presumably, as an exceptional gain. From the perspective of the statement of financial position the revaluation reserve of $20,000 is moved into accumulated profits.

Step acquisition, when an associate becomes a subsidiary, accounting for the revaluation of the prior investment

Where the step acquisition results in an associate being reclassified as a subsidiary (e.g. a prior holding of 40% followed by a purchase of 25%) then in the parent's individual accounts the investment will be at cost or fair value whilst in the group accounts equity accounting will have been applied.

From the perspective of the group accounts if the step acquisition occurs mid way through an accounting period then the preparing the group income statement will be quite tricky. First there will be a need to time apportion the results of an associate using equity accounting up to the date of the step acquisition and then also to time apportion the results of the subsidiary thereafter. In addition the gain to be reported in group income statement on the revaluation of the prior holding following the step acquisition will be the difference between the fair value at that date and the carrying value of the associate using equity accounting.

In preparing the group accumulated profits (w5) for the group statement of financial position it may be necessary to update the parent company profits for the gain on the revaluation of the prior holding following the step acquisition but this will be the difference between the fair value at that date and the carrying value of the investment in the parent's individual accounts plus the recycling of any gain previously recognised by the parent company in equity (revaluation reserve).

Question France

France has just acquired a second block of shares in Paris and as result Paris is now a subsidiary of France. Details of the first purchase of shares are as follows.

This means it is a step acquisition.

Share capital of Paris ($1)	Numbers of share acquired last year by France	Cost of that initial investment by France $
20,000	3,000	6,000

Details at the date of the second purchase of shares are as follows.

Fair value of the initial investment in Paris $	Number of extra shares acquired by France in Paris	Cost of the subsequent investment $	Fair value of the net assets of Paris $	Fair value of the non controlling interest in Paris $
9,000	12,000	25,000	10,000	9,000

Required

Calculate the gross goodwill arising.

Question Malaysia

Malaysia the parent company has owned 60% of the subsidiary KL for many years. The NCI in KL the subsidiary is currently measured at $100,000. Malaysia has just acquired a further 20% of the share capital in KL for $70,000.

It was a subsidiary so the second purchase reduces the NCI.

Required

Calculate the difference arising that will be taken to equity.

Question Greece

The statements of financial position of two companies are as follows.

	Greece $m	Athens $m
Non current assets		
Tangible	100	550
Investment in Athens	800	
Current assets	300	450
	1,200	1,000
Ordinary shares ($1)	100	200
Accumulated profits	350	500
Equity	450	700
Non current liabilities	450	270
Current liabilities	300	30
	1,200	1,000

Additional information.

1 Greece has acquired shares in Athens on three separate occasions, details of which are as follows.

	Shares acquired	Cost $m	Reserves $m
Three years ago	30m	150	100
Two years ago	80m	300	150
One year ago	90m	350	250
Total	200m	800	N/A

It looks like Athens became a subsidiary two years ago, and then one year ago there has been a purchase of the NCI shares which would have created a difference in reserves.

2   Greece has not revalued its investments in Athens and so they remain at cost. Two years ago the original investment costing $150m had a fair value of $160m.

3   The policy of the group is to calculate goodwill gross. Two years ago the fair value of the goodwill attributable to the NCI was $32.5m.

The goodwill attributable to the NCI is given so does not have to be calculated.

Required

Prepare the consolidated statement of financial position for the Greece group.

Tip – in addition to determining net assets when control was achieved (for goodwill) and at the year-end also determine net assets one year ago (for post acquisition profits).

chapter 16

Changes in the group structure due to selling shares

> **Every portrait that is painted with feeling is a portrait of the artist, not of the sitter.**

What's new?

So far we have only considered an expanding group where shares are purchased in companies that join the group. Of course in reality – and exam questions - there will come a time when shares in a subsidiary are sold.

In the group accounts the accounting for the sale of shares in a subsidiary will depend on whether or not the transaction causes control to be lost i.e. is a disposal of a subsidiary which is then derecognised, or whether after the sale the control is still maintained i.e. only represents an increase in the NCI.

Sale means the parent loses control of the subsidiary - disposal	Sale means the parent still retains control - an increase in the NCI
Where a sale of shares takes the holding of the parent to below 50%, control is lost and this means that the group has disposed of the subsidiary. This is a significant economic event.	Where the sale of shares in an existing subsidiary is such that the control is still maintained then the impact on the group accounts is minimal.
This also represents a radical change in the group structure! The sale may represent a total disposal or what was a subsidiary may now become a mere investment (if the residual holding is less than 20%) or perhaps an associate (if the residual holding is in excess of 20%).	Before the sale there was a subsidiary and afterwards it remains a subsidiary. Therefore this sale of shares is not a significant economic event. All that is really happening is that there is an increase in the NCI because there has been a partial transfer of the net assets and goodwill to the NCI.
For example where there is a 80% subsidiary and there is a sale of half of the holding leaving the parent with a residual interest of 40% then control has been lost as the residual holding of the parent dips below 50%. The relationship therefore changes from a subsidiary to an associate.	For example where there is an 80% subsidiary and there is a sale of one quarter of the holding leaving the parent holding 60%, then there has been no disposal of a subsidiary as control has been maintained. All that has happened is that the NCI has increased from 20% to 40%.

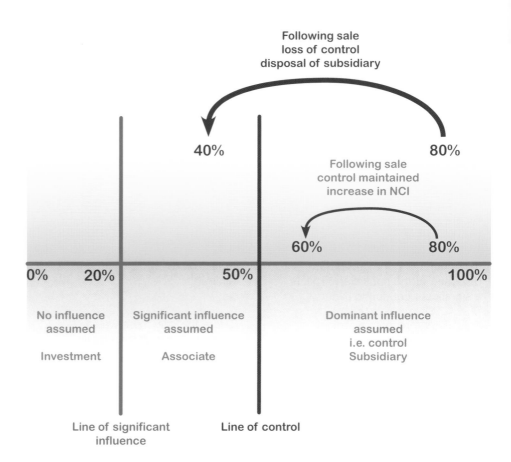

Following sale
loss of control
disposal of subsidiary

40%   80%

Following sale
control maintained
increase in NCI

60%   80%

0%   20%   50%   100%

No influence   Significant influence   Dominant influence
assumed   assumed   assumed
                                                                    i.e. control
Investment   Associate   Subsidiary

Line of significant   Line of control
influence

The distinction is very important to make, as the accounting for the sale of shares will vary depending on whether control has been lost so that there has been a disposal of a subsidiary or whether it is simply a transfer of some of the net assets and goodwill to the NCI.

This is similar in principle to the decrease in the NCI in Chapter 15 *Changes in the group structure due to buying more shares*

From the perspective of the group accounts where there is a sale of shares but control is maintained, as the parent's holding does not fall below 50%, this is not a disposal of a subsidiary rather it is an increase in the NCI. The group has not sold a subsidiary rather the parent has transferred a stake in the net assets and goodwill of the subsidiary to the NCI.

As such it is a transaction within equity. A difference arises where the proceeds received from the sale of the shares is different from the increase in the NCI.

- There is no change in the goodwill asset.
- No gain or loss arises.
- A difference will arise that will be taken to equity.

The difference is ascertained as follows.

	$
Cash received from the sale of part of the investment	X
Transfer to NCI a % of net assets and goodwill (to increase the NCI)	X
Difference to an equity reserve	X

Where the proceeds received exceeds the increase in the NCI then the difference taken to reserves will be an increase in reserves and equity.	Where the proceeds received are less than the increase in the NCI then the difference taken to reserves will be a decrease in reserves and equity.

Example

Rowe the parent has owned 80% of the subsidiary for many years. At present the net assets of the subsidiary are $300,000, the NCI $80,000 and the gross goodwill $220,000.

(i)   Rowe has just sold one quarter of the shares owned for $110,000 and thus reduces its holding from 80% to 60%.

(ii) Rowe has just sold shares for $20,000 to reduce its holding by 5% to 75%.

Required

Calculate the difference arising that will be taken to equity

(i)   First let us consider the impact when the shares are sold reducing the parent's interest to 60% and the NCI increasing to 40%

As a result of the sale of these shares the subsidiary remains a subsidiary but the NCI of 20% has increased to 40%. That is not to say that the amount of the NCI will have doubled rather the NCI will increase by 20% of the net assets and goodwill being sold.

		$
Cash proceeds received		110,000
Transfer to NCI increasing the NCI	(20% x (300,000 + 220,000))	104,000
Difference to equity (increase)		6,000

The NCI after the sale will be $184,000 ($80,000 + $104,000).

The cash received increases the assets in the top half of the statement of financial position. Where this is more than the increase in the NCI (bottom half of the statement of financial position) then the difference will also have to be taken to reserves as an increase to the reserves (equity).

Dangerous though it is to write this – if you think of the NCI as a liability – then we have received $110,000 and increased a liability by $104,000 and so have a gain of $6,000 and gains will increase equity. Of course NCI is not a liability, it is part of equity and no gain or loss arises on a increase in the NCI as it is transaction within equity – but all that might help explain why the $6,000 is an increase to equity!

(ii) Now let us consider the situation where the shares sold reduce the parent's interest by 5% and so the NCI increases to 25%. The cash being received by the parent from the NCI is for 5% of the net assets and the goodwill. The NCI will be increased and a difference taken to reserves.

		$
Cash proceeds received		20,000
Transfer to NCI increasing the NCI	(5% x (300,000 + 220,000))	26,000
Difference to equity (decrease)		6,000

The NCI after the sale will be $106,000 ($80,000 + $26,000).

The cash received increasing the net assets of the group is less than the increase in the NCI so the difference will be a decrease to the reserves (equity).

Disposals i.e. the sale means control is lost

In the group statement of financial position following the disposal of a subsidiary then the accounts of the former subsidiary are not consolidated as at the year-end there it is not a subsidiary as there is no control.

It is in the group income statement for the year that all the action takes place! Having made a disposal of the subsidiary there will a gain or loss arising and the results of the subsidiary will still need to be consolidated up to the date of disposal (i.e. time apportionment). This will be presented in a single line if the disposal of the subsidiary represents a discontinued operation per IFRS5 *Non-current Assets Held for Sale and Discontinued Operations* otherwise it will be consolidated on a line by line basis.

The gain (or loss) arising on disposal will be regarded as exceptional since the sale of the subsidiary can only take place once and it is likely to be material. The exceptional gain (or loss) will be presented on the face of the group income statement after the operating profit.

The gain on disposal is the difference between what comes into the group on the disposal of the subsidiary (in the form of the proceeds and any residual holding) and what leaves the group (in the form of the net assets, goodwill and the NCI).

The exceptional gain is determined in the following proforma

Gain to group on disposal of a subsidiary	$
Sale proceeds	X
Less all the net assets of the subsidiary at the date of disposal	(X)
Less all the goodwill remaining at the date of disposal	(X)
Plus all the NCI at the date of disposal	X
Plus the fair value of any residual holding	X
Gain to the group	X

Because the group no longer has a subsidiary it is appropriate to match the sale proceeds against the removal of all traces of the subsidiary from the accounts by removing all of the subsidiary's net assets, all its goodwill and all the NCI as well. Having removed all traces of the subsidiary if the group retains a residual holding (whether an associate or investment) then that residual holding is reintroduced at fair value.

Example

Parent purchased 60% of the shares in Baggs and the goodwill that arose on acquisition was $60,000. No goodwill has been impaired in the group accounts. At present the net assets of Baggs are $110,000 and the NCI is $22,000.

Required

Calculate the gain arising to the group on disposal of Baggs.

(i) The parent sells the entire holding for $400,000.

(ii) The parent has sold 25% leaving it with a holding of 35%. The proceeds received are $300,000 and the fair value of the residual holding of 35% is $25,000.

(i) Following the sale of all the shares Baggs is no longer a subsidiary. All the net assets, goodwill and NCI must therefore be derecognised from the group statement of financial position.

Gain to the group on the disposal of Baggs

	$
Sale proceeds	400,000
Less all the net assets of the subsidiary at the date of disposal	(110,000)
Less all the goodwill remaining at the date of disposal	(60,000)
Plus all the NCI at the date of disposal	22,000
Plus the fair value of any residual holding	Nil
Gain to the group	252,000

(ii) In the second situation by selling 25% of the shares that it owns in Baggs control is lost as the remaining holding of 35% is below the threshold (to assume control) of 50%.

Again having lost control all the net assets, goodwill and NCI must be derecognised from the group statement of financial position, as it is no longer a subsidiary. Having removed all traces the fair value of the residual holding is reintroduced at fair value.

Gain to the group on the disposal of Baggs

	$
Sale proceeds	300,000
Less all the net assets of the subsidiary at the date of disposal	(110,000)
Less all the goodwill remaining at the date of disposal	(60,000)
Plus all the NCI at the date of disposal	22,000
Plus the fair value of the residual holding	25,000
Gain to the group	177,000

These are relatively simple examples as all the data needed has already been gathered. In questions we may have to work:

- net assets at the date of disposal – and we shall use our w2 format of share capital + reserves + FVA

- goodwill at the date of disposal – and we shall use w3 format of goodwill at acquisition less any impairment loss

- NCI at the date of disposal – and we shall use our w4 format of share of net assets plus any goodwill in NCI and less NCI % of impairment loss on gross goodwill, or the FV of the NCI at acquisition as adjusted for post acquisition profits and impairment losses.

» Double entry bookkeeping

The gain to the group can be thought of in double entry terms, with the proforma being a disposal account into which all the relevant data is gathered with the resulting balancing figure on the account being the gain on disposal.

To record the cash proceeds being received is an increase in an asset and a posting of the other entry to the disposal account. When an asset is increased it is a DR.

To record the disposal of all the net assets is a decrease in the net assets and a posting of the other entry to the disposal account. When net assets are decreased it is a CR.

To record the disposal of the goodwill is a decrease in the asset of goodwill and a posting of the other entry to the disposal account. When an asset is decreased it is a CR.

To record the disposal of the NCI is a decrease in equity and a posting of the other entry to the disposal account. When equity is decreased it is a DR.

To record the introduction of the residual holding at fair value (investment in associate) is to increase an asset and a posting of the other entry to the disposal account. When an asset is increased it is a DR.

Using the numbers from the second Baggs example the entries made to transfer all the figures to disposed accounts are as follows:

Disposal account

		$	$
DR	Cash (proceeds received)	300,000	
CR	Net Assets		110,000
CR	Goodwill		60,000
DR	NCI	22,000	
DR	Associate	25,000	
CR	Income (balancing figure)		177,000

The balancing figure on the disposal represents the gain or loss to the group arising on the disposal of the subsidiary. The balancing figure is $177,000 and is a CR in the income statement and therefore a gain.

Mind Map

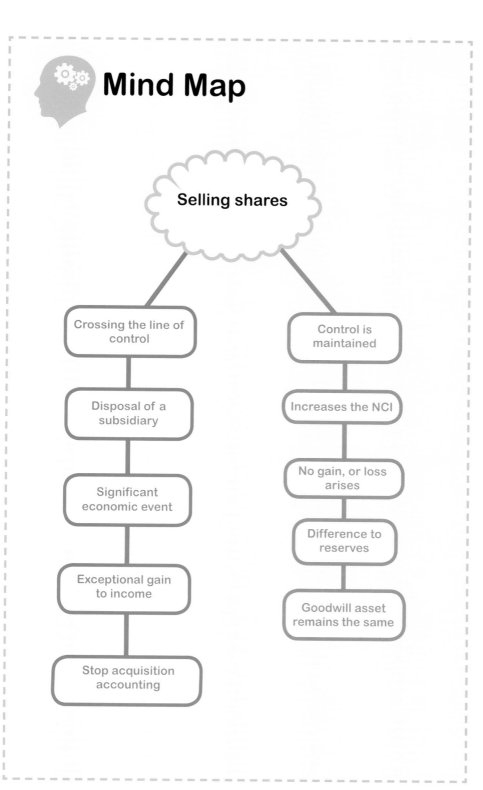

Selling shares

Crossing the line of control

Disposal of a subsidiary

Significant economic event

Exceptional gain to income

Stop acquisition accounting

Control is maintained

Increases the NCI

No gain, or loss arises

Difference to reserves

Goodwill asset remains the same

✿ Technical corner

Discontinued operations

In the group income statement, where the sale of the subsidiary has occurred during the year, basic consolidation principles will only allow the income and expenses of the subsidiary to be consolidated up to the date of disposal.

But it will also be necessary to consider how the results of the subsidiary, up to the date of the disposal are presented in the group income statement, and that will depend whether the subsidiary's activities are regarded as discontinued from a group perspective or not.

Discontinued operations	Continuing operations
Single line presentation	**Line by line consolidation**
If subsidiary that has been disposed qualifies as a discontinued operation in accordance with "IFRS5 *Non-current Assets Held for Sale and Discontinued Operations*", then the pre disposal results of the subsidiary are aggregated and presented in a single line on the face of the income statement immediately after profit for the year from continuing operations.	If the subsidiary that has been disposed of represents continuing operations of the group then the pre disposal results of the subsidiary are consolidated line by line in the same way that a subsidiary's results that had been acquired part way through the year would be consolidated.

To be classified as a discontinued operation basically means that the group must have stopped, or be about to stop, trading in a particular business activity (the sale of the subsidiary represents the groups withdrawal from say the hotel industry) or from a particular region (the sale of the subsidiary represents the group ceasing to have any operations in say Europe). Of course IFRS5 *Accounting for Non-current Assets Held for Sale and Discontinued Operations* has a precise definition and set of conditions as follows.

A discontinued operation is a component of an entity that either has been disposed of or is classified as held for sale, and:

- represents a separate major line of business or geographical area of operations

- is part of a single co-ordinated plan to dispose of a separate major line of business or geographical area of operations; or

- is a subsidiary acquired exclusively with a view to resale and the disposal involves loss of control.

For the subsidiary to qualify as being held for sale at the year-end all the following conditions must be met at the year-end:

- management is committed to a plan to sell

- the subsidiary is being actively marketed

- the subsidiary is available for immediate sale

- the subsidiary is being offered for sale at a reasonable price

- the sale is highly probable, within 12 months of classification as held for sale

- actions required to complete the plan indicate that it is unlikely that the plan will be significantly changed or withdrawn.

The rationale behind stripping out the results of a discontinued operation and reporting them in a separate line in the income statement stems from wanting to present information in such a way that will be useful to the users of the financial statements. It is a well worn criticism that the financial accounts lack a certain relevance because they are backward looking i.e. are reporting on what has happened, whereas users are living in the present and have information needs about what is going to happen in the future. By the separating out of the results of a discontinued operation the users are presented with the results from continuing operations that increases the predictive quality of the income statement and thus aids the users in their interpretation of the performance of the group.

Gain to the parent company on selling shares

As we have already seen there is a difference between the carrying value of the investment in the subsidiary in the individual accounts of the parent (cost or value) and the carrying value of the subsidiary as consolidated in the group accounts.

This chapter has so far concentrated on making sure that you can understand and determine the gain to be recognised in the group income statement (on the sale of shares in a subsidiary where there is a disposal ie. loss of control) or the difference arising in equity (because it is just a reduction in the NCI).

However from the perspective of the individual parent company there will always be a profit (or loss) arising in income on any sale. That profit will be the difference between the proceeds received and the proportion of the carrying value of the investment sold plus the recycling of any gain previously recognised by the parent company in equity (revaluation reserve).

As we are always involved in the preparation of the group accounts it is not generally necessary to actually calculate the gain to the parent. Nevertheless the gain to the parent can be used in w5 group accumulated profits when it is necessary to update the parent company profits as the parent has yet to record the gain, or to compute and then record any tax charge and liability arising on the transaction that the parent (and hence the group) will suffer.

Consider

A parent company has a 100% owned subsidiary that it acquired many years ago for $60m. The investment remains carried by the parent company at cost. The subsidiary now has net assets of $90m. All goodwill has previously been impaired. The parent has just sold its entire holding in the subsidiary for $110m. Tax is at 30% and has not been accounted for.

The gain to the individual parent company on the sale of the investment will be:

		$m
Sale proceeds		110
Less proportion of the carrying value of the investment sold	(100/100 x 60)	(60)
Plus the realisation of any gain previously recognised in equity (revaluation reserve)		(Nil)
Pre tax gain to the parent		50
Less the additional tax that arises on this gain	(30% x 50)	(15)
Post tax gain to the parent		35

The gain to the group on the disposal of the subsidiary

	$m
Sale proceeds	110
Less all the net assets of the subsidiary at the date of disposal	(90)
Less all the goodwill remaining at the date of disposal	(Nil)
Plus all the NCI at the date of disposal	Nil
Plus the fair value of any residual holding	Nil
Gain to the group	20

An additional tax charge of $15m arises on this gain that will be aggregated to the parent's tax charge and hence also increase the group tax charge.

Note also that since the group is not a legal entity - it is an artificial accounting entity - the group is not charged tax on the gain to the group of $20m. Instead the parent company, as an individual legal entity, is charged tax. Per the previous calculation, this was $15m. The tax charge in the group accounts is arrived at by simply cross-casting the parent and subsidiary's tax charges. Thus the group's tax charge will increase by $15m.

Question Ireland

The following information relates to Ireland a 60% subsidiary where goodwill is calculated in full. No goodwill has been impaired.

Net assets at acquisition	Net assets at the current date	Fair value of the NCI at acquisition	Cost of the investment	Sale proceeds
$m	$m	$m	$m	$m
500	750	300	900	3,000

Required

(i) Calculate the gain arising to the group if the sale proceeds related to a disposal of the entire shareholding held by the parent.

(ii) Calculate the difference in group equity if the sale proceeds related to a disposal of 6% leaving the parent still controlling the subsidiary by holding 54%.

Question China

The statements of comprehensive income are as follows

	China group	Beijing
Income statement	**$**	**$**
Revenue	730,000	400,000
Operating costs	(450,000)	(300,000)
Operating profits	280,000	100,000
Exceptional gain on sale of Beijing	77,500	
Profit before tax	357,500	
Tax	(150,000)	(40,000)
Profit for the year	207,500	60,000
Other comprehensive income		
Revaluation gains	10,000	
Total comprehensive income for the year	217,500	
Attributable to the parent	147,500	
Attributable to the NCI	60,000	
Profit for the year	207,500	
Attributable to the parent	157,500	
Attributable to the NCI	60,000	
Total comprehensive income for the year	217,500	

Additional information

1 The group accounts of China have been prepared except for the inclusion of the results of Beijing that have not yet been consolidated.

2 Two years ago China acquired 80% of the shares of Beijing for $145,000 when the fair value of the net assets were $140,000. The fair value of the NCI at acquisition was $20,000. Goodwill is to be calculated in full. No goodwill has been impaired.

3 In the first year Beijing reported a profit for the year of $50,000.

4   Mid way through the financial year China sells half of its holding of shares in Beijing to a third party for proceeds of $150,000. The disposal has been accounted for in the accounts of China by comparing the sale proceeds with the cost of shares sold so the gain of $77,500 has been recognised. The residual holding of 40% leaves China with significant influence over Beijing. This residual holding has a fair value of $150,000.

For six months Beijing has been a subsidiary and for six months it has been an associate so there will be a lot of time apportionment.

5   China has other subsidiaries participating in the same activities as Beijing, so the total disposal of Beijing does not represent a discontinued operation per "IFRS5 Non current assets held for sale and discontinued operations."

This means that the results of Beijing will be consolidated on a line by line basis.

6   The results of China group include the consolidation of its other group companies but not yet the results of Beijing. Profits in the current year can be assumed to accrue evenly. No group company has paid a dividend.

Required:

(i)   Prepare the consolidated statement of comprehensive income for the China group.

(ii) Prepare the consolidated statement of comprehensive income for the China group, on the basis that at mid year there was a total disposal of China's investment in Beijing for $350,000 and this represents a discontinued operation for the China group.

In the second case there will be a single presentation of the results, no associate and a need to recompute the gain to the group.

recap

on changes in the group structure

> A little sincerity is a dangerous thing, and a great deal of it absolutely fatal.

What's new?

Absolutely nothing!

Lets take this opportunity to recap on the key messages and new proformas that we have learnt in this section

Key messages - buying shares

(i) When a purchase of shares means that control is achieved, any prior investments are revalued to fair value and the gain is recognised in the income statement.

(ii) When a purchase of shares in an existing subsidiary takes place then this reduces the NCI.

- The subsidiary remains a subsidiary.

- The NCI is decreased by the proportion of the NCI acquired.

- A reduction in the NCI will not affect the goodwill asset.

- No gain or loss arises as it is a transaction within equity but the difference between the cost and the transfer from NCI is taken directly to equity.

The difference is ascertained as follows

	$
Cash paid out	X
Transfer from NCI decreasing the NCI	X
Difference to equity	X

Where the cost of the subsequent investment exceeds the decrease in the NCI then the difference taken to reserves will be a decrease in reserves and equity.

Where the cost of the subsequent investment is less than the decrease in the NCI then the difference taken to reserves will increase reserves and equity.

Key messages - selling shares

(i) When a sale of shares in a subsidiary still leaves the parent in control there has been a transfer to the NCI.

- The subsidiary remains a subsidiary.

- The NCI increases by the % of the net assets and goodwill transferred

- An increase in the NCI will not affect the goodwill asset.

- No gain or loss arises as it is transaction within equity but the difference between the proceeds and the transfer to the NCI is taken directly to equity.

The difference is ascertained as follows

	$
Cash received	X
Transfer to NCI increasing NCI	X
Difference to equity	X

Where the proceeds received exceed the increase in the NCI then the difference taken to reserves will be an increase in reserves and equity.	Where the proceeds received is less than the increase in the NCI then the difference taken to reserves will be a decrease in reserves and equity.

(ii) When a sale of shares in a subsidiary means that control is lost, this is a disposal.

- With a disposal in the group income statement the results of the subsidiary are consolidated up to the date of disposal, and an exceptional gain arises.

- The exceptional gain to the group is determined in the following proforma.

Gain to group on disposal of a subsidiary	$
Sale proceeds	X
Less all the net assets of the subsidiary at the date of disposal	(X)
Less all the goodwill remaining at the date of disposal	(X)
Plus all the NCI at the date of disposal	X
Plus the fair value of any residual holding	X
Gain to the group	X

section 7

Advanced issues: Complex group stuctures

chapter 17

Vertical group structures

❝ Life is far too important a thing ever to talk seriously about. **❞**

What's new?

So far all the group structures that we have looked at have been simple groups in that the parent company has direct ownership of the shares in its subsidiary. Now that is not always the case as it is actually possible to have a subsidiary (i.e. to control a company) without directly owning any shares in it. Let's cut to the chase and present to you with the following group structure.

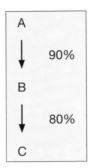

This type of group structure is known as a vertical group.

We can see here that A controls B so that B is a subsidiary of A, but we need also to consider the relationship that C has to the A group.

As it is true that A controls B
And it is true that B controls C
So it must also be true that A controls C
And because A controls C then C is a subsidiary of the A group.

This simple piece of logic is based on the principle that the definition of a subsidiary is based on the concept of control and not ownership. Let me put it another way – if my brother has a brother then my brother's brother is also my brother! So if my subsidiary has a subsidiary then my subsidiary's subsidiary is also my subsidiary!

A has no direct ownership of any shares in C, nevertheless as A is able to control B and B is able to control C so A is in control of C.

This important conclusion will mean that when we are preparing the group accounts of A, then C will be consolidated as a subsidiary i.e. goodwill will be calculated and its assets and liabilities, income and expenses consolidated and an NCI reported.

C can be referred to as a sub-subsidiary or indirect subsidiary.

Where there are vertical group structures the requirement will always be for the preparation of the ultimate parent's group accounts i.e. the A group accounts with its two subsidiary companies. Accordingly we are not interested in preparing the B group accounts.

Having established the control relationship, the second step is then to make sure that we have the correct parent's and NCI percentage interest in C the sub subsidiary. This split is essential when it comes to calculating goodwill, NCI and accumulated profits so it is pretty important!

For A the effective interest in the sub subsidiary C is

A's effective interest in C	(90% x 80%)	72%
NCI's effective interest in C	Balancing figure	28%
		100%

Thus w1 will now look like this

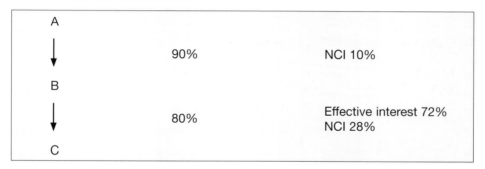

The third step is to make sure that we understand the date when A obtained control of C. The date that a subsidiary joins a group is essential as it is at that date that goodwill is calculated.

Consider the following two examples where in each case B acquired C two years ago.

Situation 1

A acquired B three years ago and B acquired C two years ago.

Here C joins the A group two years ago. When B acquires C, B is already a subsidiary of A so A has only been able to control C for the last two years.

Situation 2

A acquired B one year ago and B acquired C two years ago.

Here C only joins the A group one year ago. Whilst B acquired C two years ago, as A only acquired control of B one year ago A has only been able to control C for one year.

As A has only obtained control of C one year ago, then C's goodwill arising has to be measured as at that date. B acquired C two years ago, so where the investment in C is in B's accounts at its historic cost from two years ago, it will have to be restated to its fair value as at one year ago. The gain that arises will be recognised in income and so increase the pre acquisition profits of B.

There is a simple rule. A acquires the controlling interest in C at the latter of when A acquires B, and B acquires C.

Indirect holding adjustment

The fourth and final extra step relates to the existence of an indirect investment i.e. the cost of investment that B will have incurred in acquiring C. Let's, for the sake of argument say that was $200. As B is a 90% subsidiary of A from the perspective of A the investment in C is an indirect cost which A only bears 90% and the NCI bears 10%.

Therefore when calculating the goodwill of C, from the perspective of A an indirect holding adjustment has to be made of 10% x $200 = $20 that will reduce both the investment in C by $20 from $200 to $180 and also reduce the NCI in w4 by $20.

This adjustment needs to be seen in the context of a question – so let's go!

Example

Grandmother purchased its shareholding in Mother two years ago, and Mother purchased its shareholding in Daughter one year ago. The following financial statements relate to the Grandmother group.

Statements of financial of position	Grand-mother	Mother	Daughter
	$m	$m	$m
Investment in Mother (70% holding)	40		
Investment in Daughter (60% holding)		20	
Other assets	35	15	20
	75	35	20
Ordinary shares	40	25	10
Accumulated profits	22	7	6
Equity	62	32	16
Liabilities	13	3	4
	75	35	20
Income statements	**$m**	**$m**	**$m**
Revenue	350	50	85
Operating costs	(345)	(45)	(83)
Operating profit	5	5	2
Tax	(3)	(2)	(1)
Profit for the year	2	3	1

Additional information

1   The accumulated profits were

	Mother	Daughter
	$m	$m
One year ago	4	5
Two years ago	2	3

2   The fair value of the NCI, based on the effective shareholdings was

	Mother $m	Daughter $m
One year ago	10	12
Two years ago	6	8

3   During the year Daughter sold goods to Mother for $5m. By the year-end all the goods have been sold on by Mother to a third party.

4   The goodwill of Mother is impaired at the year-end by $2m. There were no impairment losses prior to this date. Goodwill is to be calculated in full. No dividends were paid in the year.

Required

Prepare the consolidated statement of financial position and consolidated income statement for the Grandmother group.

Let's sort out that group structure, because with a vertical group there is a lot riding on w1.

W1 Group structure

The initial working of the group structure will be

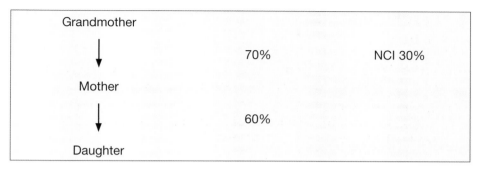

Grandmother

Mother

70%   NCI 30%

60%

Daughter

Control

From this we can establish the relationships in the group.

Grandmother controls Mother
And it is true that Mother controls Daughter
So it must also be true that Grandmother controls Daughter
And this means that Daughter is a subsidiary of the Grandmother group.

Percentages

Having established that Daughter is a subsidiary of Grandmother we can now determine its effective interest in Daughter as follows.

Grandmother's effective interest in Daughter	(70% x 60%)	42%
NCI's effective interest in Daughter	Balancing figure	58%
		100%

Don't panic that the subsidiary has a NCI in excess of 50%. It may seem strange at first, but it is correct. These proportions are for allocating net assets and profits and not for deciding control.

Dates

I note that Grandmother acquired Mother two years ago and that Mother only acquired Daughter one year ago. Accordingly Daughter has only been a member of the Grandmother group for one year so there is no need to revalue Mother's investment in Daughter. The question does contain some data about retained earnings and the fair value of the NCI on irrelevant dates and that has to be ignored e.g. details of Mother one year ago and Daughter two years ago.

To conclude Daughter has been a subsidiary of the Grandmother group for one year with an effective interest of 42% and NCI of 58% and the final presentation of this group structure will be:

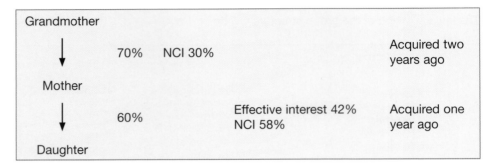

Indirect holding adjustment

As Daughter is a sub-subsidiary the investment in Daughter needs to be reduced by the indirect holding adjustment, as Grandmother did not make the investment. The indirect holding adjustment is calculated as:

The NCI in Mother		Mother's cost of investment in Daughter		
30%	x	$20m	=	$6m

W2 Net assets

The net asset working is quite straightforward as there are no fair value or other adjustments. What we have to remember when selecting the reserves at acquisition is that Mother was acquired two years ago and Daughter one year ago.

	Mother		Daughter	
	At acquisition	At year-end	At acquisition	At year-end
	$m	$m	$m	$m
Share capital	25	25	10	10
Accumulated profits	2	7	5	6
	27	32	15	16

The post acquisition profit of Mother is $5m ($32m - $27m).

The post acquisition profit of Daughter is $1m ($16m - $15m).

The goodwill calculation of Mother is as we have seen before. Mother is a directly owned subsidiary. There is an impairment loss on the gross goodwill given, and the write off will be apportioned between the parent's profits and NCI in the proportions that they normally share profits and losses.

W3 Goodwill of Mother

		$m	$m
Cost of the investment			40
Less the parent's % of the net assets at acquisition	(70% x 27)		(18.9)
Goodwill (attributable to the parent)			21.1
Fair value of the NCI at acquisition		6	
Less the NCI % of the net assets at acquisition	(30% x 27)	(8.1)	
Goodwill (attributable to the NCI)			(2.1)
Gross goodwill at acquisition			19
Less the impairment loss			(2)
Gross goodwill at year-end			17

Also don't panic that the NCI in the goodwill turns out to be a negative figure. This is possible and reflects the fact that the fair value of the shares not acquired by the parent at acquisition (i.e. the fair value of the NCI) is very low because there is a lack of demand for a non controlling interest in this company (such that the shares are trading at a discount on the fair value of its net assets).

Alternative calculation of gross goodwill

		$m
Cost of the investment		40
Fair value of the NCI at acquisition		6
Less 100% of the net assets at acquisition	(100% x 27)	(27)
Gross goodwill at acquisition		19
Less the impairment loss		(2)
Gross goodwill at year-end		17

Now for the calculation of the goodwill of Daughter in the Grandmother group accounts. It will be necessary to remember to deduct the indirect holding adjustment from Mother's cost investment in Daughter and to use Grandmother's effective interest % from NCI.

Goodwill of Daughter

		$m	$m
Cost of the investment		20	
Less the indirect holding adjustment	(30% x 20)	(6)	
Less the parent's % of the net assets at acquisition	(42% x 15)	(6.3)	
Goodwill (attributable to the parent)			7.7
Fair value of the NCI at acquisition		12	
Less the NCI % of the net assets at acquisition	(58% x 15)	(8.7)	
Goodwill (attributable to the NCI)			3.3
Gross goodwill at acquisition			11

Alternative calculation of gross goodwill

		$m
Cost of the investment		20
Less the indirect holding adjustment	(30% x 20)	(6)
Fair value of the NCI at acquisition		12
Less 100% of the net assets at acquisition	(100% x 15)	(15)
Gross goodwill at acquisition		11

Whichever way that the NCI is calculated it will be necessary to charge the NCI both with their share of the impairment loss and with the indirect holding adjustment.

W4 NCI

		$m
NCI % in Mother's year end net assets	(30% x 32)	9.6
NCI % in Daughter's year end net assets	(58% x 16)	9.3
Less the indirect holding adjustment	(30% x 20)	(6)
Plus Mother's goodwill attributable to the NCI		(2.1)
Plus Daughter's goodwill attributable to the NCI		3.3
Less the NCI % of Mother's impairment loss	(30% x 2)	(0.6)
		13.5

Or

		$m
Fair value of the Mother's NCI at acquisition.		6
Fair value of the Daughter's NCI at acquisition.		12
Less the indirect holding adjustment	(30% x 20)	(6)
Plus the NCI% of Mother's post acquisition profits w2	(30% x 5)	1.5
Plus the NCI% of Daughter's post acquisition profits w2	(58% x 1)	0.6
Less the NCI% of Mother's impairment loss	(30% x 2)	(0.6)
		13.5

W5 Accumulated profits

		$m
Parent's accumulated profits		22
Less the parent's % of Mother's impairment loss	(70% x 2)	(1.4)
Plus the parent's % of Mother's post acquisition profits w2	(70% x 5)	3.5
Plus the parent's % of Daughter's post acquisition profits w2	(42% x 1)	0.4
		24.5

Now we can prepare the group statement of financial position.

Grandmother group statement of financial position

		$m
Goodwill	w3 (17 + 11)	28
Other assets	(35 + 15 + 20)	70
		98
Ordinary shares ($1)		40
Accumulated profits	w5	24.5
Non controlling interest	w4	13.5
Equity		78
Liabilities	(13 + 3 + 4)	20
		98

Grandmother group income statement

The preparation of the group income statement is bereft of adjustments save the cancellation of an inter-company sale and purchase of $5m.

W6 NCI in profit

The only working required is the NCI in the profit for the year, as follows.

	NCI%		Profit for the year	$m
Mother	(30%	x	3)	0.9
Daughter	(58%	x	1)	0.6
				1.5

NB The indirect holding adjustment relates to an adjustment on an investment (an asset) and therefore only affects the NCI in net assets.

Grandmother group income statement

		$m
Revenue	(350 + 50 + 85 less inter company 5)	480
Operating costs	(345 + 45 + 83 less intercompany 5)	(468)
Operating profit		12
Tax	(3 + 2 + 1)	(6)
Profit for the year		6
Attributable to the parent	Balancing figure	4.5
Attributable to the NCI	w6	1.5
		6

» Double entry

The consolidation adjustment introduced by vertical group structures is the indirect holding adjustment.

We saw that Mother had incurred a cost of $20m in acquiring Daughter. From Grandmother's perspective this investment is an indirect cost that it is only responsible for 70% of, the other 30% relating to the NCI. Thus when calculating goodwill in Grandmother's group accounts the indirect investment is reduced down by 30% and the NCI charged with 30%

The indirect holding adjustment both reduces the indirect investment in Daughter and the NCI.

The indirect holding adjustment was calculated as

The NCI in Mother		Mother's cost of investment in Daughter		
30%	x	$20m	=	$6m

This indirect holding adjustment was used to reduce the equity account of NCI; to reduce equity is a DR.

This indirect holding adjustment was used to reduce down the asset of investment in Daughter; to reduce an asset is a CR.

DR	NCI	$6m	
CR	Investment in Daughter		$6m

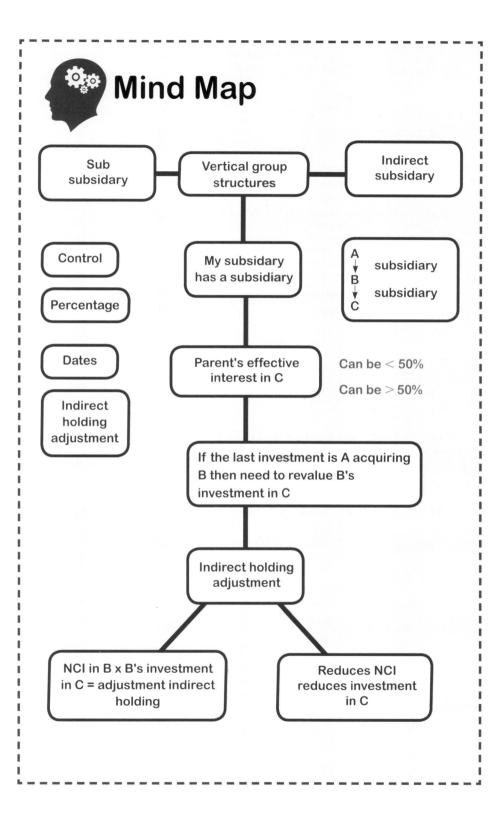

Mind Map

Sub subsidary

Vertical group structures

Indirect subsidary

Control

Percentage

Dates

Indirect holding adjustment

My subsidary has a subsidiary

A
↓
B subsidiary
↓
C subsidiary

Parent's effective interest in C

Can be < 50%

Can be > 50%

If the last investment is A acquiring B then need to revalue B's investment in C

Indirect holding adjustment

NCI in B x B's investment in C = adjustment indirect holding

Reduces NCI reduces investment in C

⚙ Technical corner

Indirect associates

What we have seen in the vertical group structure, is a subsidiary having another subsidiary so that the second subsidiary is also a subsidiary of the ultimate parent company despite no direct ownership and quite possibly the parent having an effective interest of less than 50%.

Where the subsidiary has an investment that is not a subsidiary but an associate company then the initial group structure could look like this.

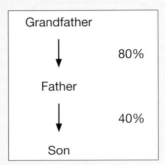

In these circumstances because Grandfather controls Father and Father has significant influence over Son it is true to say that Grandfather controls the significant influence over Son. This makes Son an associate of the Grandfather group. Son could be termed an indirect associate or a sub associate.

As an associate of the Grandfather group Son will be consolidated using equity accounting i.e. will be represented in a single line in both the group statement of financial of position and the group income statement.

Whilst ultimately the effective group interest in Son's net assets and profits will be 32% (80% x 40% = 32%) the Grandfather group (and for avoidance of any doubt by that I mean Grandfather and its subsidiary Father) is technically accountable and should report on the interest of 40% in Son and hence an NCI of 8%.

In the consolidated statement of financial position of Grandfather, Son will be recorded at cost plus 40% of Son's post-acquisition retained profits, and in the equity section, 40% of Son's retained post-acquisition profits will be allocated between equity shareholder's of Grandfather (32%) and NCI (8%).

In the consolidated income statement, 40% of Son's profit will be included in one line as the income from associate and 32% of this income will be attributable to equity shareholder's of Grandfather and 8% of this income will be attributable to NCI.

Let us put some numbers to that Grandfather example.

Subsidiary's cost of investment in associate	Fair value of associate's net assets at acquisition	Fair value of associate's net assets at year-end
$m	$m	$m
150	200	500

From this we can see that the post acquisition profits of the associate are $300m ($500m - $200m)

These post acquisition profits will increase the carrying value of the investment in the associate in the top half of the group statement of financial position. However as the parent only has an effective interest in the associate's profits of 32% (80% x 40% = 32%) giving an NCI interest of 8% (40% - 32% = 8%) this gain will be shared between the parent and the NCI's interests.

The extract of the group statement of financial position would be:

Assets		$m
Carrying value of the associate		
Cost of investment		150
Plus the parent's % of the post acquisition profits w2	(40% x 300)	120
		270
Equity		
Extract of w5 accumulated profits		
Parent's share of the associate's profits	(32% x 300)	96
Extract of w4 NCI		
NCI% of the associate's profits	(8% x 300)	24

Note that in the group accounts instead of consolidating the investment at the cost of $150m, the investment in the associate is measured at $270m, a rise in the top half of the statement of financial position of $120m, and that this rise in net assets is shared between the parent ($96m) and the NCI ($24m)

I must concede that the detailed accounting for indirect associates is not specifically illustrated in IAS28 *Investments in Associates* and that therefore arguably maybe there are other alternative ways of accounting for indirect associates.

For example it has been suggested that indirect associates should only be accounted for using the effective interest.

In our example that would lead to the carrying value of the investment being measured at $216m. The parent's effective interest in the cost (80% x $150m = $120m) would be increased by the effective interest in the profits (32% x $300m = $96m).

The extract of the group statement of financial position would therefore be:

Assets		$m
Carrying value of the associate		
Cost of investment		150
Less indirect holding adjustment	(20% x 150)	(30)
Plus the parent's % of the post acquisition profits w2	(32% x 300)	96
		216
Equity		
Extract of w5 accumulated profits		
Parent's share of the associate's profits	(32% x 300)	96
Extract of w4 NCI		
Less the indirect holding adjustment		(30)

The statement of financial position will balance as the increase in the assets from $150m to $216m is matched by the net increase in equity of $66m. ($96m - $30m).

However this results in the NCI being charged with an indirect holding adjustment and then not participating in the profits, and to me that just seems wrong!

I suppose alternatively you could ignore the indirect holding adjustment all together, so that the carrying value would be $246m, but that would result in the cost of the investment in the associate being at the full cost to the subsidiary and the increases in profits being at the effective interest to the parent, and again to me that just seems wrong!

This is another example, like dealing with associate purps, where because of limited guidance the topic is open to interpretation.

Question Primary

Primary purchased 240m shares in Secondary one year ago, and Secondary purchased 150m shares in Tertiary two years ago. The following financial statements relate to the Primary group.

As Secondary had already purchased Tertiary by the time that Primary made its acquisition then it will be necessary to restate Secondary's investment in Tertiary to fair value as at the date of primary's acquisition of Secondary and to take the gain to income.

	Primary $m	Secondary $m	Tertiary $m
Investment in Secondary	800		
Investment in Tertiary		400	
Other assets	1,200	500	600
	2,000	900	600
Ordinary shares ($1)	400	300	200
Accumulated profits	550	550	250
Equity	950	850	450
Liabilities	1,050	50	150
	2,000	900	600

The investment in Tertiary has been incurred by Secondary and not Primary, so the investment in Tertiary represents an indirect investment.

Additional information is as follows

1   The accumulated profits were:

	Secondary $m	Tertiary $m
One year ago	150	120
Two years ago	140	95

2   The fair value of the NCI, based on the effective shareholdings was:

	Secondary $m	Tertiary $m
One year ago	120	140
Two years ago	100	80

Some of this information is irrelevant; make sure you establish exactly when Tertiary joins the Primary group.

3   Impairment reviews reveal that there are no impairment losses to recognise. Goodwill is to be calculated in full.

4   At the date of acquisition the carrying values of assets and liabilities were the same as the fair values with two exceptions. Tertiary's land had a fair value in excess of its carrying value by $20m and one year ago the fair value of Secondary's investment in Tertiary was $410m. Secondary originally paid $400m for the investment in Teriary.

This is significant as the investment by Secondary in Tertiary was two years ago but it is necessary to consider when Primary obtains control of Tertiary and so at what date goodwill is being calculated.

Required

Prepare the consolidated statement of financial position for the Primary group.

With vertical group structures you can think of four steps as CPDI!

C for Control

Confirm that indeed Primary does control Secondary and Secondary controls Tertiary so that Primary does control Tertiary and Tertiary is therefore a subsidiary of Primary.

P for Percentage

Calculate Primary's effective interest in Tertiary and thus determine the NCI as a balancing figure.

Primary's interest in Secondary	X	Secondary's interest in Tertiary	= XX%	Primary's effective interest in Tertiary
		Balancing figure	XX%	NCI in Tertiary
			100%	

D for Dates

Determine when Primary acquires the controlling interest in Tertiary. This will be the later of when Primary acquires Secondary, and Secondary acquires Tertiary.

If the last investment is that Primary acquires Secondary, then Secondary investment in Tertiary will have to be revalued.

I for Indirect holding adjustment

The final twist with vertical groups is to calculate the indirect holding adjustment on the indirect investment, which is then used to reduce both Secondary's investment in Tertiary and the NCI.

NCI in Secondary	X	Secondary's investment in Tertiary	= XX

chapter 18
Mixed group structures

What's new?

Well we have seen in the previous chapter the idea of indirect investments i.e. where the subsidiary has an investment of its own that is a subsidiary, and that this is then in turn a subsidiary of the ultimate parent of the group.

Now we can explore the situation where both the parent and the subsidiary have investments in the same third company, which result in the third company becoming a subsidiary of the group.

Let me show you what a mixed groups structure looks like to illustrate the point

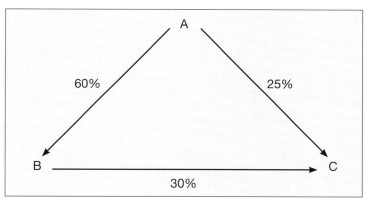

This same group structure could be portrayed instead as follows

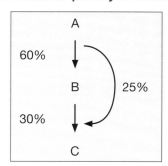

This way of drawing the group structure perhaps explains why these group structures are sometime referred to as "D" shaped groups.

As we learnt from vertical group structures it is essential to establish the relationships within the group.

By reviewing this group structure we can assume instantly that A is the parent and B is a subsidiary with a 40% NCI.

As A holds 25% of the shares in C one might think that C is an associate of A, but let us also consider the impact of the 30% shares that B holds in C.

Consider the voting rights at a share holders meeting of C. A controls B and so has power over B's voting rights of 30%. A also holds 25% of the voting rights directly. As A is able to direct the majority of the voting rights of C (i.e. 55%), C is a subsidiary of A.

This 55% is not however the effective interest in C; this is the next step.

To confirm A controls B and as A and B act together, they will be able to control C, which makes C also a subsidiary of the A group.

To establish A's effective interest in the net assets and profits of C, it is necessary to consider both the direct interest that A holds and the indirect interest held by B.

A's direct interest in C		25%
A's indirect interest (via B)	(60% x 30%)	18%
A's effective interest in C		43%
Effective non controlling interest in C	(Balancing figure)	57%
		100%

Don't be alarmed that A's effective interest in C is less than 50% and the NCI exceeds 50%. C really is a subsidiary that is controlled by A as A and its subsidiary B will act together to control C.

When tackling questions, remember to look with care at the dates to see how the group was put together and to account for the indirect holding adjustment. The technical corner explains the potential problems arising from mixed group structures that have been put together over time.

The indirect holding adjustment here would be calculated as

NCI in B	x	B's investment in C	=	Indirect holding adjustment

The indirect holding adjustment will be used to reduce both the investment in the additional subsidiary (C) and the NCI.

Lets now have a look at a question.

Example

The statements of financial position of three companies are as follows

	Alpha $000	Beta $000	Gamma $000
Investments	400	120	
Assets	1,000	680	350
	1,400	800	350
Share capital ($1)	200	100	50
Accumulated profits	800	500	200
Equity	1,000	600	250
Liabilities	400	200	100
	1,400	800	350

The following information is available

1 Alpha acquired an 80% shareholding in Beta for consideration of $350,000.

2 Beta acquired a 60% shareholding in Gamma for consideration of $120,000.

3 Alpha acquired a 20% shareholding in Gamma for consideration of $50,000.

4 All the investments were made at the same date.

5 At the date of acquisition the carrying values of the assets and liabilities were the same as the fair values.

6 Details of the accumulated profits and the fair value of the effective NCI at acquisition are as follows.

	Beta $000	Gamma $000		Beta $000	Gamma $000
Accumulated profits	200	75	Fair value of the effective NCI	90	50

7   Alpha has a policy of always calculating goodwill gross. The impairment reviews reveal no impairment losses are to be recorded. No shares have been issued since the date of acquisition.

Requirement:

Prepare the consolidated statement of financial position of the Alpha group.

W1 Group structure

It is important that we get the group structure sorted out so that we can establish the relationships and then the effective interests. All investments were made on the same date.

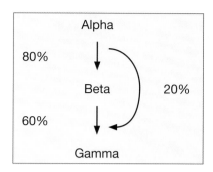

Control

In terms of the relationships Alpha is the parent of Beta, as Alpha holds a majority of the shares in Beta. The NCI of Beta is 20%

Alpha is also the parent of Gamma, Alpha controls Beta and Beta controls Gamma so it is true that Alpha controls Gamma. The indirect holding will create the need to make an indirect holding adjustment. But notice in addition to the indirect investment in Gamma, Alpha also has a direct investment in Gamma of 20%. This direct investment will be taken into account when we work out Alpha's effective interest and NCI in Gamma.

Percentages

Accordingly Alpha's effective interest in Gamma will be:

Alpha's direct interest in Gamma		20%
Alpha's indirect interest in Gamma	(80% x 60%)	48%
Alpha's effective interest in Gamma		68%
Effective NCI in Gamma	Balancing figure	32%
		100%

Dates

As all investments were made at the same date the group was all formed on the same day, so there are no nasty complications arising.

Indirect holding adjustment

There will be an indirect holding adjustment in respect of Beta's investment in Gamma.

The NCI in Beta		Beta's cost of investment in Gamma		
(20%	x	$120,000)	=	$24,000

This indirect holding adjustment will reduce both the investment in Gamma and the NCI.

W2 Net assets

The net asset calculations are straightforward as there are no fair value adjustments.

	Beta		Gamma	
	At acquisition	At year-end	At acquisition	At year-end
	$000	$000	$000	$000
Share capital	100	100	50	50
Accumulated profits	200	500	75	200
	300	600	125	250

The post acquisition profit of Beta is $300,000 ($600,000 - $300,000).

The post acquisition profits of Gamma is $125,000 ($250,000 - $125,000.

Beta's gross goodwill

		$000	$000
Cost of the investment		350	
Less the parent's % of the net assets at acquisition	(80% x 300)	(240)	
Goodwill (attributable to the parent)			110
Fair value of the NCI (at acquisition)		90	
Less the NCI % of the net assets at acquisition	(20% x 300)	(60)	
Goodwill (attributable to the NCI)			30
Gross goodwill at acquisition			140

Alternative calculation of gross goodwill for Beta

		$000
Cost of the investment		350
Fair value of the NCI at acquisition		90
Less the 100% of the net assets at acquisition	(100% x 300)	(300)
Gross goodwill at acquisition		140

The calculation of goodwill for Gamma will reflect both the direct and indirect investment and will also have to incorporate the indirect holding adjustment.

Gamma's gross goodwill

		$000	$000
Cost of the investment by Alpha		50	
Cost of the investment by Beta		120	
Less the indirect holding adjustment	(20% x 120)	(24)	
Less the parent's % of the net assets at acquisition	(68% x 125)	(85)	
Goodwill (attributable to the parent)			61
Fair value of the NCI (at acquisition)		50	
Less the NCI % of the net assets at acquisition	(32% x 125)	(40)	
Goodwill (attributable to the NCI)			10
Gross goodwill at acquisition			71

Alternative calculation of gross goodwill for Gamma

		$000
Cost of the investment by Alpha		50
Cost of the investment by Beta		120
Less the indirect holding adjustment	(20% x 120)	(24)
Fair value of the NCI (at acquisition)		50
Less 100% of the net assets at acquisition	(100% x 125)	(125)
Gross goodwill at acquisition		71

Whichever way the NCI is calculated it will be necessary to charge the NCI with the indirect holding adjustment.

W4 NCI

		$000
NCI % in Beta's year-end net assets	(20% x 600)	120
NCI % in Gamma's year-end net assets	(32% x 250)	80
Less the indirect holding adjustment	(20% x 120)	(24)
Plus Beta's goodwill attributable to the NCI		30
Plus Gamma's goodwill attributable to the NCI		10
		216

Or

		$000
Fair value of Beta's NCI at acquisition.		90
Fair value of Gamma's NCI at acquisition.		50
Less the indirect holding adjustment	(20% x 120)	(24)
Plus the NCI% of Beta's post acquisition profits w2	(20% x 300)	60
Plus the NCI% of Gamma's post acquisition profits w2	(32% x 125)	40
		216

W5 Accumulated profits

		$000
Parent's accumulated profits		800
Plus the parent's % of Beta's post acquisition profits w2	(80% x 300)	240
Plus the parent's % of Gamma's post acquisition profits w2	(68% x 125)	85
		1,125

And finally we can compile this all into a group statement of financial position.

Alpha group statement of financial position

		$000
Goodwill	(140 + 71) w3	211
Assets	(1,000 + 680 + 350)	2,030
		2,241
Share capital ($1)		200
Accumulated profits	w5	1,125
NCI	w4	216
Equity		1,541
Liabilities	(400 + 200 + 100)	700
		2,241

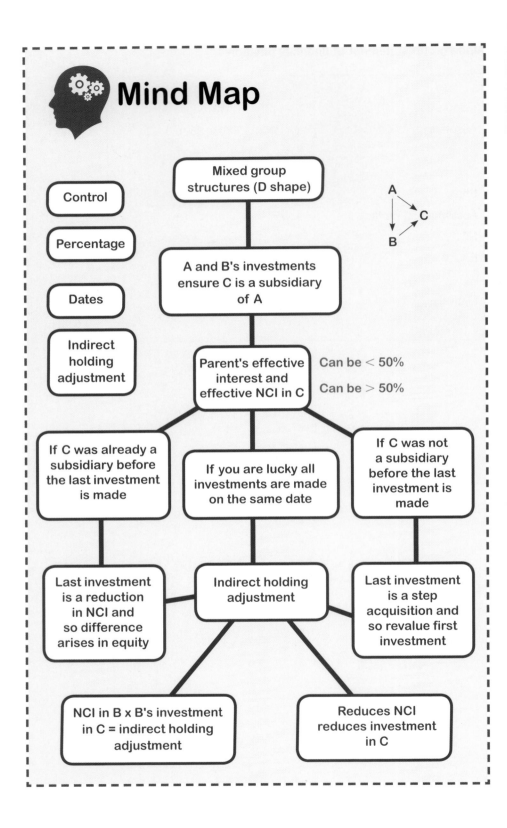

Mind Map

Mixed group structures (D shape)

Control

Percentage

Dates

Indirect holding adjustment

A → C
A → B → C

A and B's investments ensure C is a subsidiary of A

Parent's effective interest and effective NCI in C

Can be < 50%

Can be > 50%

If C was already a subsidiary before the last investment is made

If you are lucky all investments are made on the same date

If C was not a subsidiary before the last investment is made

Last investment is a reduction in NCI and so difference arises in equity

Indirect holding adjustment

Last investment is a step acquisition and so revalue first investment

NCI in B x B's investment in C = indirect holding adjustment

Reduces NCI reduces investment in C

✿ Technical Corner

Mixed groups - Step acquisition and reduction in the NCI

When we considered a vertical group, it was relevant to be aware of the order the investments were made so that the date that the ultimate parent acquired control of the sub subsidiary was correctly determined.

It is also the case that with D shaped or mixed group structures we need to be aware of the sequence that the investments were made. In our first example all investments were made at the same time, which neatly side-stepped potential complications.

We are now going to review three different group structures and in each group structure evaluate the consequences of the group being put together in a different sequence.

Group structure ABC

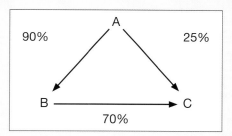

Now what is common to all of the following analysis of this ABC group is that

- A is the parent company

- B is a simple subsidiary with an NCI of 10%

- C is also a subsidiary of the A, with an effective interest of 88% and an NCI of 12%.

A's direct interest in C		25%
A's indirect interest (via B)	(90% x 70%)	63%
A's effective interest in C		88%
Non controlling interest in C	(Balancing figure)	12%
		100%

By definition group accounts are only prepared when there is a parent and a subsidiary, so in considering group accounts the starting point for the A group will always be A having acquired B.

Situation One - **the last investment is B's investment in C**

If the last investment that is made is B acquiring its investment in C (which is an indirect investment from the perspective of A) then the A group would have already existed, with A the parent, B its subsidiary and C its associate.

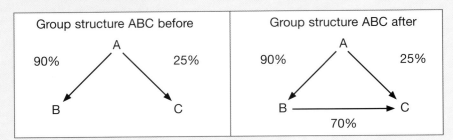

Group structure ABC before	Group structure ABC after

In such circumstances B's investment in C represents a step acquisition that gives A control over C, which becomes a new subsidiary. This means that in order to determine the goodwill arising A's original investment in C will be revalued and the gain reported in income.

All such gains are simply the difference between the new fair value and the old carrying value. In the individual parent company accounts the carrying value of C will be C as an investment. In the group accounts C is an associate and will have been equity accounted i.e. its carrying value will be as an investment in an associate and accordingly the gain reported in the group income statement will be the difference between the fair value and the carrying value of the associate. This is illustrated in the question in this chapter, Ocean.

Situation Two - **the last investment made is A's direct investment in C of 25%**

If the last investment that is made were A acquiring the direct investment in C, then there would have already existed a vertical group, with A the parent, B the subsidiary and C already having been accounted for as a sub subsidiary with an effective interest of 63% (90% x 70%) and an NCI of 37%.

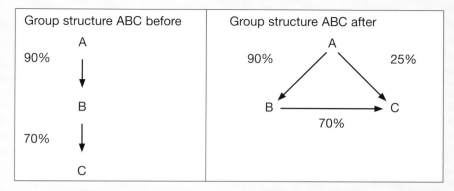

Group structure ABC before	Group structure ABC after

In such circumstances A's investment in C does not change the status of C as it was a subsidiary both before and after the investment. The acquisition therefore represents a reduction in the NCI from 37% to 12%. As per Chapter 15 *Changes in the group structure due to buying more shares*, this is accounted for as a transaction within equity, with a transfer out from the NCI of 25/37 of the NCI balance, with no change in goodwill and with no gain or loss arising but a difference going to reserves.

Group structure DEF

Lets look at a slightly different group structure.

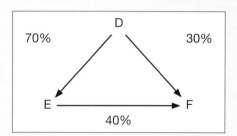

Now what we have here is

- D is the parent company

- E is a simple subsidiary with an NCI of 30%.

- F is also a subsidiary of D, with an effective interest of 58% and an NCI of 42%.

D's direct interest in F		30%
D's indirect interest (via E)	(70% x 40%)	28%
D's effective interest in F		58%
Effective NCI in F	(Balancing figure)	42%
		100%

chapter 18 Mixed group structures

Situation Three - the last investment is E's investment in F

If the last investment that is made is E acquiring its investment in F (which is an indirect investment from the perspective of the D) then there would have already been a group with D the parent, E its subsidiary and F its associate.

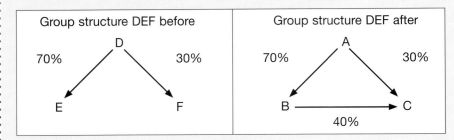

Group structure DEF before	Group structure DEF after

E's investment in F also represents a step acquisition that gives the D control over F, which becomes a new subsidiary. With step acquisitions to calculate goodwill the original investment in F that D made will have to be revalued and the gain reported in income. This follows the same principle as situation one.

Situation Four - the last investment made is D's direct investment in F

If the last investment that is made is D acquiring the direct investment in F, then there would have already existed a group, with D the parent, E the subsidiary and with F already having been accounted for as an indirect associate / sub associate (see technical corner Chapter 17 *Vertical group structures*).

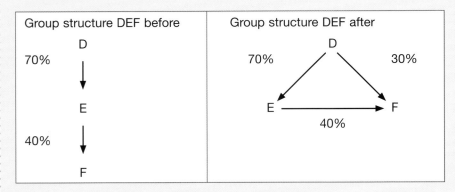

Group structure DEF before	Group structure DEF after

D's investment in F therefore represents a step acquisition that now gives the D group control over F, which becomes a new subsidiary. This means that in order to calculate the goodwill for the new subsidiary F, E's original investment in F will be revalued and a gain reported in income.

The gain in E's income will be the difference between the fair value of the investment and the cost of the investment. As the gain is made by a subsidiary of D then it will impact the NCI. However the gain reported in the group income statement will be the difference between the fair value and the carrying value of the associate. This again follows the same principle as situation one.

Group structure GHI

Let's look at yet another slightly different group structure.

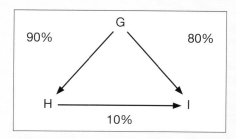

Now what we have here is

- G is the parent company

- H is a simple subsidiary with an NCI of 10%

- I is also a subsidiary of the G, with an effective interest of 89% and an NCI of 11%.

G's direct interest in I		80%
G's indirect interest (via H)	(90% x 10%)	9%
G's effective interest in I		89%
Effective NCI in I	(Balancing figure)	11%
		100%

Situation five - the last investment is H's investment of 10% in I

If the last investment that is made were H acquiring its investment in I (which is an indirect investment from the perspective of the G) then there would have already existed the G group with two directly held subsidiaries H and I.

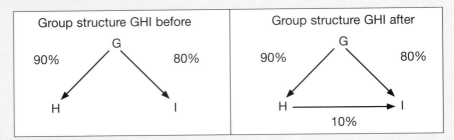

In such circumstances H's investment in I does not change the status of I as I was a subsidiary both before and after the investment. The acquisition therefore represents a reduction in the NCI from 20% to 11%. As per Chapter 15 *Changes in the group structure due to buying more shares*, this is accounted for as a transaction within equity, with a transfer out from the NCI of 9/20 of the NCI balance, with no change in goodwill and with no gain or loss arising but a difference going to reserves. This follows the same principle as situation two.

Situation six - the last investment made is G's direct investment in I of 80%

If the last investment that is made is G acquiring the direct investment in I, then there would have already existed a simple group, with H as a subsidiary and I being a simple investment.

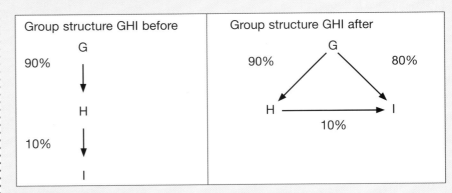

G's investment in I therefore represents a step acquisition that gives the G group control over I, which becomes a subsidiary having previously been an investment. This means that in order to calculate the goodwill for the new subsidiary I, H's original investment in I will be revalued and a pre acquisition gain reported in income of the subsidiary H and the group. As both the subsidiary H and the group will have accounted for I as an investment then the same gain will be reported in both the income of the subsidiary and the group. As this gain is being recognised in the accounts of the subsidiary H it is a gain in which the NCI will participate.

Conclusion

With a mixed (D shaped) group structure if the all the investments are made on the same date, then we are lucky, as there will be neither a reduction in the NCI nor a step acquisition! This is Alpha Example 1

With a mixed (D shape) group structure that has evolved over time there will be the need to either account for a step acquisition or to account for a reduction in the NCI.

If the third company is already a subsidiary before the last investment was made then the last investment is a reduction in the NCI. This will not affect goodwill and no gain or loss arises but there is a difference that will be accounted for in reserves. This is Unicycle Question.

If the third company was not a subsidiary before the last investment was made then the last investment is a step acquisition that creates a new subsidiary. In the calculation of goodwill arising the earlier investment in the third company is revalued with the gain being recognised in income. This is Question Ocean.

There are no new double entries introduced in complex group structures, instead there are two further questions for you to work and enjoy!

Question Unicycle

The statements of financial position of three companies are as follows

	Unicycle $000	Bicycle $000	Tricycle $000
Investment in Bicycle	400		
Investment in Tricycle	50	300	
Assets	220	340	460
	670	640	460
Share capital ($1)	300	200	200
Accumulated profits	130	250	120
Equity	430	450	320
Liabilities	240	190	140
	670	640	460

This is an indirect investment and will require an indirect holding adjustment.

Additional information

1   Three years ago Unicycle acquired a 150,000 shares in Bicycle for consideration of $400,000.

2   Two years ago Bicycle acquired a 160,000 shares in Tricycle for consideration of $300,000.

3   One year ago Unicycle acquired 10,000 shares in Tricycle for consideration of $50,000.

It looks like that Unicycle's investment of 10,000 shares (5%) will be a reduction in the NCI

4   At the date of acquisition the carrying values of the assets and liabilities were the same as the fair values, with the exception of Bicycle's inventory that had a fair value in excess of its carrying value of $10,000. This inventory was sold shortly after acquisition.

As the inventory is sold by the year-end, so at the year-end there will be no fair value adjustment.

5   Details of the fair values of the net assets and the fair value of the effective
    NCI's are as follows.

Bicycle	Net assets	NCI
	$000	$000
One year ago	400	75
Two years ago	330	60
Three years ago	300	50

Tricycle	Net assets	NCI
	$000	$000
One year ago	275	160
Two years ago	250	110
Three years ago	240	90

A lot of this information is not relevant. For example as the NCI is never revalued so the fair value of the NCI can only be relevant at the one date, i.e. the date of acquisition i.e. the date control is obtained.

6   Unicycle has a policy of always calculating goodwill gross. The impairment
    reviews reveal no impairment losses are to be recorded. No shares have
    been issued since the date of acquisition.

7   At the year end Bicycle has a financial asset of $20,000 that is receivable
    from Unicycle. This is recorded by Unicycle as financial liability at $20,000.

This is a simple cancellation of inter-company balances.

Requirement

Prepare the consolidated statement of financial position of the Unicycle
group.

Question Ocean

The financial statements of three companies are as follows.

Statements of financial position	Ocean $000	Sea $000	Lake $000
Investment in Sea (90%)	800		
Investment in Lake (40%)	500		
Investment in Lake (30%)		800	
Assets	700	250	800
	2,000	1,050	800
Share capital ($1)	500	200	80
Share premium	500	Nil	60
Accumulated profits	850	400	510
Equity	1,850	600	650
Liabilities	150	450	150
	2,000	1,050	800

This is an indirect investment!

	Ocean $000	Sea $000	Lake $000
Income statements			
Revenue	3,150	2,000	2,500
Operating costs	(2,300)	(1,820)	(2,000)
Operating profit	850	180	500
Tax	(350)	(80)	(250)
Profit for the year	500	100	250

Additional information

1 Ocean made its investment in Sea three years ago when the accumulated profits of Sea were $200,000, the fair value of the NCI was $50,000 and the fair value of the net assets $500,000. The fair value adjustment relates to the non depreciable asset of land.

2   Ocean made its investment in Lake two years ago when the accumulated profits of Lake were $100,000. The initial investment gave Ocean significant influence over the financial and operating policies of Lake. At that date the book value of the net assets were not materially different from their fair value.

This means that when Ocean acquired Lake it became an associate.

3   Sea made its investment in Lake six months ago. At that date the book value of the net assets were not materially different from their fair value. At that date the fair value of the Ocean's investment in Lake was $700,000 and the fair value of the effective NCI in Lake was $700,000.

When Sea makes its investment in Lake this creates a subsidiary, there is a step acquisition. There will need to be time apportionment in the income statement as Lake will be a an associate for 6 months and a subsidiary for 6 months.

4   Ocean has a policy always to calculate goodwill gross on the acquisition of a subsidiary. The impairment reviews reveal no impairment losses are to be recorded. No dividends have been paid in the current year. No group company has issued any shares in the last three years. Profits are assumed to accrue evenly.

Thank goodness for these small mercies, as there is enough going on in this question already!

Requirement

Prepare the consolidated statement of financial position and the consolidated income statement of the Ocean group.

recap

on complex group structures

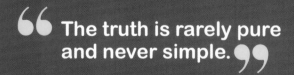

The truth is rarely pure and never simple.

What's new?

Absolutely nothing!

Let's take this opportunity to recap on the key messages when preparing group accounts with indirect holdings and the steps that have to be taken.

Vertical groups

A vertical group looks like this

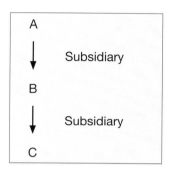

In reviewing this type of group structure remember:

- the definition of a subsidiary is based on control
- if my subsidiary has a subsidiary then that is also my subsidiary
- CPDI.

C for Control

Confirm that indeed A does control B and B controls C so that A does control C and C is therefore a subsidiary of A.

P for Percentage

Calculate the A's effective interest in C and thus determine the NCI as a balancing figure.

A's interest in B	x	B's interest in C	=	XX%	A's effective interest in C
		Balancing figure		<u>XX%</u>	Effective NCI in C
				<u>100%</u>	

D for Dates

Determine when A acquires the controlling interest in C. This will be the latter of when A acquires B, and B acquires C.

If the last investment is that A acquires B, then B's investment in C will have to be revalued.

I for Indirect holding adjustment

The final twist with vertical groups is to calculate the indirect holding adjustment on the indirect investment, which is then used to reduce both B's investment in C and the NCI.

| NCI% in B | x | B's investment in C | = | XX |

Mixed Groups

A mixed group looks like this.

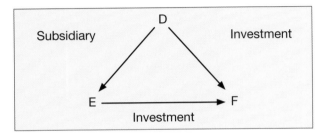

In reviewing this type of group structure remember:

- the definition of a subsidiary is based on control
- CPDI.

C is for Control

Having identified that E is a subsidiary of D, confirm that D and E's combined investments in F means that D also controls F so F is therefore a subsidiary of D.

P is for Percentage

Calculate the D's effective interest in F, which will comprise both its direct and indirect investment, and thus determine the NCI as a balancing figure.

D's direct interest in F		XX%
D's indirect interest in F (via E)	(% x %)	XX%
D's effective interest in F		XX%
Effective NCI in F	(Balancing figure)	XX%
		100%

D is for Dates

If F was already a subsidiary before the last investment was made then the last investment is a reduction in the NCI. This will not affect goodwill and no gain or loss arises but there is a difference that will be accounted for in equity.

If F was not a subsidiary before the last investment was made then the last investment is a step acquisition that creates a new subsidiary. In the calculation of goodwill arising the earlier investment in F will be revalued with the gain being recognised in income.

If all the investments are made on the same date, then we are lucky, as there will be neither a reduction in the NCI nor a step acquisition!

I is for Indirect holding adjustment

The final twist with mixed group structures is to calculate the indirect holding adjustment on the indirect investment, which will then be used to reduce both E's investment in F and the NCI.

NCI% in E	x	E's investment in F	=	XX

section 8

Advanced issues:
Foreign currency

chapter 19

Foreign currency at the individual company stage

> **Most people are other people. Their thoughts are someone else's opinions, their lives a mimicry, their passions a quotation.**

What's new?

So far all the accounting we have done is in $ (dollars). This has been on the (silent) assumption that all the group companies we have looked at to date have had the $ as their functional currency – that is to say they have been setting prices, paying wages and generally entering into transactions in $ and as a result have naturally kept their accounting records and prepared their financial statements in $.

From an individual company perspective we are now going to consider what happens when a company enters into the occasional transaction in a foreign currency and then how to deal with the year-end balances and the foreign exchange differences that arise as a result.

This is an unusual chapter, as it doesn't involve looking at group accounts! Nevertheless it is essential to plough through if you are going to be able to prepare group accounts with overseas subsidiaries that prepare their financial statements in a foreign currency.

There are four rules that have to be followed when accounting for foreign currency at the individual company stage.

Rule 1	Transactions in a foreign currency	All transactions entered into in a foreign currency must be translated into the functional currency (i.e. the $) using the exchange rate ruling on the date of the transaction.

The exchange rate ruling on the date of transaction is often called the spot rate – though in reality may be a weekly or monthly average.

Rule 2	Year-end foreign currency monetary balances	Year-end foreign currency monetary balances are retranslated into the functional currency (i.e. the $) at the closing rate.

Examples of monetary balances are receivables, cash, payables and loans.

Rule 3	Year-end foreign currency non-monetary balances	Year-end foreign currency non-monetary balances are not retranslated i.e. they remain recorded at their original (historic) rate.

Examples of non-monetary balances are property plant and equipment and inventory.

Rule 4	Foreign currency exchange differences	Exchange differences arising at the individual company stage are recognised immediately as operating expenses in the income statement unless they relate to loans, in which case they are finance costs or income.

Exchange differences can be gains or losses.

Example

On the 15 March Woolams a company whose functional currency is the dollar imports an item of plant on 30 days credit and is invoiced for DN72,000, the Dinar (DN) being the functional currency of the exporter.

At 31 March Woolams has a year-end and has to prepare a statement of financial position.

On 15 April Woolams settles the liability of DN72,000.

The relevant exchange rates are as follows

15 March	Exchange rate	DN9: $1
31 March	Exchange rate	DN8: $1
15 April	Exchange rate	DN10: $1

With the exchange rate being expressed in this way, with more DN than $, then when a transaction is expressed in DN and has to be translated into $ we divide!

Required

Show the accounting entries required in the accounts of Woolams in respect of the foreign currency transaction.

NB The other company, who functions in DN, has no foreign currency transaction to worry about as the transaction was entered into in DN, which is its functional currency.

At 15 March Woolams has a transaction that has been entered into in a foreign currency to record in its accounting records.

The transaction of buying an item of plant on credit terms has been entered into at DN72,000 but as the company functions in dollars the transaction will have to be translated into $ using the exchange rate ruling on the date of the transaction.

15 March	DN72,000	÷ 9	= $8,000

The transaction can then be recorded in the accounts

Increase asset of plant	DR	Plant	$8,000	
Increase liability of payable	CR	Payable		$8,000

At 31 March the company has a year-end and has a statement of financial position to prepare.

The plant is a non-monetary asset so will remain recorded at $8,000 at the historic rate. I am happy that the plant remains recorded at its historical rate - after all we are using historical cost accounting.

The liability is however a monetary amount and requires retranslating at the closing rate with the resulting exchange difference being taken to the income statement. I am happy that the liability is retranslated. After all what we owe at the year is DN72,000 and the best way of reporting that at the year end is to use the closing rate.

15 March	DN72,000	÷ 9	= $8,000
31 March	DN72,000	÷ 8	= $9,000
	Exchange difference		$1,000

The exchange difference arises on the retranslation of the liability. The exchange difference increases the liability. To increase a liability is to record a loss in the income statement.

Recording a loss	DR	Income statement	$1,000	
Increase liability of payable	CR	Payable		$1,000

The extract from the statement of financial position will show

	$
Non current asset	8,000
Accumulated profits	(1,000)
Current liabilities	9,000

On 15 April there is a further foreign currency transaction to record.

The transaction of settling a liability for DN72,000 has been made but as the company functions in dollars the transaction will have to be translated into $ using the exchange rate ruling on the date of the transaction.

15 April	DN72,000	÷ 10	= $7,200

The transaction can then be recorded in the accounts

Decrease liability of payable	DR	Payable	$7,200	
Decrease asset of cash	CR	Cash at bank		$7,200

But note that this transaction wholly extinguishes the liability, which was last seen recorded in the accounts at $9,000. Therefore there is a further exchange difference arising.

31 March	DN72,000	÷ 8	= $9,000
15 April	DN72,000	÷10	= $7,200
	Exchange difference		$1,800

The exchange difference arises on the settlement of the liability. The exchange difference decreases the liability. To decrease a liability is to record a gain in the income statement.

Decrease liability of payable	DR	Liability	$1,800	
Recording a gain	CR	Income statement		$1,800

» Double entry

We have seen the double entries integrated into the explanation, so there are no new double entries to show. Instead let's see how those double entries would look in the Payables account in the accounting records of Woolams presented as a T account.

Payable account

		$			$
31 March	Balance c/d	9,000	15 March	Plant	8,000
			31 March	Income statement exchange loss	1,000
		9,000			9,000
15 April	Cash	7,200	31 March	Balance b/d	9,000
15 April	Income statement exchange gain	1,800			
		9,000			9,000

As a CR balance brought down at the year-end this is a liability in the statement of financial position.

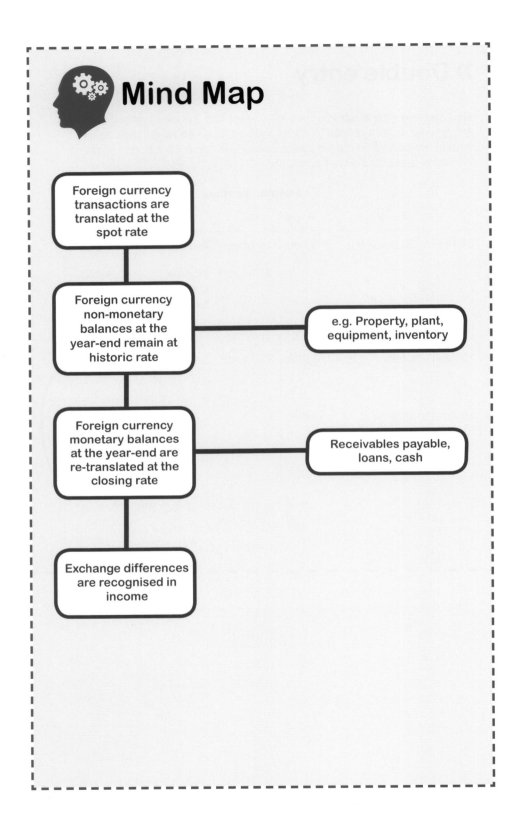

Mind Map

Foreign currency transactions are translated at the spot rate

Foreign currency non-monetary balances at the year-end remain at historic rate

e.g. Property, plant, equipment, inventory

Foreign currency monetary balances at the year-end are re-translated at the closing rate

Receivables payable, loans, cash

Exchange differences are recognised in income

⚙ Technical corner

Accounting for pre acquisition dividends received

By the way this technical corner has nothing to with foreign currency – but it is to do with the individual company stage i.e. how the parent should account for dividends received from the subsidiary.

When a subsidiary company makes a distribution of profit and pays a dividend to its parent company this is normally regarded as coming from the post acquisition profits of the subsidiary. Whilst the subsidiary profits will strictly comprise both pre and post acquisition profits, a last in first out approach is always adopted in identifying the profit that is being distributed.

The parent company naturally records such post acquisition dividends as income. This is because the post acquisition dividend represents a return *on* the investment i.e. it is income. In the group income statement this dividend income is eliminated, as it is inter-company.

There can arise a situation where the subsidiary makes a distribution out of the pre acquisition profits. For example a dividend paid by the subsidiary immediately after the acquisition or in excess of post acquisition profits will be a pre acquisition dividend.

When the parent is in receipt of a pre acquisition dividend then this is not a return *on* the investment rather the pre acquisition dividend represents a return *of* the investment i.e. capital. The pre acquisition dividend should therefore be accounted for by the parent as a reduction in the investment rather than as income.

The payment of a pre acquisition dividend will not however ultimately impact on the group accounts as like all inter company dividends it will be cancelled out on consolidation. Specifically although the cost of the investment has been reduced the measurement of goodwill will not change, as the pre acquisition dividends will represent both a reduction in the parent's investment and the net assets of the subsidiary that were acquired.

Consider an example

Awais, the parent company has just acquired 100% of the shares of Amar by paying consideration with a fair value of $800m. The fair value of the identifiable net assets at acquisition of Amar are represented by equity capital of $100m, accumulated profits of $250m and fair value adjustments of $150m.

The fair value of the net assets of Amar the subsidiary at acquisition is therefore $500m as determined as follows.

	$m
Share capital	100
Accumulated profits	250
Fair value adjustments	150
	500

The goodwill arising in Awais's group accounts on the acquisition of Amar is $300m as determined as follows.

		$m
Cost of investment		800
Less net assets acquired	(100% x 500)	(500)
Goodwill		300

Now let us suppose that at acquisition Amar has a large cash balance and one week after acquisition Amar pays a dividend of $100m all of which therefore is received by Awais. This is a pre acquisition dividend, which should be accounted for by the parent company as a deduction from its investment in the subsidiary. The investment in Amar will be reduced from $800m to $700m.

However the net assets of Amar at acquisition are now $100m less as well, since the pre acquisition profits have been distributed and the cash paid out.

The calculations of the net assets and the goodwill after the pre acquisition dividend will now be as follows.

		$m
Share capital		100
Accumulated profits	(250 less the pre acquisition dividend of 100)	150
Fair value adjustments		150
		400

		$m
Cost of investment	(800 less the pre acquisition dividend 100)	700
Less net assets acquired	(100% x 400)	(400)
Goodwill		300

Note that the goodwill arising in Awais's group accounts on the acquisition of Amar is still $300m.

Question Rosa Parks

On the 10 March Rosa, whose functional currency is the dollar, lends Parks $60,000. Parks has the functional currency of the Dinar (DN). Parks converts the cash advanced into DN immediately.

At 31 March Parks has a year-end and has to prepare a statement of financial position.

On 10 April Parks repays Rosa DN60,000.

The relevant exchange rates are as follows.

10 March	Exchange rate	DN10: $1
31 March	Exchange rate	DN8: $1
10 April	Exchange rate	DN9: $1

With the exchange rate being expressed in this way, with more DN than $, then when a transaction is expressed in $ and has to be translated into DN we multiply.

Required:

Show for Parks the accounting entries required in respect of the foreign currency transaction.

NB Parks functions in DN.

chapter 20
Overseas subsidiaries

" There are only two kinds of people who are really fascinating: people who know absolutely everything, and people who know absolutely nothing. "

What's new?

Well if a subsidiary is located overseas then it is reasonable to expect that it will probably have a different functional currency to its parent company. As a result the subsidiary's financial statements will have been drawn up in what from the parent's perspective, is a foreign currency. Therefore as part of the consolidation process the subsidiary's financial statements will have to be translated into the currency that the group will choose to present its group accounts i.e. the presentational currency.

There are four rules that have to be followed when translating the financial statements of an overseas subsidiary into the presentational currency of the group (assumed to be the $).

Rule 1	The statement of financial position	All the **assets and liabilities** of the overseas subsidiary are translated at the **closing rate**. This will also apply to any consolidation adjustments to those assets and liabilities e.g. fair value adjustments, additional depreciation and purps.
Rule 2	The statement of comprehensive income	All the **income and expenses** of the overseas subsidiary are translated at the **average rate**. This will also apply to any consolidation adjustments to those income and expenses e.g. additional depreciation on the fair value adjustments, impairment losses and purps.
Rule 3	Goodwill	For the group statement of financial position the asset of **goodwill** is translated at the **closing rate**, but for the group income statement any **impairment loss** will be translated at the **average rate**.
Rule 4	Group foreign exchange differences	The **group exchange difference** is recognised in **equity** (and so will appear in the other comprehensive income section of the statement of comprehensive income) and will be apportioned between the parent and the NCI.

The share capital and reserves of the overseas subsidiary will be dealt with as normal in w2, which will be prepared in the local currency.

Arguably the goodwill of an overseas subsidiary relates to such unquantifiable factors as customer loyalty, hard working staff and the general reputation of the business. As these factors exist in the overseas market it is appropriate to regard goodwill as an overseas asset. All of the other assets of the overseas subsidiary are translated at the closing rate, so it is naturally consistent that the goodwill arising on consolidation is also translated at the closing rate.

Strictly income and expenses should be translated at the exchange rate ruling at the date of the transaction, but the standard does allow that average rates can be used where there is no great fluctuation in the exchange rates. Clearly it is impractical for an exam question to provide both a breakdown of income and expenses into 365 different parts and 365 rates of exchange, so the assumption is that income and expenses accrue evenly and the given average rate will be used to translate.

Exchange differences at the individual company stage

For accounting purposes there are two types of exchange differences that arise. One type is those that arise at the individual company stage. We have discussed these in Chapter 19 *Foreign currency at the individual company stage*. These arise on individual transactions and balances and the exchange difference is recognised in the income statement. When preparing the group accounts it is probable that there will have been inter-company transactions and as such the parent and or the subsidiary will have individual exchange differences recognised in their income statements, which will then be consolidated into the group income statement.

For example the parent company will have a foreign currency transaction in respect of the dividend income from the overseas subsidiary, as from the perspective of the parent company the dividend will be declared and paid in a foreign currency. If the parent company records the dividend receivable at a different rate from when it is received then the parent company will have an exchange difference arising that will be taken to the income statement.

In practical terms such exchange differences on inter-company dividends can be avoided all together if the parent company simply only records the dividend when it is actually received and when translating the subsidiary's financial statements the subsidiary's distribution is translated at that same rate of exchange.

An unavoidable exchange difference arises when the overseas subsidiary borrows $ from its parent company. To the overseas subsidiary, borrowing in $ represents a foreign currency transaction as the subsidiary will have a different functional currency. On receipt of the loan the subsidiary will translate the transaction at the exchange rate ruling at the date of the transaction. At the year-end the $ loan will represent a foreign currency monetary balance to the overseas subsidiary that will have to be retranslated thus giving rise to an exchange difference in the income statement that will form part of group income.

Exchange differences at the group accounts stage

The second type of exchange difference arises as a result of the translation necessary to convert the overseas subsidiary's financial statements into the presentational currency so that they are in a fit state for consolidation. This difference is recognised in equity and not in income.

The exchange difference in the group accounts arises on the retranslation of the subsidiary's

- opening net assets
- profit for the year
- goodwill.

The subsidiary's assets and liabilities are translated at the closing rate each year and that rate will change year on year. The opening net assets will have been translated previously at last year's closing rate and are now being retranslated at this year's closing rate, thus an exchange difference will arise.

With the subsidiary's profit for the year it is originally translated in the income statement at the average rate, but the assets that are created by the profit are being translated at the closing rate, thus an exchange difference arises. Consider that a sale creates revenue in the income statement that is translated at the average rate but the corresponding receivable that is created is translated at the closing rate.

The goodwill arising is regarded as an overseas asset and as such is translated at the closing rate each year, so as with the subsidiary's net assets an exchange difference will arise.

The group exchange difference is unrealised but is realised on the disposal of the subsidiary. It is recycled to the income statement by being included as part of the gain or loss on disposal of the subsidiary. (See the technical corner for an example).

The whole of the group exchange difference will be recognised in the other comprehensive income section in the statement of comprehensive income, with the NCI element being reported separately. The parent's share of the exchange difference will be taken to a foreign currency reserve. The parent and the NCI share the exchange difference arising on the net assets and profit in their normal proportion, but this will not necessarily apply to gross goodwill as the NCI attributable to gross goodwill is usually in a different proportion.

To recap the group exchange difference is calculated on the retranslation of the subsidiary's

- opening net assets (last year's closing rate to this year's closing rate)
- profit for the year (this year's average rate to this year's closing rate)
- goodwill (last year's closing rate to this year's closing rate).

				Total	Parent %	NCI %
			$	$	$	$
Opening net assets	@	Last year's closing rate	X			
Opening net assets	@	This year's closing rate	X̲			
Difference				X	X	X
Profits for the year	@	The average rate for the year	X			
Profits for the year	@	This year's closing rate	X̲			
Difference				X	X	X
Goodwill attributable to the parent	@	Last year's closing rate	X			
Goodwill attributable to the parent	@	This year's closing rate	X̲			
Difference				X	X	
Goodwill attributable to the NCI	@	Last year's closing rate	X			
Goodwill attributable to the NCI	@	This year's closing rate	X̲			
Difference				X		X
Total				X̲	X̲	X̲

The group exchange difference numbers are presented in an answer as follows.

- The total group exchange difference is reported in the other comprehensive income section of the statement of comprehensive income.

- The parent's share of the total group exchange difference is reported in the group statement of financial position in a separate foreign currency exchange reserve.

- The NCI share of the total group exchange difference is part of the NCI in the total comprehensive income.

Quite frankly all of this explanation of the group exchange difference can be rather off putting. I would encourage not obsessing about it!

Well that's it for now! Let's get on with a question.

Example

The following are the summarised accounts of Nigeria and Lagos.

	Nigeria	Lagos
Statement of financial position	**$**	**DN**
Tangible non current assets	218,000	100,000
Financial assets	22,000	Nil
Investment in Lagos	100,000	Nil
Current assets	90,000	209,600
	430,000	309,600
Ordinary shares ($1 / DN1 shares)	175,000	50,000
Share premium	50,000	10,000
Revaluation reserve	40,000	Nil
Accumulated profits	125,000	150,000
Equity	390,000	210,000
Non current liabilities	15,000	88,000
Current liabilities	25,000	11,600
	430,000	309,600
Statement of comprehensive income		
Income statement		
Revenue	500,000	300,000
Operating costs	(400,000)	(150,000)
Operating profit	100,000	150,000
Finance cost	(6,100)	(3,300)
Interest receivable	1,100	Nil
Profit before tax	95,000	146,700
Tax	(20,000)	(46,700)
Profit for the year	75,000	100,000
Other comprehensive income		
Revaluation surplus	10,000	Nil
Total comprehensive income	85,000	100,000

Additional information

1   Nigeria acquired 40,000 shares in Lagos on the first day of the accounting period for DN400,000 when the accumulated profits were DN50,000 and the fair value of the NCI was DN30,000

2   At the date of acquisition the fair value of Lagos's non current assets, which at that time had a remaining useful life of ten years, exceeded their book value by DN10,000.

3   The annual impairment review in respect of the goodwill arising reveals that no impairment losses have arisen.

4   Since the date of acquisition no dividends have been paid and no shares issued.

5   At acquisition Nigeria made a long-term loan of $22,000 to Lagos with a coupon rate and an effective rate of interest of 5%. Nigeria has recognised the loan as a separate financial asset. All of the finance cost recognised in Lagos's income statement and all of the interest receivable recognised in Nigeria's income statement relates to the interest on this loan which was paid and accounted for when the exchange rate was DN3 to $1. Lagos incorrectly continues to carry the loan in its accounting records translated at the historic rate.

6   Exchange rates to $1.

	DN
Start of the year	4.0
Average rate	3.0
End of the year	2.0

Required

Prepare the consolidated statement of financial position and the consolidated statement of comprehensive income for the Nigeria group.

First of all let us think about what is new in this question.

Lagos, a company that functions in the currency DN has borrowed in $ and the liability it has at the year-end is a monetary balance which remains incorrectly recorded at the historic rate. Accordingly it is necessary to process a correction in the accounts of Lagos. It is simply inappropriate to begin the translation and consolidation of the subsidiary where the figures in the subsidiary's accounts are incorrect. And of course when we start adjusting the accounts of the subsidiary then the effect on profit will have to be shared between the parent and the NCI. If we pick up such adjustments early enough then we can directly incorporate them into the net assets schedule.

As you will recall from looking at foreign currency transactions from an individual company perspective, transactions have to be translated using the exchange rate ruling on the date of the transaction, and at the year-end monetary items have to be retranslated at the closing rate, with exchange differences being taken to the income statement.

In the accounts for Lagos the $22,000 loan should have been accounted for as follows.

When the loan was made	$22,000	x 4	DN88,000
At the year end	$22,000	x 2	DN44,000
Exchange difference (gain)			DN44,000

In fact if we look again at the statement of financial position then we can see the non current liability is shown as DN88,000, whereas it should be only DN44,000. The exchange difference that needs to be recorded reduces the loan in DN that Lagos has and so represents a gain to Lagos.

The exchange gain therefore should be recorded by Lagos.

Gain reduces the liability	DR	Non current liabilities	DN44,000	
Gain is income – interest receivable	CR	Income		DN44,000

From the perspective of Nigeria, who functions in $ and has made the loan in $, there is no foreign currency exchange difference arising, since it is not a foreign currency transaction.

In passing it should be noted that the inter-company loan and asset and the inter-company interest will be eliminated on consolidation, as they do not represent external items.

It is also true to say that being faced with a subsidiary with its assets and liabilities all expressed in DN is new and they will all need to be translated into $ using the closing rate – lets get this out of the way now and then we can refer back to it in the preparation of the group statement of financial position.

	Lagos DN	Closing rate	$
Tangible non current assets	100,000	÷ 2	50,000
Current assets	209,600	÷ 2	104,800
Non current liabilities	44,000*	÷ 2	22,000
Current liabilities	11,600	÷ 2	5,800

* As updated – but ultimately not part of the final answer as it is inter-company so will be eliminated.

On the same basis all the income and expenses of Lagos as they are also expressed in DN also need to be translated into $ this time using the average rate – let's get this out of the way now and then we can refer back to it in the preparation of the group statement of comprehensive income.

	Lagos DN	Average rate	$
Revenue	300,000	÷ 3	100,000
Operating costs	150,000	÷ 3	50,000
Finance costs	3,300	÷ 3	1,100
Interest receivable*	44,000	÷ 3	14,667
Tax	46,700	÷ 3	15,567

*As updated i.e. this is the exchange gain enjoyed by Lagos as an individual company – and so is to be reported as part of the group income. As the exchange gain relates to a loan it is appropriate to report this as a financing item.

Now you can argue that the group exchange difference on the retranslation of the subsidiary's net assets, goodwill and profit is also new – but I would recommend that because it can be tricky it is always initially left blank or regarded as a balancing figure, with a proof only calculated at the end of the question.

Let's now turn attention to drawing up the group structure.

W1 Group structure

Nigeria

↓

Lagos

Parent's interest 40,000 / 50,000
80%

NCI is 20%

The acquisition was one year ago, so there will be no need to time apportion in the income statement.

Let us as far possible do all the workings as they relate to Lagos in its local currency of the DN, and only actually translate the goodwill and NCI at the last hurdle.

W2 Net assets of Lagos

	At acquisition DN	At year-end DN
Share capital	50,000	50,000
Share premium	10,000	10,000
Accumulated profits	50,000	150,000
Exchange gain on the loan	N/A	44,000
Fair value adjustment	10,000	10,000
Depreciation	N/A	(1,000)
	120,000	263,000

The asset subject to depreciation has a remaining life of ten years.
The subsidiary was acquired one year ago, so the additional depreciation is DN10,000 x 1/10 = DN1,000.

The post acquisition profits, including the updating of the exchange gain on the loan and net of the excess depreciation on the fair value adjustment is DN143,000 (DN263,000 - DN120,000).

W3 Goodwill

The goodwill arising needs to be calculated in the local currency first and then translated at the closing rate.

		DN	DN
Cost of the parent's investment		400,000	
Less the parent's % of the net assets at acquisition	(80% x 120,000)	(96,000)	
Goodwill (attributable to the parent)			304,000
Fair value of the NCI at acquisition		30,000	
Less the NCI % of the net assets at acquisition.	(20% x 120,000)	(24,000)	
Goodwill (attributable to the NCI)			6,000
Gross goodwill at acquisition			310,000

Alternative calculation of gross goodwill

		DN
Cost of the parent's investment		400,000
Fair value of the NCI at acquisition		30,000
Less 100% of the net assets at acquisition	(100% x 120,000)	(120,000)
Gross goodwill at acquisition		310,000

There is no impairment loss so we can proceed to translating the goodwill at the closing rate.

DN310,000	÷ 2	=	$155,000

W4 NCI

		DN
NCI % in the subsidiary's year-end net assets	(20% x 263,000)	52,600
Plus the goodwill attributable to the NCI		6,000
		58,600
Or		
Fair value of the NCI at acquisition.		30,000
Plus the NCI% of the post acquisition profits w2	(20% x 143,000)	28,600
		58,600

The NCI translated at the closing rate

DN58,600	÷ 2	=	$29,300

W5 Accumulated profits

		$
Parent's accumulated profits		125,000
Plus the parent's % of the post acquisition profits of the subsidiary Lagos w2 as translated at the average rate	(80% x 143,000 ÷ 3)	38,133
		163,133

If the subsidiary had been acquired more than one year ago, then each year's post acquisition profits would be translated at the average rate for each year.

Finally we can draw up the group statement of financial position. The figures that are expressed in $ are those of the subsidiary that have already been translated. The parent's share of the group exchange difference can be left as a balancing figure and proved at the end.

The non current liabilities of Lagos and the financial asset of Nigeria represent the inter-company loan so are not reported as group assets or liabilities.

The group revaluation reserve is the parent only as the subsidiary has no change in its revaluation reserve post acquisition.

Nigeria's group statement of financial position

		$
Intangible – goodwill	w3	155,000
Tangible non current assets	(218,000 + $50,000 + fair value adjustment (DN10,000 less DN1,000 ÷ 2) $4,500)	272,500
Current assets	(90,000 + $104,800)	194,800
		622,300
Ordinary shares		175,000
Share premium		50,000
Revaluation reserve		40,000
Foreign currency exchange	(Balancing figure – but proved below)	119,067
Accumulated profits	w5	163,133
Non controlling interest	w4	29,300
Equity		576,500
Non current liabilities		15,000
Current liabilities	(25,000 + $5,800)	30,800
		622,300

In looking at the preparation of the group income statement the figures that are expressed in $ are those of the subsidiary that have already been translated.

There is no inter-company sales to be eliminated – but there is the inter-company interest payable and receivable of $1,100 to exclude.

The subsidiary has an exchange gain on its loan that will need to be included, translated at the average rate and this will impact on the NCI.

There is no impairment of goodwill, but there is an additional depreciation following on from the fair value adjustment which will have to be translated at the average rate, and this will impact on the NCI.

Nigeria group statement of comprehensive income

		$
Income statement		
Revenue	(500,000 + $100,000)	600,000
Operating costs	(400,000 + $50,000 depreciation on the fair value adjustment (DN1,000 ÷ 3) $333)	(450,333)
Operating profit		149,667
Finance cost		(6,100)
Interest receivable	(the exchange gain on the loan)	14,667
Profit before tax		158,234
Tax	(20,000 + $15,567)	(35,567)
Profit for the year		122,667
Other comprehensive income		
Revaluation surplus		10,000
Group exchange difference	(See below)	131,333
Total comprehensive income		264,000
Attributable to parent	Balancing figure	113,134
Attributable to the NCI	w6	9,533
Profit for the year		122,667
Attributable to parent	Balancing figure	242,200
Attributable the NCI	(9,533 + 12,267) w7	21,800
Total comprehensive income		264,000

W6 NCI in the subsidiary's profits

		DN		$
NCI in the subsidiary's profits for the year	20% x	100,000	÷ 3	6,667
Less the NCI % in the depreciation on the FVA	20% x	(1,000)	÷ 3	(67)
Plus the NCI% in the exchange gain on the loan	20% x	44,000	÷ 3	2,933
	20% x	143,000	÷ 3	$9,533

The NCI is in the subsidiary's updated and adjusted profit as translated at the average rate.

Hopefully you recognise the figure of DN143,000 – because having owned the subsidiary for one year this profit is also the post acquisition profits per w2

There was no impairment on goodwill – but had there been, as goodwill is gross then the NCI share would have been charged as well.

W7 Group exchange difference

Finally let's number crunch our way through the group exchange difference for this year.

The group exchange difference for this year arises on the retranslation of the subsidiary's

- opening net assets (last year's closing rate to this year's closing rate) per w2

- profit for the year (this year's average rate to this year's closing rate) per the NCI calculation in the subsidiary's profit for the year

- goodwill (last year's closing rate to this year's closing rate) per w3.

It is necessary to split the exchange difference between the parent and the NCI. For the net assets and profit that is done in the normal proportions, but not for the gross goodwill.

					Total	Parent	NCI
Opening net assets				$	$	$	$
DN120,000	÷	4	=	30,000			
DN120,000	÷	2	=	60,000			
80/20 split					30,000 gain	24,000	6,000
Profits for the year							
DN143,000	÷	3	=	47,667			
DN143,000	÷	2	=	71,500			
80/20 split					23,833 gain	19,066	4,767
Goodwill attributable to the parent							
DN304,000	÷	4	=	76,000			
DN304,000	÷	2	=	152,000			
					76,000 gain	76,000	
Goodwill attributable to the NCI							
DN6,000	÷	4	=	1,500			
DN6,000	÷	2	=	3,000	1,500 gain		1,500
Total					131,333	119,066	12,267

The exchange difference on the opening net assets represents a gain as the net assets are higher and that is good news. Mind you it is not an operating gain and it is unrealised so it no surprise that these exchange differences are not included in income.

The exchange difference on the profit for the year also represents a gain as the year-end net assets generated exceed that of the profit reported.

The exchange difference on the goodwill represents a gain as it increases the goodwill. Note that it is easier to calculate the exchange difference on the goodwill attributable to the parent and the NCI separately as the split is not in the proportion 80/20.

In this question the overseas subsidiary had only been acquired for one year, and so there is only an exchange difference arising for this year. If the overseas subsidiary had been acquired four years ago then either this calculation has to be repeated another four times, or the question would have to have given the brought forward accumulative foreign exchange balance.

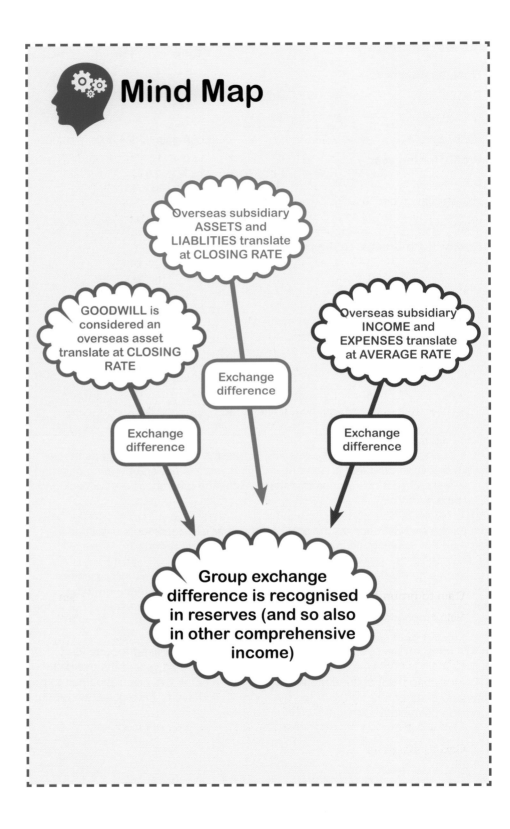

Mind Map

Overseas subsidiary ASSETS and LIABLITIES translate at CLOSING RATE

GOODWILL is considered an overseas asset translate at CLOSING RATE

Overseas subsidiary INCOME and EXPENSES translate at AVERAGE RATE

Exchange difference

Exchange difference

Exchange difference

Group exchange difference is recognised in reserves (and so also in other comprehensive income)

⚙ Technical corner

Accounting for the disposal of foreign subsidiaries

As we have seen when consolidating an overseas subsidiary, there will be an exchange difference that is recognised in reserves. Arguably the reason why it is recognised in a foreign currency reserve (therefore also included in other comprehensive income), and not as part of profit in the income statement, is because it is an unrealised gain or loss and doesn't arise from the operating activities of the group. Rather the group exchange difference is a paper gain or loss that arises from fluctuations in exchange rates.

On the disposal of the subsidiary we have seen how it has been necessary to wash out and remove all traces of the subsidiary from the group accounts. So in calculating the gain to the group on the disposal of a subsidiary the proceeds are netted off against all the subsidiary's net assets, all the goodwill and all the NCI. When a foreign subsidiary is disposed of it is also necessary to remove the balance on the foreign currency exchange reserve. The balance on the foreign currency exchange reserve is transferred to income as part of the gain to the group.

It can be explained that the disposal of the subsidiary has caused the balance on the group exchange difference to become realised and so the balance is recycled to the income statement as part of the gain to the group on disposal.

Consider

A parent company Tanna is selling all of its holding in a subsidiary for $100m when the net assets are $25m, the goodwill $20m the NCI $10m and the cumulative gains in the foreign currency exchange reserve $6m.

The gain to the group on disposal would be calculated as follows.

Gain to group on disposal of an overseas subsidiary	$m
Sale proceeds	100
Less all the net assets of the subsidiary at the date of disposal	(25)
Less all the goodwill remaining at the date of disposal	(20)
Plus all the NCI at the date of disposal	10
Plus the fair value of any residual holding	Nil
Plus the group foreign exchange gain reserve at date of disposal	6
Gain to the group	71

If the balance of the foreign currency reserve had represented losses then the $6m would not have been added rather it would have been deducted giving an exceptional gain to the group of $59m.

Recycling previously recognised gains

You may have noticed that the group foreign currency gain was said to have been recycled to the income statement on realisation. This means that in clearing out the foreign currency reserves the balance is transferred to the income statement to increase the gain on disposal. It can be argued that this is wholly appropriate as the gain is now realised in nature and the natural traditional place to report realised gains and losses is in profit.

Now what I would point out is that this recycling is a form of double counting so far as reporting total comprehensive income is concerned. The group foreign exchange difference has already been included in the comprehensive income statement i.e. it has already been reported in total comprehensive income in the year that it arose, so to recycle it and report it again as part of the exceptional gain on disposal in the income statement is to double count it.

Now when I was first learning about accounting, I was taught by a wonderful teacher – Peter Bruff – who explained to me that gains can only be recognised once. The approach taken with the group foreign currency exchange difference does mean gains are being recognised twice, once on the recording of the foreign currency exchange difference and then again on the disposal of the subsidiary. This treatment is inconsistent with the accounting for realisation of unrealised gains on the sale of revalued assets accounted for under IAS16 *Property Plant and Equipment* where gains are only recognised once and not recycled on disposal.

Consider that land accounted for under IAS16 *Property Plant and Equipment* cost $30 and was then revalued to $35. On revaluation the unrealised gain would be recognised in reserves of $5 and this gain of $5 would be reported in total comprehensive income as part of the other comprehensive income and not as part of the income statement as it is both unrealised and not of an operating nature. That all seems logical and consistent to me.

Now when this asset is subsequently sold for say $36, the rules in IAS16 *Property Plant and Equipment* require that the gain on disposal is the difference between the sale proceeds ($36) and the carrying value ($35). so the gain recognised as the exceptional gain in the income statement will be $1! The revaluation reserve of $5 will be realised but it is not recycled to the income statement, as gains can only be recognised once. Rather a movement in reserves transferring the balance on the revaluation reserve to the accumulated profits cleans out the revaluation reserve. To me this is logical, but is inconsistent with the manner in which the realisation on disposal of the group exchange difference is dealt with.

Mind you the principle of recycling is not unique to the group stage foreign exchange gains – you may recall we saw this in Chapter 15 *Changes in the group structure due to buying more shares* when we looked at step acquisitions. When a subsequent investment gives the parent control the revaluation surplus of a prior holding accounted for under IAS39 *Financial Instruments: Recognition and Measurement* sitting in revaluation reserves having already been recognised as part of total comprehensive income is then recognised as a gain in the income statement.

Question Greenland

One year ago Greenland acquired 80% of Nuuk, whose functional currency is the Dinar (DN) for DN7,500. The financial statements of both companies are as follows.

	Greenland	Nuuk
Statements of financial position		
Non current assets	$	DN
Investment in Nuuk	5,000	–
Tangible	15,000	2,500
Current assets	10,000	3,000
	30,000	5,500
Share capital ($1 / DN1)	8,000	1,000
Share premium	6,000	800
Revaluation reserve	2,000	200
Accumulated profits	4,000	2,500
Equity	20,000	4,500
Liabilities	10,000	1,000
	30,000	5,500
Statements of comprehensive income		
Income	$	DN
Revenue	45,000	70,000
Cost of sales	(20,000)	(54,250)
Gross profit	25,000	15,750
Operating costs	(15,000)	(7,000)
Profit before tax	10,000	8,750
Tax	(8,000)	(7,450)
Profit for the year	2,000	1,300
Other comprehensive income		
Revaluation gain	150	Nil
Total comprehensive income	2,150	1,300

The assets and liabilities will be translated at the closing rate. The income and expenses will be translated at the average rate. There will also be an exchange difference in other comprehensive income.

1 At the date of acquisition the accumulated profits of Nuuk were DN1,200 and the balance on the revaluation reserve was DN200. Nuuk has not issued any shares since the date of acquisition. At the date of acquisition the fair value of the net assets of Nuuk were DN4,200. The increase in the fair value is attributable to plant with a remaining life of two years.

The fair value adjustment will be the balancing figure in the net assets calculation, which will be prepared in DN. The additional depreciation is an extra expense to be translated at the average rate in income..

2 Goodwill is to be calculated gross. The fair value of the NCI at the date of acquisition was DN1,000. In preparation for the impairment review the recoverable amount of Nuuk was DN9,000.

Calculate the goodwill and the impairment loss all in DN and then translate the residual asset into $. The impairment loss will be an additional expense translated in the income at the average rate.

3 Throughout the year Greenland sold goods for $1,000 to Nuuk. At the year end there is no balance remaining on the current accounts.

The inter company sale will be eliminated – but so will the cost of sales as well.. There is no purp.

Exchange rates to $1.

	DN
Start of the year	1.50
Average rate	1.75
End of the year	2

As there are more DN to $1 so to translate from DN to $ divide.

Required

Prepare the group statement of financial position and the group statement of comprehensive income for the Greenland group.

recap
on foreign currency

What's new?

Absolutely nothing! Let's just recap our key messages.

A foreign currency is a currency other than the company's functional currency.

The functional currency is the currency that the company will operate in i.e. the predominate currency in which it sets prices, pays wages, invoices and raises finance.

Individual company stage

Individual companies with transactions and balances in a foreign currency need to follow four rules.

Rule 1	Transactions in a foreign currency	Translate at the spot rate
Rule 2	Year-end foreign currency monetary balances	Retranslate at the closing rate
Rule 3	Year-end foreign currency non-monetary balances	Remain at historic rate
Rule 4	Foreign currency exchange differences	Income statement

Group accounts stage

A parent with an overseas subsidiary will have to translate the financial statements of an overseas subsidiary into the presentational currency of the group following four rules.

Rule 1	Assets and liabilities and their adjustments	Translate at the closing rate
Rule 2	Income and expenses and their adjustments	Translate at the average rate
Rule 3	Goodwill is regarded as an overseas asset	Translate asset at closing rate Translate impairment loss at average rate
Rule 4	Group foreign exchange differences	Equity

Prepare the net assets workings in the local currency and so goodwill and the NCI in the net assets are in the local currency and they can then be translated into the presentational currency at the closing rate.

The group exchange difference is calculated on the retranslation of the subsidiary's:

- opening net assets (last year's closing rate to this year's closing rate)
- profit for the year (this year's average rate to this year's closing rate)
- goodwill (last year's closing rate to this year's closing rate).

				Total	Parent %	NCI %
			$	$	$	$
Opening net assets	@	Last year's closing rate	X			
Opening net assets	@	This year's closing rate	X̲			
Difference				X	X	X
Profits for the year	@	The average rate for the year	X			
Profits for the year	@	This year's closing rate	X̲			
Difference				X	X	X
Goodwill attributable to the parent	@	Last year's closing rate	X			
Goodwill attributable to the parent	@	This year's closing rate	X̲			
				X	X	
Goodwill attributable to the NCI	@	Last year's closing rate	X			
Goodwill attributable to the NCI	@	This year's closing rate	X̲			
				X		X
Total				X̲	X̲	X̲

The group exchange difference numbers are presented in an answer as follows.

- The total group exchange difference is reported in the other comprehensive income section of the statement of comprehensive income.

- The NCI share of the total group exchange difference is part of the NCI in the total comprehensive income.

- The parent's share of the total group exchange difference is reported in the group statement of financial position in a separate foreign currency exchange reserve.

The group exchange difference, is unrealised but is realised on disposal and recycled to the income statement by being included as part of the profit or loss when the gain or loss on disposal of the subsidiary is recognised.

section 9

An overview of recent changes

chapter 21

An overview of recent changes

> " There are only two
> kinds of people who
> are really fascinating:
> people who know
> absolutely everything,
> and people who know
> absolutely nothing. "

What's new?

Well if you have read the book then not a lot really, but this final chapter takes a step back, to have an overview of the changes introduced following the revision to IFRS3 *Business Combinations* and IAS27 *Consolidated and Separate Financial Statements* and to explain some of the changes that it introduced in the context of a number of conceptual themes.

IFRS3 *Business Combinations* and IAS27 *Consolidated and Separate Financial Statements* were revised in January 2008 and are to be applied prospectively to all business combinations occurring in the first accounting period beginning on or after 1 July 2009. Retrospective application to earlier business combinations is not permitted.

The revisions radically changed the measurement and accounting for goodwill, NCI, step acquisition, transactions with the NCI and disposals. These changes were driven by three themes as set out below.

The economic entity concept

Prior to the revisions it was true to say that group accounts were prepared very much using a parent company or proprietary approach i.e. it was assumed that the group accounts were prepared for the benefit of, and from the perspective of the parent company shareholders. For example under the parent company approach prior to the revisions, only the goodwill attributable to the parent was ever accounted for. Here are three consequences of the economic entity approach.

1   Because the revised standards adopt an economic entity approach all providers of equity share capital are treated as shareholders of the group, even when they are not shareholders in the parent company. This is a more inclusive approach towards the NCI. The revised standards unequivocally regard the NCI as much as shareholders of the group as the parent company shareholders and so requires the NCI to be presented as such i.e. within equity.

2   A further practical example of the economic entity concept is that when NCI is measured at acquisition at fair value this results in the full goodwill of the whole subsidiary being accounted for as a group asset. Even though the subsidiary may be partially owned, it is fully controlled so this is consistent with the way all the subsidiary's other assets and liabilities are accounted for. The subsidiary's goodwill is recognised in full on the group statement of financial position and the NCI are attributed a share in it.

3   On the group statement of financial position the NCI is presented within equity. Where at the end of an accounting period the subsidiary reports retained profits the NCI increases by its share of those retained profits and where the subsidiary incurs losses, the NCI will decrease by its share of those losses.

If the losses are so great that the NCI becomes a deficit balance (i.e. representing the NCI in the net liabilities of the subsidiary) then the NCI is reported as a negative figure. After all the NCI is part of equity, and equity shares in both profits and losses.

Control gained and control lost as significant economic events

Prior to the revisions of the standards, goodwill was accounted for by reference to the historic cost of investments so further investments after control had been achieved resulted in more goodwill arising.

Prior to the revisions of the standards any sale of the parent's interest in a subsidiary was accounted for as a separate transaction with goodwill being proportionately reduced and gains or losses arising in income (even if control was maintained).

The revised standards introduces the principle that only a change in control is a significant economic event that requires recognition or derecognition of goodwill. This new principle has a number of practical consequences.

1   A business combination only occurs, (and so acquisition accounting applied with and goodwill recognised) when control is achieved. Obtaining control is a significant economic event. See Chapter 15 *Changes in the group structure due to buying more shares.*

2   Once control has been achieved, subsequent transactions with the NCI (both further acquisitions and disposals that do not result in a loss of control) do not impact on the measurement of income or goodwill. These transactions with the NCI are not significant economic events, but in tune with the economic entity concept are transactions within equity. See Chapters 15 *Changes in the group structure due to buying more shares* and Chapter 16 *Changes in the group structure due to selling shares.*

3   A gain on a disposal only occurs and goodwill derecognised when control is lost. The loss of control is a significant economic event. See Chapter 16 *Changes in the group structure due to selling shares.*

Fair values

It has long been established that at acquisition the net assets of the subsidiary have to be adjusted to their fair value but the revised standards have introduced a greater use of fair values into accounting for business combinations.

Here are four specific examples.

1   On a step acquisition in measuring the total investment in the newly acquired subsidiary, the previously held interests in the new subsidiary are remeasured to fair value with the gain being reported in income. Goodwill arises and the investments are measured at the fair value at the date control was achieved. In substance the original investment is being sold and then reacquired. This follows the principle that a change in control is a significant

economic event. See Chapter 15 *Changes in the group structure due to buying more shares.*

2   Similarly on a disposal of a controlling interest, any residual interest is remeasured to fair value and reflected in income as part of the gain to the group on disposal. In substance the whole of the investment is being sold and then partially reacquired. This follows the principle that a change in control is a significant economic event. See Chapter 16 *Changes in the group structure due to selling shares.*

3   The contingent consideration given, as part of the cost of the investment in the subsidiary must be recorded at fair value. Previously such contingent consideration was only accounted for when it was probable. Recording contingent consideration at fair value ensures that all consideration given for the investment is recorded at fair value. See Chapter 4 *Recording the fair value of the investment in the subsidiary.*

4   Where the NCI at acquisition is measured at fair value, then goodwill is arrived at with all the possible component parts being at fair value. Measuring the NCI at fair value at acquisition follows the economic entity concept as then goodwill is measured in full See Chapter 5 *Non controlling interest at fair value and gross goodwill.*

Answers

Chapter 1

Answer Zambia

The first step is to show the group structure.

W1 Group structure

Zambia		
↓	Parent interest 100%	The acquisition was today
	Non controlling interest nil	
Lusaka		

From this we can see that Zambia is the parent company of Lusaka as it controls Lusaka by virtue of owning a majority, in fact a 100%, of the shares of Lusaka. This means that Lusaka is the subsidiary company. Because Zambia, the parent owns 100% of the shares of Lusaka this means there is no non controlling interest in the subsidiary's net assets.

The second step is to consider what the net assets of Lusaka really are at the date of acquisition and at the year-end.

W2 Net assets of the subsidiary

	At acquisition	At year-end
	$m	$m
Share capital	200	200
Accumulated profits	300	300
	500	500

Because the date of acquisition and the year-end are the same, the net assets are the same.

The third step is to determine whether any goodwill arose on the acquisition by comparing the cost of Zambia's investment in Lusaka with the parent's share of the nets assets at acquisition using column 1 of working 2.

W3 Goodwill

		$m
Cost of the parent's investment		500
Less the parent's % of the subsidiary's net assets at acquisition from w2 column 1	(100% x 500)	(500)
Goodwill		Nil

The fourth step would be work out any non controlling interest but as the subsidiary is 100% owned there will be no non controlling interest.

W4 Non controlling interest

		$m
NCI% of the subsidiary's net assets at year-end from w2 column 2	(0% x 500)	Nil

The fifth working considers what the accumulated profits belonging to the parent should be. This will just be the accumulated profits of Zambia since Lusaka has made no profit since the acquisition.

W5 Group accumulated profits

	$m
Parent's accumulated profits	400
Plus the parent's % of the subsidiary's post acquisition profits from w2	Nil
	400

Finally the group statement of financial position can be prepared.

Zambia group statement of financial position

	Zambia $m	Lusaka $m		Group $m
Goodwill			None arises w3	Nil
Investment in Lusaka	500		Cancelled out in w3	Nil
Assets	600	650	Simple cross cast	1,250
	1,100	650		1,250
Ordinary shares ($1)	400	200	Parent only	400
Accumulated profits	400	300	w5	400
Non controlling interest			w4	Nil
Equity	800	500		800
Liabilities	300	150	Simple cross cast	450
	1,100	650		1,250

Chapter 2

Answer Trinidad

The first working will be the group structure, then w2 the net assets of the subsidiary (as represented by the share capital and reserves) at acquisition and year-end (which are the same date), then w3 calculate goodwill, then w4 the non controlling interest, before finally w5 group accumulated profits.

W1 Group structure

Trinidad is the parent company of Tobago as it controls Tobago by virtue of owning a majority of the shares.

Trinidad		
↓	Parent's interest (225/300) 75% Non controlling interest 25%	The acquisition was today
Tobago		

W2 Net assets of the subsidiary

	At acquisition $m	At year-end $m
Share capital	300	300
Accumulated profits	400	400
	700	700

As the acquisition occurred today the net assets at acquisition and at the year-end are the same.

Thirdly let us compare the cost of investment made by Trinidad with the share of the net assets that were acquired to calculate the goodwill on acquisition.

W3 Goodwill

		$m
Cost of the parent's investment		800
Less the parent's % of the subsidiary's net assets at acquisition from w2 column 1	(75% x 700)	(525)
Goodwill		275

The goodwill arising is capitalised as an intangible asset.

Fourthly the non controlling interest in the subsidiary's net assets at the year-end can be calculated.

W4 Non controlling interest

		$m
NCI % of the subsidiary's net assets at the year-end from w2 column 2	(25% x 700)	175

Finally let us consider accumulated profits. As the subsidiary Tobago has only just been acquired and no goodwill has been written off it will be that of the parent only.

W5 Group accumulated profits

	$m
Parent's accumulated profits	500
Plus the parent's % of the subsidiary's post acquisition profits	Nil
	500

Finally the group statement of financial position can be prepared, with the assets and liabilities cross cast, the goodwill replacing the investment in the subsidiary and the share capital of the group being that of the parent only.

Trinidad group statement of financial position

		$m
Goodwill	w3	275
Assets	(1,000 + 900)	1,900
		2,175
Ordinary shares ($1)	Parent only	400
Accumulated profits	w5	500
Non controlling interest	w4	175
Equity		1,075
Liabilities	(900 + 200)	1,100
		2,175

Chapter 3

Answer Croatia

The group structure is always the place to start. It a very good habit to note here the parent's % and the non controlling interest as well as how long the subsidiary has been a member of the group.

W1 Group structure

Croatia

↓   Parent's interest (60/100) 60%   The acquisition was one year
       Non controlling interest 40%   ago

Zagreb

W2 Net assets

	At acquisition	At year end
	$m	$m
Share capital	100	100
Accumulated profits	60	400
	160	500
	Used to calculate goodwill in w3	Used to calculate the non controlling interest in w4

The increase in the net assets of $340m ($500m - $160m) in the post acquisition period represents the profits the subsidiary has made since acquisition and the parent's % is taken to group accumulated profits in w5.

W3 Goodwill

		$m
Cost of the parent's investment		600
Less the parent's % of the subsidiary's net assets at acquisition	(60% x 160)	(96)
Goodwill		504

The goodwill will appear as an intangible asset in the group accounts.

W4 Non controlling interest

		$m
NCI% in the net assets of the subsidiary w2	(40% x 500)	200

The non controlling interest in the net assets will be part of the group equity.

W5 Group accumulated profits

		$m
Parent's accumulated profits		750
Plus the parent's % of the subsidiary's post acquisition profits	(60% x (500 - 160))	204
		954

Croatia group statement of financial position

		$m
Non current assets		
Goodwill	w3	504
Tangible	(1,000 + 800)	1,800
Current assets	(400 + 200)	600
		2,904
Ordinary shares ($1)		800
Accumulated profits	w5	954
Non controlling interest	w4	200
Equity		1,954
Non current liabilities	(250 + 300)	550
Current liabilities	(200 + 200)	400
		2,904

Chapter 4

Answer Russia

(i) Fair value of consideration

The cost of the investment that Russia gave for its investment in Moscow can be ascertained by aggregating the fair value of the consideration given.

Cost of Investment in Moscow (at fair value)

		$
Cash		62,963
Shares	Russia has issued 100,000 shares each being worth $3 (50,000 x 100% x 2/1 x $3)	300,000
Deferred consideration	The cash that will be paid in the future of $40,000 will have to be discounted to reflect the time value of money. (80 cents x 50,000 x 1/1.08)	37,037
		400,000

(ii) Goodwill arising on consolidation

The cost of investment will be used to calculate goodwill as follows.

		$
Cost of the parent's investment (at fair value)		400,000
Less the parent's % of the net assets at acquisition	(100% x 150,000)	(150,000)
Goodwill of Moscow		250,000

As an aside, the parent's and group's income statement in the first year will recognise a finance cost of 8% x $37,037 = $2,963. The movement on the liability account can be summarised as follows.

	Opening balance	Plus the finance cost charged to income statement at 8%	Less the cash paid	Closing balance
	$	$	$	$
Year 1	37,037	2,963	(40,000)	Nil

Chapter 5

Answer Thames

In this question, the NCI will be 25%. The fair value of the NCI at acquisition is stated and given the requirement of the question. We can move straight to w3 goodwill and w4 NCI to answer the question.

(i)   W3 Goodwill

		$	$
Cost of the parent's investment (at fair value)		1,000	
Less the parent's % of the net assets at acquisition	(75% x 800)	(600)	
Goodwill (attributable to the parent)			400
Fair value of the NCI at acquisition		300	
Less the NCI % of the net assets at acquisition	(25% x 800)	(200)	
Goodwill (attributable to the NCI)			100
Gross (or full) goodwill at acquisition			500

Or W3 Goodwill

		$
Cost of the parent's investment (at fair value)		1,000
Fair value of the NCI at acquisition		300
Less 100% of the net assets at acquisition	(100% x 800)	(800)
Gross (or full) goodwill at acquisition		500

(ii)   W4 NCI at the year-end

		$
NCI% in the net assets in the subsidiary at the year-end	(25% x 3,000)	750
Plus the goodwill attributable to the NCI		100
		850

The NCI at the year-end can be determined in another way. As we are given the fair value of the NCI at the date of acquisition (which includes the NCI in the goodwill) then at the year end this will have risen by the NCI% in the post acquisition profits. That is to say the NCI% in the subsidiary profits will increase the NCI in the net assets. The net assets at acquisition have risen from $800 to $3,000 so the post acquisition profit is $2,200.

Alternative W4 NCI at the year-end

		$
Fair value of the NCI at acquisition.		300
Plus the NCI% of the post acquisition profits	(25% x 2,200)	550
		850

You may in the long run prefer to use this alternative method, it's my preferred method.

Answer Yangtze

In this question, the NCI is 40%. The fair value of the NCI at acquisition is again stated and given the requirement of the question. We can again move straight to w3 goodwill and w4 NCI to answer the question.

(i) W3 Goodwill

		$	$
Cost of the parent's investment		500	
Less the parent % of the net assets at acquisition	(60% x 400)	(240)	
Goodwill (attributable to the parent)			260
Fair value of the NCI at acquisition		200	
Less the NCI % of the net assets at acquisition	(40% x 400)	(160)	
Goodwill (attributable to the NCI)			40
Gross (or full) goodwill at acquisition			300

Or W3 Goodwill

		$
Cost of the parent's investment		500
Fair value of the NCI at acquisition		200
Less 100% of the net assets at acquisition	(100% x 400)	(400)
Gross (or full) goodwill at acquisition		300

(ii) W4 NCI at the year-end

		$
NCI% of the net assets at year-end	(40% x 600)	240
Plus the goodwill attributable to the NCI		40
		280
OR		
Fair value of the NCI at acquisition		200
Plus the NCI% of the post acquisition profits	(40% x 200)	80
		280

The alternative method of calculating the NCI at the year-end is to take the fair value of the NCI at acquisition and increase it by the NCI's share in the post acquisition profits of the subsidiary. The post acquisition profits are $200 as the net assets have risen from $400 at acquisition to $600 at the year-end.

Answer Ganges

In this example, the NCI is 20%. The fair value of the NCI at acquisition is again stated and given the requirement of the question, and we can again move straight to w3 goodwill and w4 NCI to answer the question.

(i)   W3 Goodwill

		$	$
Cost of the parent's investment		300	
Less the parent % of the net assets at acquisition	(80% x 400)	(320)	
Goodwill (attributable to the parent)			(20)
Fair value of the NCI at acquisition		86	
Less the NCI % of the net assets at acquisition	(20% x 400)	(80)	
Goodwill (attributable to the NCI)			6
Gross goodwill at acquisition			(14)

Or

		$
Cost of the parent's investment		300
Fair value of the NCI at acquisition		86
Less 100% of the net assets at acquisition	(100% x 400)	(400)
Gross goodwill at acquisition		(14)

Now this gross goodwill is a discount arising on consolidation i.e. negative goodwill in respect of a bargain purchase. The $14 will be immediately recognised in income as a gain.

(ii)   W4 NCI at the year-end

		$
NCI% of the net assets at year-end	(20% x 620)	124
Plus the goodwill attributable to the NCI		6
		130
OR		
Fair value of the NCI at acquisition		86
Plus the NCI% of the post acquisition profits	(20% x 220)	44
		130

The alternative method of calculating the NCI at the year-end is to take the fair value of the NCI at acquisition and increase it by the NCI's share in the post acquisition profits of the subsidiary. The post acquisition profits are $220 as the net assets have risen from $400 at acquisition to $620 at the year-end.

Chapter 6

Answer Barbados

As always we should look at doing the big five workings of group structure, net assets, goodwill, NCI and group accumulated profits.

W1 Group structure

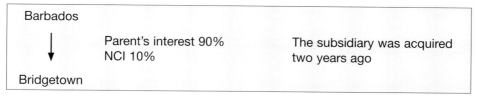

Barbados
↓
Bridgetown

Parent's interest 90%
NCI 10%

The subsidiary was acquired two years ago

The fair value adjustment of $100m on the plant increases the net assets both at acquisition and at the year-end because the plant is still an asset at the year-end. But also at the year-end there will be an adjustment for the additional depreciation.

W2 Net assets

	At acquisition $m	At year-end $m
Share capital	100	100
Accumulated profits	250	500
Fair value adjustment	100	100
Additional depreciation (1/4 x $100m x 2 years)	___	(50)
	450	650
	Used to calculate goodwill in w3	Used to calculate the NCI in w4

In this example two years have passed between the date of acquisition and the year-end. Therefore it is necessary to adjust for two years of additional depreciation at the year-end (column 2).

The increase in the net assets since acquisition is $200m ($650 - $450) and this represents the profits of the subsidiary since acquisition. The parent's % of this will be taken to the group accumulated profits in w5. The post acquisition profits of $200m, reflects the additional depreciation that has been charged.

W3 Goodwill

		$m
Cost of the investment		1,000
Less the parent's % of the net assets at acquisition	(90% x 450)	(405)
Goodwill (attributable to the parent)		595

Because goodwill is calculated using the proportionate approach there is no NCI in goodwill, and no fair value of the NCI at acquisition.

W4 NCI

		$m
NCI% of the net assets at year-end	(10% x 650)	65

W5 Group accumulated profits

		$m
Parent profits		250
Plus the parent's % of the post acquisition profits	(90% x (650 -450))	180
		430

Barbados group statement of financial position

		$m
Goodwill	w3	595
Assets	(600 + 800) plus the fair value adjustment 100 less the additional depreciation 50	1,450
		2,045
Ordinary shares ($1)		650
Accumulated profits	w5	430
Non controlling interest	w4	65
Equity		1,145
Liabilities	(700 + 200)	900
		2,045

Answer Mauritius

W1 Group structure

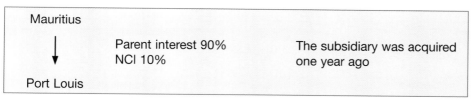

Mauritius		
↓	Parent interest 90% NCI 10%	The subsidiary was acquired one year ago
Port Louis		

Because the fair value of the net assets has been given at $2,000m, so the actual fair value adjustment on the plant is not known. The fair value adjustment will be the balancing figure in w2 column 1.

The accumulated profits of the subsidiary at acquisition are not given either. As the year-end accumulated profits are $1,000m, and the subsidiary was acquired one year ago during which profits of $250m were retained, then the profits at the date of acquisition must have been $750m.

W2 Net assets

	At acquisition $m	At year end $m
Share capital	200	200
Share premium	500	500
Accumulated profits	750	1,000
Fair value adjustment (bal fig)	550	550
Depreciation (550 x 1/5)	Nil	(110)
	2,000	2,140
	As the total of the fair value of the net assets was given so the FVA becomes the balancing figure. The net assets at acquisition will be used to calculate goodwill in w3.	This will be used to calculate the NCI in W4

In passing you may always assume that the share capital and share premium do not change i.e. there has not been an issue of shares after acquisition.

The asset subject to the fair value adjustment has a life of five years, and is presumed to still be there after one year.

The depreciation is a post acquisition adjustment. One year has passed since the date of acquisition, so the additional depreciation is $550m x $1/5$ x 1 year = $110m.

W3 Goodwill

		$m	$m
Cost of the investment		3,000	
Less the parent's % of the net assets at acquisition	(90% x 2,000)	(1,800)	
Goodwill (attributable to the parent)			1,200
Fair value of the NCI at acquisition		260	
Less the NCI % of the net assets at acquisition	(10% x 2,000)	(200)	
Goodwill (attributable to the NCI)			60
Gross (or full) goodwill			1,260

Or

		$m
Cost of the investment		3,000
Fair value of the NCI at acquisition		260
Less 100% of the net assets at acquisition	(100% x 2,000)	(2,000)
Gross (or full) goodwill at acquisition		1,260

W4 NCI

		$m
NCI% of the net assets year-end w2	(10% x 2,140)	214
Plus the goodwill attributable to the NCI w3		60
		274
OR		
Fair value of the NCI at acquisition.		260
Plus the NCI% of the post acquisition profits	(10% x 140)	14
		274

The difference of $140m between the net assets at acquisition and at the year-end represents the post acquisition profits of the subsidiary. The $140m post acquisition profit can also be thought of as the $250m profit that the subsidiary originally reported less the additional depreciation of $110m charged on the fair value adjustment.

The parent's share will be used to calculate the overall group accumulated profits in W5 and the NCI's share can be used to prove the NCI at the year-end.

Answer Bangladesh

W1 Group structure

Bangladesh		
↓	Parent's interest 80% NCI 20%	The subsidiary was acquired three years ago
Dhaka		

W2 Net assets

	At acquisition	At year end
	$m	$m
Share capital	400	400
Share premium	800	800
Accumulated profits	250	600
FVA on inventory	10	Nil
FVA on plant	110	110
Depreciation		(33)
	1,570	1,877
	This will be used to calculate goodwill in w3.	This will be used to calculate the NCI in w4.

Three years have passed since the date of acquisition, so the additional depreciation is $110m x 1/10 x 3 years = $33m.

The inventory is subject to a fair value adjustment at acquisition, but has since been sold so does not feature as an adjustment three years later. There will no adjustment to group inventory on the group statement of financial position.

As the actual fair value adjustments were given, both net assets figures are simple totals.

W3 Goodwill

		$m	$m
Cost of the investment		2,000	
Less the parent % of the net assets at acquisition	(80% x 1,570)	(1,256)	
Goodwill (attributable to the parent)			744
Fair value of the NCI at acquisition		400	
Less the NCI % of the net assets at acquisition	(20% x 1,570)	(314)	
Goodwill (attributable to the NCI)			86
Gross goodwill			830

Or

		$m
Cost of the investment		2,000
Fair value of the NCI at acquisition		400
Less 100% of the net assets at acquisition	(100% x 1,570)	(1,570)
Gross (or full) goodwill at acquisition		830

W4 NCI at the year-end

		$m
NCI% in the net assets at year-end	(20% x 1,877)	375
Plus the goodwill attributable to the NCI w3		86
		461
OR		
Fair value of the NCI at acquisition		400
Plus the NCI% of the post acquisition profits	(20% x (1,877 − 1,570))	61
		461

Chapter 7

Answer Singapore

The impairment review has to be calculated after the goodwill has been calculated. After the impairment loss has been calculated the gross goodwill is reduced and the impairment loss is split between the parent shareholders and the NCI in the normal proportions that they share profits and losses.

		$m	$m
Cost of the investment			800
Less the parent's % of the net assets at acquisition	(60% x 500)		(300)
Goodwill attributable to the parent			500
Fair value of the NCI at acquisition		250	
Less the NCI % of the net assets at acquisition	(40% x 500)	(200)	
Goodwill attributable to the NCI			50
Gross goodwill arising at acquisition			550

Or

		$m
Cost of the investment		800
Fair value of the NCI at acquisition		250
Less 100% of the net assets at acquisition	(100% x 500)	(500)
Gross goodwill arising at acquisition		550

Impairment review	$m
Carrying value	
Net assets of the subsidiary at year-end	600
Goodwill	550
	1,150
Recoverable amount	(1,000)
Impairment loss	150

The goodwill that will appear as an asset in the group statement of financial position at the year-end will be $550m less the impairment loss of $150m = $400m.

The parent's share of the gross impairment loss of $150m is 60% x $150 = $90m and will be deducted from group accumulated profits at w5.

The NCI's share of the gross impairment loss of $150m is 40% x $150m = $60m and will be deducted from the NCI at w4.

Answer Hong Kong

In conducting the impairment review of proportionate goodwill it is first necessary to gross it up.

Proportionate goodwill	Grossed up	Goodwill including the notional unrecognised
$300 x	100/60 =	$500

Now for the purposes of the impairment review of the subsidiary the goodwill of $500 together with the net assets of $250 forms the carrying value of the cash-generating unit.

Impairment review

Carrying value	$
Net assets of the subsidiary at year-end	250
Goodwill	500
	750
Recoverable amount	(700)
Impairment loss	50

The impairment loss does not exceed the artificially grossed up goodwill so therefore it is only the goodwill that has been impaired, and as proportionate goodwill is only attributable to the parent the impairment loss will not impact NCI and the other net assets.

Only the parent's share of the goodwill impairment loss $30 (60% x $50) will be recorded.

The impairment loss will be applied to write down the goodwill, so that the intangible asset of goodwill that will appear on the group statement of financial position will be $270 ($300 - $30).

In the group statement of financial position the group accumulated profits will be reduced by $30. There is no impact on the NCI.

As an aside, in the group income statement the impairment loss of $30 will be charged as an extra operating expense. There is no impact on the NCI.

Chapter 8

Answer Turkey

The current accounts must be eliminated on consolidation as neither the current account receivable of $25m in the parent's accounts or the current account payable of $12m in the subsidiary accounts actually represents external group items.

Further the goods in transit of $5m and the cash in transit of $8m both need to be included in group inventory and cash respectively.

			$m
Less	Receivable in current assets	by the current account balance of	25
Less	Payables in current liabilities	by the current account balance of	12
Plus	Inventory in current assets	by the goods in transit	5
Plus	Cash in current assets	by the cash in transit	8

Extract of Turkey's group statement of financial position

		$m
Current assets		
Inventory	(200 + 250 plus the goods in transit 5)	455
Receivables	(100 + 140 less the current account 25)	215
Cash at bank	(50 + 160 plus the cash in transit 8)	218
		888
Current liabilities	(100 + 160 less the current account 12)	248

Always exclude any inter-company current account balance and always include any goods and cash in transit.

Chapter 9

Answer Thomas

(i)

Unsold inventory		Mark-up		Purp
(500 – 300) = 200	X	25/125	=	40

(ii) Where the parent is the seller the consolidation adjustment for this purp is to:

less $40 from inventory in cross casting current assets

less $40 from the accumulated profits (w5) (100% as the parent is the seller).

(iii) Where the subsidiary is the seller the consolidation adjustment for this purp is to:

less $40 from inventory in cross casting current assets

less $32 (80% x $40) from accumulated profits (w5) (only the parent's % as the subsidiary is the seller)

less $8 (20% x $40) from the NCI (w4).

This ensures both the parent and the NCI are charged with their relative share of the purp.

Answer Felix

(i)

Unsold inventory		Margin		purp
(500 x ¾) = 375	X	10%	=	37.5

(ii) Where the parent is the seller the consolidation adjustment for this purp is to:

less $37.5 from inventory in cross casting current assets

less $37.5 from the accumulated profits (w5) (all as the parent is the seller).

(iii) Where the subsidiary is the seller then 40% of the purp (40% x 37.5 = 15) will be deducted from the NCI and only 60% of the purp (60% x 37.5 = 22.5) from accumulated profits. The consolidation adjustment is to:

less $37.5 from inventory in cross casting current assets

less $22.5 from the accumulated profits (w5) (only the parent's % as the subsidiary is the seller)

less $15 from the NCI (w4).

Answer Alice

(i)

Unsold inventory		Margin		purp
$(500 \times 2/3) = 333$	X	50%	=	167

(ii) Where the parent is the seller the consolidation adjustment for this purp is to;

less $167 from inventory in cross casting current assets

less $167 from the accumulated profits (w5) (100% as the parent is the seller)

(iii) Where the subsidiary is the seller then 25% of the purp (25% x 167 = 42) will be deducted from the NCI and only 75% of the purp (75% x 167 = 125) from accumulated profits. The consolidation adjustment is to:

less $167 from inventory in cross casting current assets

less $125 from the accumulated profits (w5) (only the parent's % as the subsidiary is the seller)

less $42 from the NCI (w4).

Chapter 10

Answer to England

Ok, let's deal with the current accounts and the cash in transit and the purp now but in future it will just be picked up as an adjustment on the face of the statement of financial position.

To adjust for the inter-company accounts we need to eliminate both balances and to include the cash in transit.

> Less Payables $6m when cross casting
>
> Plus Cash $4m when cross casting
>
> Less Receivables $10m when cross casting

To adjust for the purp the margin of 10% on the unsold inventory of $20m gives a purp of $2m that is both deducted from the accumulated profits (the parent is the seller so there is no charge to the NCI) and to inventory on the face of the statement of financial position.

> Less accumulated profits $2m
>
> Less inventory $2m

Remember that the first proper working will be to sort out the group structure. England is the parent company that controls London by virtue of owning a majority of its shares. Having purchased 36m of the 60m shares this is a 60% subsidiary and so the non controlling interest is 40%.

W1 Group structure

The second working is to establish the net assets of the subsidiary both at the date of the acquisition and at the year-end. The net assets of the subsidiary will be represented by its share capital, reserves and fair value adjustments. The reason for determining the net assets at the date of acquisition is to calculate the goodwill arising on consolidation. The reason for determining the net assets at the year-end is to determine the NCI and for the impairment review.

W2 Net assets

	At acquisition $m	At year-end $m
Share capital	60	60
Share premium	140	140
Accumulated profits	38	100
Fair value adjustment	12	12
Depreciation (12 x ¼ x 1 year)	___	(3)
	250	309
	Used to calculate goodwill in w3.	Used to calculate the non controlling interest in w4 and relevant for the impairment review.

The increase in the net assets in the post acquisition period of $59m ($309m – $250m) represents the profits of the subsidiary made since acquisition. This is used in group accumulated profits w5, and in NCI w4.

The post acquisition profits $59m of the subsidiary can be proved as follows

	$m
Subsidiary's accumulated profits at year-end	100
Less the subsidiary's accumulated at acquisition	(38)
Less the additional depreciation charged on the fair value adjustment	(3)
Post acquisition profits of the subsidiary	59

The third working is to determine the goodwill arising on consolidation. Almost inevitably when the parent buys the investment in the subsidiary it will pay a premium over and above the fair value of the net assets acquired. This premium arising on consolidation is termed goodwill and is required to be capitalised as an intangible asset in the group accounts. Goodwill will be subject to an annual impairment review and so be written down should it suffer a fall in value. As goodwill is to be calculated gross the impairment loss will be charged against the accumulated profits and the NCI in the proportions of 60/40.

When calculating gross goodwill we match the cost of the parent's investment and the fair value of the NCI's at acquisition with the fair value of the net assets of the subsidiary at the date of acquisition.

W3 Goodwill

		$m	$m
Cost of the parent's investment		350	
Less the parent's % of the net assets at acquisition w2	(60% x 250)	(150)	
Goodwill (attributable to the parent)			200
Fair value of the NCI at acquisition		150	
Less the NCI % of the net assets at acquisition w2	(40% x 250)	(100)	
Goodwill (attributable to the NCI)			50
Gross goodwill at acquisition			250
OR			
Cost of the parent's investment			350
Fair value of the NCI at acquisition			150
Less 100% of the net assets at acquisition w2	(100% x 250)		(250)
Gross goodwill at aquisition			250

Impairment review of gross goodwill

	$m	$m
Carrying value		
Net assets of the subsidiary at year-end w2	309	
Goodwill w3	250	559
Recoverable amount		(499)
Impairment loss		60

The goodwill remaining at the year-end will be $190m ($250m less $60m).

The accumulated profits will be charged with $36m (60% x $60m).

The NCI will be charged with $24m (40% x $60m).

As always the fourth working is the non controlling interest. However it is calculated it will be net of the impairment loss of gross goodwill.

W4 NCI

		$m
NCI % of the net assets of the subsidiary at year-end w2	(40% x 309)	123.6
Plus the goodwill attributable to the NCI w3		50
Less the NCI% of the impairment loss w3	(40% x 60)	(24)
		149.6
OR		
Fair value of the NCI at acquisition.		150
Plus the NCI% of the post acquisition profits w2	(40% x 59)	23.6
Less the NCI% of the impairment loss w3	(40% x 60)	(24)
		149.6

The last working is the group accumulated profits. This will comprise three basic elements. The starting point is the profits of the parent at the year-end from its statement of the financial position as adjusted here for all of the purp as the parent was the seller. As the gross goodwill has been impaired then the parent's share of this will have been written off and thus profits will have been reduced. Now when it comes to the subsidiary's profits that are attributable to the parent, there are two constraints that prevent a simple inclusion of all of their profits by a simple cross cast.

One constraint is that the subsidiary has only been a member of the group for a certain period – in this case one year – i.e. the group can only include the post acquisition profits.

The second constraint is that the parent is only entitled to its share of those profits in this case 60%. The increase in the net assets of the subsidiary from the date of acquisition to the year-end is the post acquisition profits (which will include the additional depreciation from the fair value adjustment) and is to be found as the difference in the columns in w2.

W5 Group accumulated profits

		$m
Parent's accumulated profits		350
Less all the purp (as parent is the seller)	(100% x 2)	(2)
Less the parent's % of the impairment loss	(60% x 60) w3	(36)
Plus the parent's % of the post acquisition profits of the subsidiary w2	(60% x 59) w2	35.4
		347.4

England group statement of financial position

		$m
Non current assets		
Intangible (goodwill)	w3 (250 less impairment loss 60)	190
Tangible	(500 + 300 plus the FVA 12 less the depreciation 3)	809
Current Assets		
Inventory	(30 + 110 less the purp 2)	138
Receivables	(20 +105 less the current account 10)	115
Cash at bank	(50 + 35 plus the cash in transit 4)	89
		1,341
Ordinary shares	(parent only)	200
Share premium	(parent only)	50
Accumulated profits	w5	347.4
Non controlling interest	w4	149.6
Equity		747
Non current liabilities	(230 + 140)	370
Current liabilities	(120 + 110 less the current account 6)	224
		1,341

Answer Wales

W1 Group structure

Wales

$\downarrow$

Cardiff

Parent's interest 60% (1,800 / 3,000)   The acquisition was six
NCI 40%   months ago

Before proceeding on to the net asset working it is worth noting that the accounts of Wales are out of date because it has not yet properly recorded the investment in the subsidiary Cardiff at the fair value of the consideration given.

The shares issued by Wales need to be recorded. The 500m shares with a nominal value of $1 need to be recorded at their market value of $3 each.

	$m	$m
Increase in Wales's investment in Cardiff	1,500	
Increase in the share capital of Wales		500
Increase in the share premium of Wales		1,000

The deferred consideration also needs to be recorded. At the date of acquisition the liability to pay $2,000m in three years' time needs to be discounted so that it is measured at the present value of the future cash flow at the date of acquisition. The discounting will reduce the size of the liability.

$$\$2,000m \times \frac{1}{1.1^3} = \$1,503m$$

	$m	$m
Increase in Wales's investment in Cardiff	1,503	
Increase in the non current liabilities of Wales		1,503

This means that the investment in the Cardiff is

	$m
Per original question	4,000
Shares issued at market value	1,500
Deferred consideration at present value	1,503
	7,003

But the liability in respect of the deferred consideration needs to be increased at the date of preparing the statement of financial position because it is being prepared six months further on from the date of acquisition. Accordingly the liability to pay the deferred consideration needs to be increased to reflect the fact it is only two and half years away and not three years. There will be an unwinding of the discount that will increase the size of the liability and create a finance cost.

$1,503m x 10% x 6/12 = $75m

The annual rate of interest is 10% but the time lapse is only six months, thus the use of 6/12.

	$m	$m
Decrease in the accumulated profits of Wales due to the finance cost	75	
Increase in the non current liabilities of Wales		75

The extra non current liability will therefore be $1,503m plus $75m = $1,578m.

There is also a provision for unrealised profit (purp) to calculate. The subsidiary Cardiff is the seller so this will be charged against to the profits attributable to the parent and the NCI in the ratio of 60/40.

Unsold inventory		Profit margin		purp
$20m	X	25%	=	$5m

W2 Net assets

When considering the net asset calculations the pre acquisition profits of Cardiff are not stated. The date of acquisition is exactly half way through the current accounting period. Following the assumption that the profits accrue evenly and that the current years profits are $2,500m the accumulated profits mid year can be ascertained, as:

		$m
Cardiff's accumulated profits at the year-end		3,500
Less 6/12 of the profits made in the current accounting period	(6/12 x 2,500)	(1,250)
Cardiff's accumulated profits at acquisition		2,250

Now we can prepare the net asset workings, remembering also to include the fair value adjustment on the brand.

	At acquisition	At year-end
	$m	$m
Share capital	3,000	3,000
Accumulated profits	2,250	3,500
Fair value adjustment	500	500
Less the amortisation (500 x 1/10 x 6/12)		(25)
	5,750	6,975

The increase in the adjusted net assets representing the post acquisition profits are ($6,975m – $5,750m) = $1,225m. This is after taking into account the amortisation of the brand Bay but before the provision for unrealised profit and the impairment loss.

W3 Goodwill

		$m	$m
Cost of the parent's investment		7,003	
Less the parent's % of the net assets at acquisition	(60% x 5,750)	(3,450)	
Goodwill (attributable to the parent)			3,553
Fair value of the NCI at acquisition		3,000	
Less the NCI % of the net assets at acquisition	(40% x 5,750)	(2,300)	
Goodwill (attributable to the NCI)			700
Gross goodwill at acquisition			4,253
Less impairment loss (as given)			(300)
Gross goodwill at the year-end			3,953

or

		$m
Cost of the parent's investment		7,003
Fair value of the NCI at acquisition		3,000
Less 100% of the net assets at acquisition	(100% x 5,750)	(5,750)
Gross goodwill at acquisition		4,253
Less impairment loss (as given)		(300)
Gross goodwill at the year-end		3,953

The impairment loss of the gross goodwill $300m will be charged between the profits attributable to the parent and the NCI in the proportion of 60/40.

W4 NCI

		$m
NCI of the net assets at year-end w2	(40% x 6,975)	2,790
Plus the goodwill attributable to the NCI w3		700
Less the NCI % of the impairment loss	(40% x 300)	(120)
Less the NCI % of the purp (subsidiary's seller)	(40% x 5)	(2)
		3,368
OR		
Fair value of the NCI at acquisition.		3,000
Plus the NCI % of the post acquisition profits of the subsidiary, w2	(40% x 1,225)	490
Less the NCI % of the impairment loss	(40% x 300)	(120)
Less the NCI % of the purp (subsidiary's seller)	(40% x 5)	(2)
		3,368

W5 Group accumulated profits

		$m
Parent's profits		6,000
Less the finance cost unwinding the discount on the deferred consideration (as not recorded previously by the parent)		(75)
Less parent's % of the impairment loss of gross goodwill w3	(60% x 300)	(180)
Plus the parent's % of the post acquisition profits of the subsidiary w2	(60% x 1,225)	735
Less parent's % of the purp (subsidiary is seller)	(60% x 5)	(3)
		6,477

The statement of financial position of the Wales group

		$m
Non current assets		
Intangible - goodwill	w3	3,953
Intangible - brand	(500 less the amortisation 25)	475
Tangible	(10,000 + 5,000)	15,000
Current assets	((3,000 + 4,000) less the purp 5)	6,995
		26,423
Ordinary shares	(5,000 plus the new shares 500)	5,500
Share premium	On the new shares	1,000
Accumulated profits	w5	6,477
Non controlling interest	w4	3,368
Equity		16,345
Non current liabilities	((4,000 + 2,000) plus new deferred consideration 1,578))	7,578
Current liabilities	(2,000 + 500)	2,500
		26,423

Chapter 11

Answer Bahamas

W1 Group structure

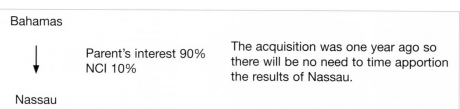

Bahamas

↓

Nassau

Parent's interest 90%
NCI 10%

The acquisition was one year ago so there will be no need to time apportion the results of Nassau.

There are two inter-company sales transactions to eliminate where both revenue and cost of sales will be reduced. The elimination of the inter company transactions can be done on the face of the income statement and has no impact on the NCI.

Both however create an unrealised profit arising from the unsold goods following the inter-company sale at a transfer price.

Unsold inventory at the year-end		Gross profit margin		
(1/4 x $100m)	X	20%	=	$5m

Unsold inventory at the year-end		Gross profit mark-up		
(½ x $180m)	X	50 / 150	=	$30m

With the second purp of $30m, Nassau, the subsidiary is the seller so this will impact the NCI. These purps are both extra expenses (reduces profits by increasing cost of sales).

W2 Net assets

	At acquisition $m	At year-end $m
Share capital	1,000	1,000
Accumulated profits	800	2,200
Fair value adjustment	200	200
Depreciation (1/4 x 200)		(50)
Total	2,000	3,350

The additional depreciation is an extra expense (reduces profits by increasing cost of sales). It relates to the subsidiary's profits so will impact the NCI.

The post acquisition profits of the subsidiary are $1,350m (before dealing with the purp).

W3 Goodwill

		$m
Cost of the parent's investment		4,000
Less the parent's % of the net assets at acquisition w2	(90% x 2,000)	(1,800)
Goodwill		2,200

Goodwill is not being calculated gross. There is no impairment loss.

W4 NCI

		$m
NCI % of the net assets at year-end w2	(10% x 3,350)	335
Less the NCI % of the purp (subsidiary's seller)	(10% x 30)	(3)
		332

Goodwill is not being calculated gross so there is no goodwill attributable to the NCI, and there is no fair value of the NCI at acquisition.

W5 Group accumulated profits

		$m
Parent's accumulated profits		15,690
Less the purp (parent is seller)	(100% x 5)	(5)
Less the purp (subsidiary is seller)	(90% x 30)	(27)
Plus the parent's % of the post acquisition profits	(90% x 1,350)	1,215
		16,873

We can now proceed to preparing the group statement of financial position. The workings for assets are quite busy, so instead of being shown on the face of the accounts it is presented in a working below.

W6 Assets

Assets	$m
Parent	20,000
Subsidiary	5,000
Fair value adjustment	200
Less depreciation	(50)
Less purp (parent is seller)	(5)
Less purp (subsidiary is seller)	(30)
	25,115

Bahamas group statement of financial position

		$m
Goodwill	w3	2,200
Assets	w6	25,115
		27,315
Share capital ($1)		5,000
Accumulated profits	w5	16,873
NCI	w4	332
Equity		22,205
Liabilities	(3,310 + 1,800)	5,110
		27,315

Before moving on to to prepare the group income statement, there are the further workings to undertake of cost of sales and the NCI in the subsidiary's profits. The finance costs and the exceptional item can be simply cross cast like the other income and expenditure, but the investment income of the parent comes directly from the subsidiary and so is eliminated from the group income statement.

W7 Cost of sales

Cost of sales	$m
Parent	12,000
Subsidiary	2,000
Less the inter-company	(100)
Less the inter-company	(180)
Plus the purp (parent is seller)	5
Plus the purp (subsidiary is seller)	30
Plus the additional depreciation	50
	13,805

W8 NCI in the subsidiary's profits

		$m
NCI % of the subsidiary's profits as given	(10% x 1,500)	150
Less the NCI % of depreciation on FVA	(10% x 50)	(5)
Less the NCI % of the purp (subsidiary is seller)	(10% x 30)	(3)
		142

Finally we can now proceed to prepare the group income statement.

Bahamas group income statement

		$m
Revenue	(20,000 + 4,000 less inter-company (100 + 180))	23,720
Cost of sales	w7	(13,805)
Gross profit		9,915
Distribution costs	(2,100 + 300)	(2,400)
Administration expenses	(1,400 + 500)	(1,900)
Operating profit		5,615
Exceptional gain	(0 + 580)	580
Investment income	(90 less inter-company 90)	Nil
Finance costs	(600 + 150)	(750)
Profit before tax		5,445
Tax	(700 + 130)	(830)
Profit for the year		4,615
Attributable to the parent	Balancing figure	4,473
Attributable to the NCI	w8	142
Profit for the year		4,615

Bahamas group statement of changes in equity

	Share capital	Accumulated profits	NCI	Total Equity
	$m	$m	$m	$m
Opening balance	5,000	12,600	200	17,800
Profits for the year		4,473	142	4,615
Less dividends		(200)	(10)	(210)
Closing balance	5,000	16,873	332	22,205

The share capital of the group is that of the parent company only and the parent has issued no shares in the period.

The opening accumulated profits are that of the parent only. This is because the subsidiary was acquired one year ago. Accumulated profits increase by the profits attributable to the parent from the group income statement and decrease by the parent's dividend.

The opening NCI is based only the net assets at the start of the year as goodwill is not gross. (10% x net assets $2,000m = $200m). NCI increases by its share of the profit for the year and decreases by the NCI in the subsidiary's dividend (10% x $100m = $10m). The parent has received the other 90% of the subsidiary's dividend that has been distributed, which is then eliminated in the consolidated income statement as an inter-company item.

The total column is acting as a proof, a double check if you like, that all is well between the group income statement and the group statement of financial position as it all agrees with the answer.

Chapter 12

Answer Kenya

It is massively significant to note that Nairobi was acquired during the year. This will mean that only its post acquisition results are consolidated, though all of the other comprehensive income is post acquisition.

W1 Group structure

Kenya

Parent's interest 75%
NCI 25%

The acquisition was six months ago so there will be the need for time apportionment.

Nairobi

The question tells us that the parent has not correctly recorded the investment i.e. that the liability in respect of the deferred consideration has not been discounted. It is necessary to do this in order to work out the finance cost that will need to be charged in respect of the unwinding of the discount as well as the goodwill arising which is subject to an impairment review.

The fair value of the consideration will be the present value of the deferred consideration. The liability is due to be paid two years after the date of acquisition, but the discount rate quoted in the question is 4% every six months and not per annum. Therefore as there are four lots of six months between the date of acquisition and the payment date the calculation of the fair value of the liability and the cost of the investment will be.

$$\$1{,}000m \times \frac{1}{1.1^3} = \$855m$$

The finance cost reflecting the unwinding of the discount in the first six months that the parent company has not yet recorded and should have recorded as an additional finance cost is

$$4\% \times \$855m = \$34m$$

It will be necessary to determine the net assets of the subsidiary at the year-end in order for the impairment review.

W2 Net assets

	At acquisition $m	At year-end $m
Share capital	100	100
Accumulated profits (see below)	400	500
Fair value adjustment (bal fig)	100	100
Depreciation (1/5 x 6/12 x 100)		(10)
	600	690

		$m
Nairobi's accumulated profits at the start of the accounting period		300
Plus 6/12 of the current year's profits	(6/12 x 200)	100
Nairobi's accumulated profits at the date of acquisition		400
Plus 6/12 of the current year's profits	(6/12 x 200)	100
Nairobi's accumulated profits at year-end		500

W3 Goodwill

		$m	$m
Cost of the parent's investment (at fair value)		855	
Less the parent's % of the net assets at acquisition	(75% x 600)	(450)	
Goodwill (attributable to the parent)			405
Fair value of the NCI at acquisition		250	
Less the NCI % of the net assets at acquisition	(25% x 600)	(150)	
Goodwill (attributable to the NCI)			100
Gross goodwill			505

Of course gross goodwill can be calculated using the alternative presentation.

		$m
Cost of the parent's investment (at fair value)		855
NCI at acquisition at fair value		250
Less the 100% of the net assets at acquisition	(100% x 600)	(600)
Gross goodwill		505

W4 Impairment review for gross goodwill

	$m	$m
Carrying value of Nairobi		
Net assets of the subsidiary at year-end w2	690	
Goodwill w3	505	
		1,195
Recoverable amount		(900)
Impairment loss		295

W5 Cost of sales

		$m
Parent		2,000
Subsidiary (time apportioned)	(6/12 x 200)	100
Less the inter-company		(100)
Plus the impairment loss on the goodwill w4		295
Plus the purp		Nil
Plus the depreciation on the FVA (time apportioned)	(1/5 x 6/12 x 100)	10
		2,305

There is no need to time apportion the impairment loss or any purp (if there were any) as they both arose in the post acquisition period i.e. at the year-end.

W6 NCI in the subsidiary's profits

		$m
NCI % of subsidiary's profits as given BUT time apportioned	(25% x 6/12 x 200)	25
Less NCI % of the depreciation on FVA	(25% x 10)	(2.5)
Less NCI % of the purp (subsidiary is seller)		Nil
Less the NCI % of the impairment loss w4	(25% x 295)	(74)
		(51.5)

Clearly it is unusual to have a NCI in a loss for the year rather than an NCI in the profit for the year.

W7 NCI in the subsidiary's total comprehensive income

		$m
NCI in the subsidiary's profit (as above)		(51.5)
NCI in the subsidiary's other comprehensive income	(25% x 100)	25
		(26.5)

Kenya group statement of comprehensive income

Income statement		$m
Revenue	(10,000 + (6/12 x 1,000) less the inter-company (100))	10,400
Cost of sales	w5	(2,305)
Gross profit		8,095
Operating costs	(1,500 + (6/12 x 450))	(1,725)
Operating profit		6,370
Finance cost		(34)
Profit before tax		6,336
Tax	(2,500 + (6/12 x 150))	(2,575)
Profit for the year		3,761
Other comprehensive income		
Revaluation gains	(1,000 + 100)	1,100
Total comprehensive income		4,861
Attributable to the parent	Balancing figure	3,812.5
Loss attributable to the NCI	w6	(51.5)
Profit for the year		3,761
Attributable to the parent	Balancing figure	4,887.5
Loss attributable to the NCI	w7	(26.5)
Total comprehensive income		4,861

Chapter 13

Answer Sierra

Sierra Leone Freetown

W1 Group structure

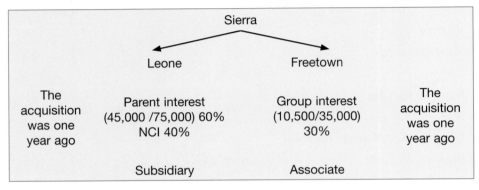

	Sierra		
	Leone	Freetown	
The acquisition was one year ago	Parent interest (45,000 /75,000) 60% NCI 40%	Group interest (10,500/35,000) 30%	The acquisition was one year ago
	Subsidiary	Associate	

Before we go any further let's sort out what is going on with the inter-company transactions as detailed in the question at points 3, 4 and 5.

Leone is a subsidiary selling to its parent company Sierra goods for $10,000. This is an inter-company transaction and must be eliminated on consolidation. As result in the group income statement.

Less	revenue	$10,000	
Less	cost of sales		$10,000

There is a provision for unrealised profit needed in respect of the unsold inventory at the year-end.

80% has been sold on	Unsold inventory at the year end	Multiplied by the gross profit margin	Gives us the purp
(20% x $10,000)	= $2,000	x 40%	= $800

As the subsidiary is the seller the NCI will be charged with their share of the adjustment in both the income statement and the statement of financial position.

In the group statement of financial position the purp will need to reduce the inventory.

Less	Group accumulated profits w5	(60% x 800)	$480	
Less	NCI w4	(40% x 800)	$320	
Less	Inventory			$800

Freetown is an associate selling to its parent company goods for $15,000. This sale and purchase is not eliminated on consolidation as only the share of the associates profits are reported in the group accounts. The revenue figure of the associate is not included in group revenue.

However the group share of the provision for unrealised profit is needed in respect of the unsold inventory at the year-end.

Unsold at the year end is 20% of the sales	Multiplied by the gross profit margin	Gives us the purp	Of which the parent's % of the associate is 30%	Consolidation adjustment
(20% x $15,000) = 3,000	x 50%	= $1,500	x 30% =	$450

As the seller is the associate so the associate's profits are reduced as well as the group inventory.

Less	Group accumulated profits w5	$450	
Less	Inventory		$450

In respect of point 5, the inter-company balances and interest is between the parent and the subsidiary and requires simple elimination.

less	Payables (liability)	$5,000	
less	Receivables (asset)		$5,000
less	Interest receivable (income)	$10,000	
less	Finance cost (expense)		$10,000

Now back to net assets etc !!

The question tells us the fair value of the net assets at acquisition, which means that it is the fair value adjustment that becomes the balancing figure. For Leone the asset subject to depreciation has a five year life and as the acquisition took place one year ago so one years depreciation is required in the post acquisition period. For Freetown the fair value adjustment related to land and as land is not consumed or used up it is not subject to depreciation.

W2 Net assets

| | Leone | | Freetown | |
| | Acq | Y/e | Acq | Y/e |
	$	$	$	$
Share capital	75,000	75,000	35,000	35,000
Revaluation reserve	Nil	1,000	Nil	2,000
Accumulated profits	30,000	49,000	25,000	38,000
Fair value adjustments (balancing figure)	45,000	45,000	10,000	10,000
Depreciation ($1/5 \times 45,000$)		(9,000)		
Total	150,000	161,000	70,000	85,000

The increase in the net assets of Leone since acquisition is $11,000. ($161,000 - $150,000).

This is partly attributable to a revaluation gain ($1,000) and partly to profits ($10,000).

The parent's share of the revaluation gain will be taken to the group's revaluation reserves. (60% x $1,000 = $600).

The parent's share of the post acquisition profits of $10,000 will be taken to accumulated profits w5. (60% x $10,000 = $6,000).

The increase in the net assets of Freetown (the associate) since acquisition is $15,000 ($85,000 - $70,000) and this will be taken to increase the carrying value of the investment in the associate.

This is partly attributable to a revaluation gain ($2,000) and partly to profits ($13,000).

The parent's share of the revaluation gain will be taken to the group's revaluation reserves. (30% x $2,000 = $600).

The parent's share of the post acquisition profits of $13,000 will be taken to accumulated profits w5 (30% x $13,000 = $3,900).

The investment in the associate

		$
Cost of the investment of Freetown		30,000
Plus the parent's post acquisition profits (including the revaluation gain) w5	(30% x (85,000 – 70,000))	4,500
Carrying value of the associate		34,500

W3 Goodwill

Leone		$	$
Cost of the parent's investment		100,000	
Less the parent's % of the net assets at acquisition	(60% x 150,000)	(90,000)	
Goodwill (attributable to the parent)			10,000
Fair value of the NCI at acquisition		63,000	
Less the NCI % of the net assets at acquisition	(40% x 150,000)	(60,000)	
Goodwill (attributable to the NCI)			3,000
Gross goodwill at acquisition			13,000

Or

		$
Cost of the parent's investment		100,000
Fair value of the NCI at acquisition		63,000
Less 100% of the net assets at acquisition	(100% x 150,000)	(150,000)
Gross goodwill at acquisition		13,000

No goodwill is impaired.

The goodwill of the subsidiary has been calculated gross, so the NCI will participate and the NCI will rise by $3,000 as well.

W4 NCI in the subsidiary's net assets

		$
NCI % of the net assets at year end w2	(40% x 161,000)	64,400
Plus the goodwill attributable to the NCI w3		3,000
Less the NCI % of the subsidiary's purp (subsidiary is seller)	(40% x 800)	(320)
		67,080
Or		
Fair value of the NCI at acquisition.		63,000
Plus the NCI% of the post acquisition profits	(40% x 11,000)	4,400
Less the NCI% of the purp (subsidiary is seller)	(40% x 800)	(320)
		67,080

W5 Group accumulated profits

		$
Parent's accumulated profits		150,000
Less the parent's % of the purp (subsidiary is seller)	(60% x 800)	(480)
Less the parent's % of the purp (associate is seller)	(30% x 1,500)	(450)
Plus the parent's % of the post acquisition profits of the Leone subsidiary (w2)	(60% x 10,000)	6,000
Plus the parent's % of the post acquisition profits of the Freetown associate (w2)	(30% x 13,000)	3,900
		158,970

W6 Revaluation reserve

		$
Parent's revaluation reserve		50,000
Plus the parent's % of the post acquisition gain of the subsidiary (w2)	(60% x 1,000)	600
Plus the parent's % of the post acquisition gain of the associate (w2)	(30% x 2,000)	600
		51,200

Sierra group statement of financial position

Non current assets			$
Intangible	w3		13,000
Tangible	(100,000 + 80,000	plus 45,000 FVA less depreciation (9,000)) (w2)	216,000
Investment in associate	w2		34,500
			263,500
Current assets			
Inventory	(22,000 + 30,000	less purps (800 + 450))	50,750
Receivables	(58,000 + 10,000	less inter-company (5,000))	63,000
Cash at bank	(40,000 + 20,000)		60,000
			437,250
Share capital			100,000
Revaluation reserve	w6		51,200
Accumulated profits	w5		158,970
Non controlling interest	w4		67,080
Equity			377,250
Liabilities	(50,000 + 15,000	less inter-company (5,000))	60,000
			437,250

Sierra group statement of comprehensive income

In order to prepare the group statement of comprehensive income there are several additional workings that will need to be done. For example cost of sales, the income from the associate and the NCI in the subsidiary's profit for the year. The adjustments for eliminating the inter-company sales and interest can be achieved on the face of the answer.

W7 Cost of sales

		$
Parent		300,000
Subsidiary		140,000
Less the inter-company		(10,000)
Plus all the purp (subsidiary is seller)		800
Plus the depreciation	(1/5 x 45,000)	9,000
		439,800

No mention of the associate is made in the cost of sales – the impact of the associate will be restricted to a single line.

W8 Income from the associate

		$
Parent's % of the associate's profits for the year	(30% x 15,000)	4,500
Less the Parent's % of the purp (associate is seller)	(30% x 1,500)	(450)
		4,050

W9 NCI in the subsidiary's profits

		$
NCI % of the subsidiary's profits for the year as given	(40% x 20,000)	8,000
Less the NCI % of the depreciation on the subsidiary's FVA (1/5 x 45,000 = 9,000)	(40% x 9,000)	(3,600)
Less the NCI % of purp (subsidiary is seller)	(40% x 800)	(320)
		4,080

As the subsidiary is the seller with the purp so there is an impact on the NCI as the adjustment to profit relates to the subsidiary and the subsidiary's profits and losses are shared between the parent and the NCI.

The additional depreciation on the fair value adjustment creates an adjustment to the profit of the subsidiary that will also impact on the NCI.

There was no impairment on goodwill – but as goodwill is gross, if there had been then the NCI share would have been charged as well.

W10 NCI in the subsidiary's comprehensive income

		$
NCI % of the subsidiary's profits for the year	w9	4,080
Plus the NCI % of in the revaluation gain	(40% x 1,000)	400
		4,480

Sierra group statement of comprehensive income

Income statement		$
Revenue	(500,000 + 200,000 but less inter company 10,000))	690,000
Cost of sales	w7	(439,800)
Gross profit		250,200
Administration expenses	(50,000 + 10,000)	(60,000)
Operating profit		190,200
Interest receivable	(10,000 but less 10,000 as all inter-company)	Nil
Interest payable	(10,000 but less 10,000 as all inter-company)	Nil
Income from associate	w8	4,050
Profit before tax		194,250
Tax	(60,000 + 20,000)	(80,000)
Profit for the year		114,250
Other comprehensive income		
Revaluation gains	(10,000 + 1,000 + (30% x 2,000))	11,600
Total comprehensive income		125,850
Attributable to parent	Balancing figure	110,170
Attributable the NCI	w9	4,080
Profit for the year		114,250
Attributable to parent	Balancing figure	121,370
Attributable the NCI	w10	4,480
Total comprehensive income		125,850

Chapter 15

Answer France

France	3,000/20,000	15% acquired last year
		NCI 25%
Paris	12,000/20,000	60% acquired now

The first acquisition gave France 3,000 / 20,000 shares in Paris i.e. 15%. This holding is not a majority so does not give control. It is on the subsequent acquisition of the 12,000 / 20,000 shares in Paris i.e. the 60% that control is achieved with a total holding now of 75% and therefore a NCI of 25%. On the second investment the original investment is revalued to fair value giving a gain that is reported in the income statement of $3,000.

	$
Fair value of the original investment	9,000
Less the cost of the original investment	(6,000)
Gain to the income statement	3,000

In this example there is no need to do w2 net assets, as the figure is given, so we can proceed straight to w3 goodwill.

W3 Goodwill

		$	$
Fair value of the original investment		9,000	
Fair value of the consideration given for the second investment		25,000	
Cost of parent's investment			34,000
Less the parent's % of the net assets at acquisition	(75% x 10,000)		(7,500)
Goodwill (attributable to the parent)			26,500
Fair value of the NCI		9,000	
Less the NCI % of the net assets at acquisition	(25% x 10,000)	(2,500)	
Goodwill (attributable to the NCI)			6,500
Gross goodwill at acquisition			33,000

Alternatively the gross goodwill can be calculated as follows

		$
Fair value of the original investment		9,000
Fair value of the consideration given for the second investment		25,000
Fair value of the NCI		9,000
Less 100% of the net assets at acquisition	(100% x 10,000)	(10,000)
Gross goodwill at acquistion		33,000

Answer Malaysia

The cost of reducing the NCI is $70,000 and this will be compared with the reduction in the NCI. The NCI of 40% has been halved so the new NCI of 20% will represent half that of the original $100,000 and will be measured at $50,000, thus a transfer decreasing the NCI is required of $50,000.

	$
Cash paid out	70,000
Transfer to NCI decreasing the NCI	50,000
Difference reduces equity	20,000

As the cost of the subsequent investment exceeds the decrease in the NCI the difference taken to equity will be a reduction in reserves.

The cash paid out reduces the assets in the top half of the statement of financial position. Where this is more than the reduction in the NCI (bottom half of the statement of financial position) then the difference will also have to be deducted from reserves (equity).

Again, dangerous though it is to write this – if you think of the NCI as a liability – then we have paid out $70,000 to settle a liability of $50,000. This is not good! There is a loss of $20,000 and losses decrease equity. But remember that the NCI is not a liability – this just might help explain why the $20,000 difference is a decrease in equity.

Answer Greece

The first thing is as always to sort out the group structure.

Greece currently owns all (200/200) of the shares in Athens so has a 100% subsidiary – but this investment has been acquired in steps.

W1 Group structure

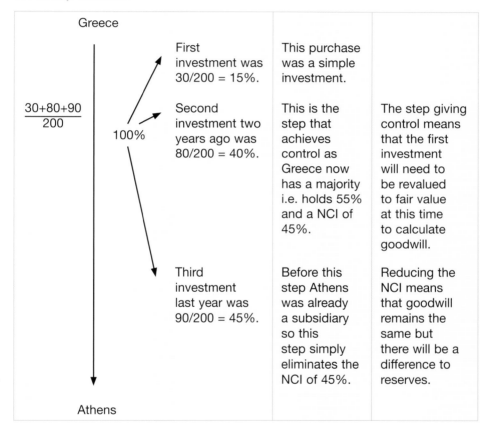

Greece

$$\frac{30+80+90}{200}$$

100%

Athens

First investment was 30/200 = 15%.

This purchase was a simple investment.

Second investment two years ago was 80/200 = 40%.

This is the step that achieves control as Greece now has a majority i.e. holds 55% and a NCI of 45%.

The step giving control means that the first investment will need to be revalued to fair value at this time to calculate goodwill.

Third investment last year was 90/200 = 45%.

Before this step Athens was already a subsidiary so this step simply eliminates the NCI of 45%.

Reducing the NCI means that goodwill remains the same but there will be a difference to reserves.

W2 Net assets

There is a need for net assets at three dates in this example – to ensure that we have all the information necessary to calculate goodwill and reserves.

Net assets of Athens

| | Acquisition | | |
| | Two years ago | One year ago | Year-end |
	$m	$m	$m
Share capital	200	200	200
Accumulated profits	150	250	500
	350	450	700

From two years to one year ago the post acquisition profits are ($450 - $350) = $100m during which time the parent's interest was 55%.

From one year ago to the year-end the post acquisition profits are ($700- $450) = $250m during which time the parent's interest was 100%.

W3 Goodwill

The goodwill is calculated when control was achieved two years ago. For consolidation purposes the first investment of $150m three years ago is revalued by $10m to $160m at that time. This gain is recognised in income and thus will increase the accumulated profits in w5.

		$m	$m
Fair value of the original investment		160	
Fair value of second investment		300	
		460	
Less the parent's % of the net assets at acquisition	(55% x 350)	(192.5)	
Goodwill (attributable to the parent)			267.5
Goodwill (attributable to the NCI)			32.5
Gross goodwill at acquisition			300

No goodwill has been impaired, so this is the goodwill that will be reported on the statement of financial position.

The subsequent acquisition of the remaining 45% one year ago for $350m does not create any extra goodwill as goodwill is only calculated for a subsidiary once that is say when control is acquired. Buying up the extra shares in an existing subsidiary instead reduces the NCI and creates a difference that is taken to reserves but is neither a gain nor loss.

The NCI at the time the step acquisition was made to reduce the NCI to nil one year ago was as follows.

		$m
NCI % of the net assets one year ago w2	(45% x 450)	202.5
Plus the goodwill attributable to the NCI w3		32.5
		235

Reduction in the NCI

	$m
Cash paid out (cost of the third investment)	350
Transfer from NCI to decrease NCI (45/45 x 235)	235
Difference to equity (decrease)	115

This difference is taken to reserves as a deduction. The asset of cash has been reduced down by more than the NCI so there remains a further deduction to make from equity. Whilst technically this not a loss (as it is a transaction within equity) it has cost more to buy out the NCI than its carrying value so it feels like a loss!

W4 NCI

The NCI at the year-end will be based on the NCI % at the year-end, and as it is now a 100% owned entity there will be no NCI!

W5 Group accumulated profits

		$m
Parent's profits		350
Plus the gain recognised in income from revaluing the first investment	(160 - 150)	10
Plus the parent's % of the post acquisition profits of the subsidiary whilst 55% owned w2	(55% x 100)	55
Plus the parent's % of the post acquisition profits of the subsidiary whilst 100% owned w2	(100% x 250)	250
		665

Greece group statement of financial position

Non current assets		$m
Tangible	(100 + 550)	650
Goodwill	w3	300
Current assets	(300 + 450)	750
		1,700
Ordinary shares ($1)		100
Accumulated profits	w5	665
Difference when decreasing NCI	w3	(115)
Non controlling interest		Nil
Equity		650
Non current liabilities	(450 + 270)	720
Current liabilities	(300 + 30)	330
		1,700

I suppose the difference of ($115m) could be presented as a deduction from accumulated profits, to show net group reserves of $550m but taking a purist perspective the difference is not a loss as it has arisen from a transaction within equity and so to mix it up with accumulated profits sends a confused message.

Chapter 16

Answer Ireland

(i) In order to calculate the gain to the group on the disposal of Ireland we have to calculate the gross goodwill.

		$m	$m
Cost of the investment		900	
Less the parent's % of the net assets at acquisition	(60% x 500)	(300)	
Goodwill (attributable to the parent)			600
Fair value of the NCI		300	
Less the NCI % of the net assets at acquisition	(40% x 500)	(200)	
Goodwill (attributable to the NCI)			100
Gross goodwill arising at acquisition			700

Gross goodwill can be calculated in an alternative way.

		$m
Cost of the parent's investment		900
Fair value of the NCI at acquisition		300
Less 100% of the net assets at acquisition	(100% x 500)	(500)
Gross goodwill at acquisition		700

Of course in order to calculate the gain to the group we also have to calculate the NCI at the date of disposal.

W4 NCI

		$m
NCI % of the net assets at disposal w2	(40% x 750)	300
Plus the goodwill attributable to the NCI w3		100
		400
OR		
Fair value of the NCI at acquisition		300
Plus the NCI% of the post acquisition profits of the subsidiary, as represented by the post acquisition increase in the net assets.	((40% x (750 – 500))	100
		400

Gain to the group

Now so long as we can remember the proforma we can calculate the gain to the group.

	$m
Sale proceeds	3,000
Less all the net assets of the subsidiary at the date of disposal	(750)
Less all the goodwill remaining at the date of disposal	(700)
Plus all the NCI at the date of disposal	400
Plus the fair value of any residual holding	Nil
Gain to the group	1,950

(ii) As a result of the sale of these shares the subsidiary remains a subsidiary but the NCI of 40% has increased to 46%. Where there has been a reduction in the NCI a difference arises that is taken to equity. The difference is between the proceeds received and the transfer increasing the NCI. The transfer to the NCI represents 6% of the net assets and the goodwill.

		$m
Cash proceeds received		3,000
Transfer to NCI increasing the NCI	(6% x (750 + 700))	87
Difference increases equity		2,913

The NCI after the sale will be $184,000.

The cash received increases the assets in the top half of the statement of financial position. Where this is more than the increase in the NCI (bottom half of the statement of financial position) then the difference will also have to be taken to reserves as an addition to the reserves (equity).

Answer China

The group structure changes during the year.

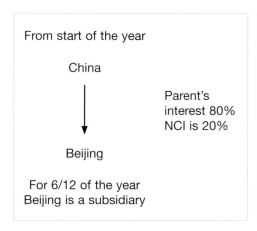

From start of the year

China

Parent's
interest 80%
NCI is 20%

Beijing

For 6/12 of the year
Beijing is a subsidiary

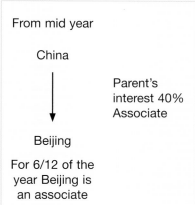

From mid year

China

Parent's
interest 40%
Associate

Beijing

For 6/12 of the
year Beijing is
an associate

Because of the change in the group structure that has taken place during the year it will be necessary to do a lot of time apportionment! Beijing was a subsidiary for half the year and was also an associate for half the year.

But the first thing to get sorted is the exceptional gain to the group arising on the disposal of the subsidiary. The question suggests that the gain is $77,500 that was determined by comparing the sale proceeds with the cost of shares sold (see below) but this is the gain to the parent company and not to the group.

W2 Gain to the parent

		$
Proceeds		150,000
Less cost of shares sold	(40/80 x 145,000)	(72,500)
Gain to the parent company		77,500

Knowing the proforma to compute the gain to the group means that we have to start to gather our ingredients together of net assets, goodwill and NCI at disposal.

W3 Goodwill

With no impairment loss the goodwill at disposal can be determined as follows.

			$
Cost of the investment		145,000	
Less the parent's % of the net assets at acquisition	(80% x 140,000)	(112,000)	
Goodwill (attributable to the parent)			33,000
Fair value of NCI at acquisition		20,000	
Less the NCI% of the net assets at acquisition	(20% x 140,000)	(28,000)	
Goodwill (attributable to the NCI)			(8,000)
Gross goodwill			25,000

Or

		$
Cost of the parent's investment		145,000
Fair value of the NCI at acquisition		20,000
Less 100% of the net assets at acquisition	(100% x 140,000)	(140,000)
Gross goodwill		25,000

The net assets of the subsidiary at the date of disposal cannot be readily ascertained in the normal way. However we know that at acquisition the net assets were $140,000 and that they would have been increased by the post acquisition profit in the first year of $50,000 and then in the second year up to the date of disposal by 6/12 of $60,000. Therefore the net assets at disposal were $220,000 ($140,000 + $50,000 + $30,000).

W4 NCI at disposal

		$
NCI% in the net assets at disposal	(20% x 220,000)	44,000
Plus the goodwill attributable to the NCI (which is a negative figure!)		(8,000)
		36,000
Or		
Fair value of the NCI at acquisition.		20,000
Plus the NCI% of the post acquisition profits of the subsidiary.	(20% x 50,000 + (6/12 x 60,000))	16,000
		36,000

W5 Gain to the group

	$
Sale proceeds	150,000
Less all the net assets of the subsidiary at the date of disposal	(220,000)
Less all the goodwill remaining at the date of disposal w3	(25,000)
Plus all the NCI at the date of disposal w4	36,000
Plus the fair value of any residual holding	150,000
Gain to the group	91,000

Finally we can begin to put together the group income statement.

Remembering though that

- Beijing was only a subsidiary for the first six months and as such its results are consolidated on a time apportionment basis. Its revenue and expenses are consolidated on a line by line basis as it is a continuing operation

- the exceptional gain on disposal is inserted after operating profit

- for the latter six moths Beijing is an associate and so its results are equity accounted for in the income statement. Equity accounting means bringing in the results in one line!

China group statement of comprehensive income

Income statement		$
Revenue	(730,000 + (6/12 x 400,000))	930,000
Operating costs	(450,000 + (6/12 x 300,000))	(600,000)
Operating profit		330,000
Exceptional gain	w5	91,000
Income from associate	(40% x 60,000 x 6/12)*	12,000
Profit before tax		433,000
Tax	(150,000 + (6/12 x 40,000))	(170,000)
Profit for the year		263,000
Other comprehensive income		
Revaluation gains		10,000
Total comprehensive income		273,000
Attributable to the parent	Balancing figure	197,000
Attributable to the NCI	(60,000 + 20% x (6/12 x 60,000))#	66,000
Profit for the year		263,000
Attributable to the parent	Balancing figure	207,000
Attributable to the NCI	(60,000 + 20% x (6/12 x 60,000))#	66,000
Total comprehensive income		273,000

*The working represents the parent's % of the associate's profit for the year as time apportioned. There is no impairment loss or purp or additional depreciation to worry about.

#The existing NCI's share of group profits is increased by the 20% of the time apportioned profit for the year generated by Beijing.

(ii) In answer to the second part of the question, if there was a complete disposal of Beijing and it represented a discounted operation, then the results of Beijing would be shown in a single line as "profit from discontinued operations".

The gain to the group will be calculated with no residual holding.

W6 Gain to the group

	$
Sale proceeds	350,000
Less all the net assets of the subsidiary at the date of disposal	(220,000)
Less all the goodwill remaining at the date of disposal w3	(25,000)
Plus all the NCI at the date of disposal w4	36,000
Gain to the group	141,000

China Group statement of comprehensive income

Income statement		$
Revenue	Per the question	730,000
Operating costs	Per the question	(450,000)
Operating profit		280,000
Exceptional gain	w6	141,000
Profit before tax		421,000
Tax	Per the question	(150,000)
Profit for the year from continuing operations		271,000
Profit from discontinued operations	(6/12 x 60,000)	30,000
Profit for the year		301,000
Other comprehensive income		
Revaluation gains		10,000
Total comprehensive income		311,000
Attributable to the parent	Balancing figure	235,000
Attributable to the NCI	(60,000 + 20% x (6/12 x 60,000))	66,000
Profit for the year		301,000
Attributable to the parent	Balancing figure	245,000
Attributable to the NCI	(60,000 + 20% x (6/12 x 60,000))	66,000
Total comprehensive income		311,000

Chapter 17

Answer Primary

W1 Group structure

Let's sort out that group structure, because with a vertical group there is a lot riding on w1.

The initial working of the group structure will be

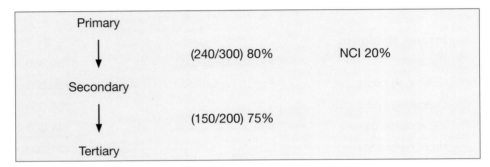

Primary		
↓	(240/300) 80%	NCI 20%
Secondary		
↓	(150/200) 75%	
Tertiary		

Control

Secondary is a simple subsidiary that is directly controlled by Primary. Tertiary is also a subsidiary of Primary as Primary controls Secondary and Secondary controls Tertiary.

Percentages

The effective interest in the sub subsidiary Tertiary is.

Effective Primary interest in Tertiary	80% x 75%	=	60%
Effective NCI interest in Tertiary	Balancing figure		40%
			100%

These are the proportions for allocating the net assets and profits of Tertiary.

Dates

Primary only acquired control of Secondary one year ago, so that is when Tertiary also joined the group. Therefore the information about Tertiary's retained earnings, the fair value of the NCI and the cost of the investment two years ago are all irrelevant.

The fair value of Secondary's investment in Tertiary is $410m, some $10m more than Secondary has recorded in its statement of financial of position. As such there is a fair value adjustment required by Secondary of $10m increasing both the investment and creating a pre acquisition revaluation reserve.

Indirect holding adjustment

Their investment holding adjustment is therefore.

20% x $410m = $82m

To conclude Tertiary has been a subsidiary of the Primary group for one year with an effective interest of 60%, a NCI of 40% and the final presentation of this group structure will be:

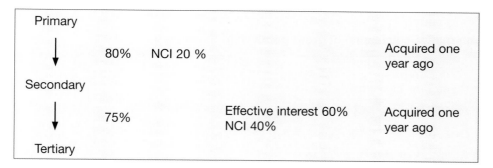

The net assets working for Secondary has to include the fair value adjustment on its investment in Tertiary and Tertiary has to include the fair adjustment on the land.

W2 Net assets

	Secondary		Tertiary	
	At acquisition	**At year-end**	**At acquisition**	**At year-end**
	$m	**$m**	**$m**	**$m**
Share capital	300	300	200	200
Accumulated profits	150	550	120	250
Fair value adjustment	10	10	20	20
	460	860	340	470

The post acquisition profit of Secondary is $400m ($860m - $460m).

The post acquisition profit of Tertiary is $130m ($470m - $340m).

W3 Goodwill of Secondary

		$m	$m
Cost of the investment		800	
Less the parent's % of the net assets at acquisition	(80% x 460)	(368)	
Goodwill (attributable to the parent)			432
Fair value of the NCI at acquisition		120	
Less the NCI % of the net assets at acquisition	(20% x 460)	(92)	
Goodwill (attributable to the NCI)			28
Gross goodwill at acquisition			460

Alternative calculation of gross goodwill of Secondary

		$m
Cost of the investment		800
Fair value of the NCI at acquisition		120
Less 100% of the net assets at acquisition	(100% x 460)	(460)
Gross goodwill at acquisition		460

Goodwill of Tertiary – the sub subsidiary

		$m	$m
Cost of the investment		400	
Plus the fair value adjustment at acquisition		10	
Less the indirect holding adjustment	(20% x 410)	(82)	
Less the parent's % of the net assets at acquisition	(60% x 340)	(204)	
Goodwill (attributable to the parent)			124
Fair value of the NCI at acquisition		140	
Less the NCI % of the net assets at acquisition	(40% x 340)	(136)	
Goodwill (attributable to the NCI)			4
Gross goodwill at acquisition			128

Alternative calculation of gross goodwill of Tertiary

		$m
Cost of the investment		400
Plus the fair value adjustment at acquisition		10
Less the indirect holding adjustment	(20% x 410)	(82)
Fair value of the NCI at acquisition		140
Less 100% of the net assets at acquisition	(100% x 340)	(340)
Gross goodwill at acquisition		128

W4 NCI

		$m
NCI % in Secondary's year-end net assets	(20% x 860)	172
NCI % in Tertiary's year-end net assets	(40% x 470)	188
Less the indirect holding adjustment	(20% x 410)	(82)
Plus Secondary's goodwill attributable to NCI		28
Plus Tertiary's goodwill attributable to NCI		4
		310
Or		
Fair value of Secondary's NCI at acquisition.		120
Fair value of Tertiary's NCI at acquisition.		140
Less the indirect holding adjustment	(20% x 410)	(82)
Plus the NCI% of Secondary's post acquisition profits w2	(20% x 400)	80
Plus the NCI% of Tertiary's post acquisition profits w2	(40% x 130)	52
		310

W5 Group accumulated profits

		$m
Parent profits		550
Plus the parent's % of Secondary's post acquisition profits w2	(80% x 400)	320
Plus the parent's % of Tertiary's post acquisition profits w2	(60% x 130)	78
		948

Now we can prepare the group statement of financial position.

Primary group statement of financial position

		$m
Goodwill	(460 + 128) w3	588
Other assets	(1,200 + 500 + 600 + land FVA 20)	2,320
		2,908
Ordinary shares ($1)		400
Accumulated profits	w5	948
Non controlling interest	w4	310
Equity		1,658
Liabilities	(1,050 + 50 + 150)	1,250
		2,908

Chapter 18

Answer Unicycle

W1 Group structure

It is important that we get this mixed group structure sorted out at the date that the group statement of financial position is drawn up so that we can establish the relationships and then the effective interests.

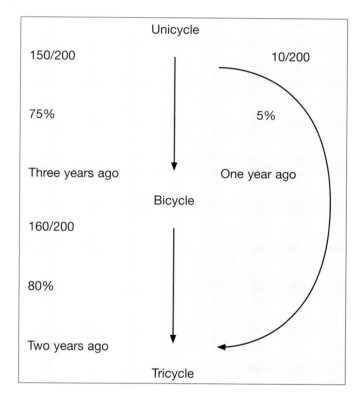

Control

In terms of the relationships, Unicycle has been the parent of Bicycle for three years, as Unicycle holds a majority of the shares in Bicycle. The NCI of Bicycle is 25%.

Unicycle was the parent of Bicycle when two years ago Bicycle acquired control of Tricycle making Tricycle a subsidiary of Unicycle and Bicycle at the same time. Therefore on the consolidation of Tricycle into the Unicycle group there will be no need to revalue Bicycle's investment in Tricycle.

Percentages

Now at the year-end when we work out Unicycle's effective interest and NCI in Tricycle we shall take all the investments into account as all the investments have taken place by the year-end.

Unicycle's direct interest in Tricycle		5%
Unicycle's indirect interest in Tricycle	(75% x 80%)	60%
Unicycle's effective interest in Tricycle		65%
Effective NCI in Tricyle	(Balancing figure)	35%
		100%

Dates

Before the Unicycle's direct investment in Tricycle the effective interest in Tricycle was only 60% and accordingly the NCI 40%. So as a result of Unicycle's direct acquisition of 5% last year the NCI reduced from 40% to 35%.

One year ago, in addition to the indirect investment in Tricycle, Unicycle acquired a direct investment in Tricycle of 5%. This further investment did not change the status of Tricycle, as it was a subsidiary of Unicycle both before and after the investment. The acquisition therefore represents a reduction in the NCI.

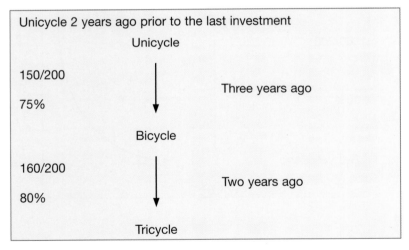

As per Chapter 15 *Changes in the group structure due to buying more shares*, this is accounted for as a transaction within equity, with a transfer out from the NCI, with no change in goodwill and with no gain or loss arising but a difference going to reserves. But let's work out that difference once we know the NCI and that requires net assets and goodwill to be sorted first.

Indirect holding adjustment

There will be an indirect holding adjustment in respect of Bicycle's investment in Tricycle that will reduce both the investment in Tricycle and the NCI as follows.

The NCI in Bicycle	Bicycle's cost of investment in Tricycle		$000
25%	X 300	=	75

W2 Net assets

You might argue that doing a full net asset working is superfluous as all the net asset numbers are given in the question itself, but the working does make clear the post acquisition profits. Unicycle's % of Tricycle's post acquisition profits increased last year, thus for Tricycle net assets at three dates are shown. Note that the fair value adjustment on Bicycle's inventory at acquisition is not included at the year-end as it has been sold so will not exist at the year-end.

	Bicycle		Tricycle		
	At acquisition	At year-end	At acquisition of (60%)	At purchase of 5%	At year-end
	3 years ago		2 years ago	1 year ago	
	$000	$000	$000	$000	$000
Share capital	200	200	200	200	200
Accumulated profits	90*	250	50*	75*	120
Fair value adjustment	10	Nil	Nil	Nil	Nil
	300	450	250	275	320

*Balancing figures

The post acquisition profit of Bicycle is $150,000 ($450,000 - $300,000).

The post acquisition profit of Tricycle is $25,000 whilst a 60% subsidiary ($275,000 - $250,000).

The post acquisition profit of Tricycle is $45,000 whilst a 65% subsidiary ($320,000 - $275,000).

W3 Bicycle's gross goodwill

		$000	$000
Cost of the investment		400	
Less the parent's % of the net assets at acquisition	(75% x 300)	(225)	
Goodwill (attributable to the parent)			175
Fair value of the NCI at acquisition		50	
Less the NCI % of the net assets at acquisition	(25% x 300)	(75)	
Goodwill (attributable to the NCI)			(25)
Gross goodwill at acquisition			150

Don't worry that the goodwill attributable to NCI is negative. The overall goodwill is positive so goodwill is an asset. Had the overall goodwill been negative i.e. a discount arising on consideration rather than a premium, then it would have been recognised as a gain in group income.

Alternative calculation of gross goodwill for Bicycle

		$000
Cost of the investment		400
Fair value of the NCI at acquisition		50
Less 100% of the net assets at acquisition	(100% x 300)	(300)
Gross goodwill at acquisition		150

The calculation of goodwill for Tricycle will only reflect the indirect investment, as that was the only investment at the time when control was achieved. Being an indirect investment an indirect holding adjustment will be made. When calculating goodwill Bicycle's investment in Tricycle should not include the additional 5% as this relates to the reduction in the NCI. Goodwill is not affected by the decrease in the NCI, as it is a transaction within equity.

Tricycle's gross goodwill

		$000	$000
Cost of the investment by Bicycle		300	
Less the indirect holding adjustment	(25% x 300)	(75)	
Less the parent's % of the net assets at acquisition	(60% x 250)	(150)	
Goodwill (attributable to the parent)			75
Fair value of the NCI at acquisition		110	
Less the NCI % of the net assets at acquisition	(40% x 250)	(100)	
Goodwill (attributable to the NCI)			10
Gross goodwill at acquisition			85

Alternative calculation of gross goodwill for Tricycle

		$000
Cost of the investment by Unicycle		300
Less the indirect holding adjustment	(25% x 300)	(75)
Fair value of the NCI at acquisition		110
Less the 100% of the net assets at acquisition	(100% x 250)	(250)
Gross goodwill at acquisition		85

W4 NCI

Whichever way you wish to present the NCI in the subsidiaries' net assets the NCI% in Tricycle at the year-end is 35% and there will an indirect holding adjustment.

If we calculate NCI at the year-end then we are just looking at calculating what is left of the NCI at the year-end, so the share of the net assets in Tricycle can be reduced down to 35% but the NCI in the gross goodwill of $10,000 is reduced down by 5/40 i.e. by $1,250 to $8,750.

		$000
NCI % in the Bicycle's year-end net assets	(25% x 450)	112.5
NCI % in the Tricycle's year-end net assets	(35% x 320)	112
Less the indirect holding adjustment	(25% x 300)	(75)
Plus Bicycle's goodwill attributable to the NCI		(25)
Plus Tricycle's goodwill attributable to the NCI	(10 – (5/40 x 10))	8.75
		133.25

If we calculate the NCI by reconciling the fair value of the NCI at acquisition with the current balance of the NCI then we see that the full transfer out of the NCI of the transfer to equity is the NCI's share of the net assets and gross goodwill at the date of purchase. The difference between the cost and the transfer out of NCI is taken directly to equity as it does not impact on goodwill nor is it a gain or loss.

NCI of Tricycle prior to reduction

		$
NCI % in net assets one year ago (w2)	(40% x 275)	110
Plus goodwill attribuable to the NCI (w3)		10
		120

Transfer reducing the NCI

$$^{5}/_{40} \times \$120,000 = \$15,000$$

The difference is ascertained as follows

	$000
Cash paid out (cost of the investment)	50
Transfer from NCI decreasing the NCI	15
Difference to equity (decrease)	35

Where the cost of the subsequent investment exceeds the decrease in the NCI then the difference taken to reserves will be a decrease in reserves and equity. More assets have been reduced than NCI so in order to make the statement of financial position balance there has to be a further deduction in equity.

As the difference is not technically a loss I prefer to show this as a negative reserve separate from accumulated profits.

Or NCI

		$000
Fair value of the Bicycle's NCI at acquisition.		50
Fair value of the Tricycle's NCI at acquisition.		110
Less the indirect holding adjustment	(25% x 300)	(75)
Plus the NCI% of Bicycle's post acquisition profits w2	(25% x 150)	37.5
Plus the NCI% of Tricycle's post acquisition profits w2	(40% x 25)	10
Plus the NCI% of Tricycle's post acquisition profits w2	(35% x 45)	15.75
Less the transfer decreasing the NCI		(15)
		133.25

W5 Group accumulated profits

		$000
Parent accumulated profits		130
Plus the parent's % of Bicycle's post acquisition profits w2	(75% x 150)	112.5
Plus the parent's % of Tricycle's post acquisition profits w2	(60% x 25)	15
Plus the parent's % of Tricycle's post acquisition profits w2	(65% x 45)	29.25
		286.75

And finally we can compile this all into a group statement of financial position.

Unicycle group statement of financial position

		$000
Goodwill	w3 (150 + 85)	235
Assets	(220 + 340 + 460 less inter-company 20)	1,000
		1,235
Share capital ($1)		300
Difference		(35)
Accumulated profits	w5	286.75
NCI	w4	133.25
Equity		685
Liabilities	(240 + 190 + 140 less inter-company 20))	550
		1,235

Answer Ocean

W1 Group structure

The group structure at the year-end is as follows

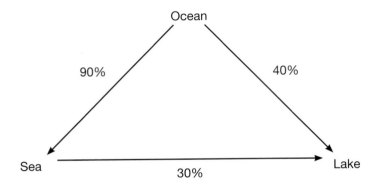

Ocean

90%   40%

Sea   Lake
              30%

Control

This shows us that Ocean is the parent and Sea is a subsidiary with a 10% NCI, and that Ocean is able to control Lake so that Lake is a subsidiary of Ocean.

To confirm this analysis consider the voting rights at a shareholders meeting of Lake. Ocean would hold 40% of the voting rights, and Ocean would also have power over its subsidiary Sea's voting rights of 30%. As Ocean is able to direct the majority of the voting rights of Lake (i.e. 70%) Lake is a subsidiary of Ocean. This 70% is not however the effective interest in Lake; this is the next step.

Percentages

Ocean's effective interest in the net assets and profits of Lake will comprise both its direct interest and the indirect interest held by Sea.

Ocean's direct interest in Lake		40%
Ocean's indirect interest (via Sea)	(90% x 30%)	27%
Effective interest in Lake		67%
Effitive NCI in Lake	(Balancing figure)	33%
		100%

Dates

But whilst this is the group structure that exists at the year-end and is relevant for preparing the group statement of financial position, it has only existed in this form since Sea made its investment in Lake six months ago. In order to prepare the group income statement we need to establish what the group structure was for the first six months of the accounting period.

At the start of the accounting period the group structure is as follows

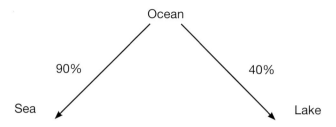

Ocean

90%   40%

Sea   Lake

This again shows us that Ocean is the parent and Sea is a subsidiary with a 10% NCI.

As Ocean holds 40% of the shares in Lake then Lake is an associate of Ocean. The information in the question confirms this conclusion as it is stated that the investment gives Ocean significant influence. Lake will therefore be equity accounted for the first six months of the year in the income statement.

Further this means that when, in the middle of the accounting period Sea acquires its 30% investment in Lake, Ocean obtains control of Lake so that Lake becomes a subsidiary of the Ocean group. As Ocean already has a 40% interest in Lake it means that the acquisition of Lake is a step acquisition that achieves control.

From an individual company perspective Ocean's original investment in Lake of $500,000 will be remeasured to its fair value of $700,000 with the $200,000 gain being recognised by the parent as income.

From a group perspective the carrying value of Lake the associate will be remeasured to the fair value of $700,000 with the gain being recognised in group income. In the group accounts equity accounting will be used to determine the carrying value of Lake as an associate. Six months before the year-end this can be determined by updating the cost of the investment by the share of the post acquisition profits.

Lake's profits six months before the year-end are the accumulated profits at the year-end less 6/12 of the current years profits.

		$000
Accumulated profits at the year-end		510
Less the profits in the last six months of the year	(6/12 x 250)	(125)
		385

The post acquisition profits to be considered here are those between the date of Ocean's original acquisition two years ago ($100,000) and six months before the year-end.

Investment in associate Lake		$000
Cost of investment		500
Plus Ocean's % of the post acquisition profits	(40% x (385 – 100))	114
Carrying value of the associate		614

So from a group perspective the carrying value of Lake the associate of $614,000 will be remeasured to the fair value of $700,000 with a gain being recognised in group income of $86,000

Indirect holding adjustment

In calculating the goodwill of Lake, since part of the investment is an indirect holding there will be an indirect holding adjustment.

Sea's investment in Lake cost $800,000. From the perspective of calculating goodwill in Ocean's group accounts this has to be reduced down as Ocean only has a 90% interest in Sea and so only a 90% interest in the cost of the investment in Lake. Sea's investment in Lake of $800,000 is, from Ocean's perspective, an indirect cost of which the NCI of Sea is responsible for 10%.

The indirect holding adjustment in respect of Sea's investment in Lake is:

The NCI in Sea		Sea's cost of investment in Lake		
(10%	X	$800,000)	=	$80,000

W2 Net assets

Lets now get on with the rest of the answer, starting with the net assets.

	Sea		Lake	
	At acquisition	At year-end	At acquisition (6 months ago)	At year-end
	$000	$000	$000	$000
Share capital	200	200	80	80
Share premium	Nil	Nil	60	60
Accumulated profits	200	400	385	510
Fair value adjustment (bal fig)	100	100	Nil	Nil
	500	700	525	650

The post acquisition profit of Sea is $200,000 ($700,00 - $500,000)

The post acquisition profit of Lake is $125,000 ($650,000 - $525,000)

W3 Goodwill

As a directly owned subsidiary then the goodwill calculation of Sea is relatively straightforward.

Sea's gross goodwill

		$000	$000
Cost of investment		800	
Less parent's % of the net assets at acquisition	(90% x 500)	(450)	
Goodwill (attributable to the parent)			350
Fair value of the NCI at acquisition		50	
Less NCI % of the net assets at acquisition	(10% x 500)	(50)	
Goodwill (attributable to the NCI)			Nil
Gross goodwill at acquisition			350

Alternative calculation of gross goodwill for Sea

		$000
Cost of the investment		800
Fair value of the NCI at acquisition		50
Less 100% of the net assets at acquisition	(100% x 500)	(500)
Gross goodwill at acquisition		350

The calculation of goodwill for Lake will reflect both the direct and indirect investment (and so incorporate the indirect holding adjustment) and the revaluation of the first investment, as it is a step acquisition.

Lake's gross goodwill

		$000	$000
Fair value of the original investment	(500 + 200)		700
Cost of the investment by Sea			800
Less the indirect holding adjustment	(10% x 800)		(80)
Less the parent's % of the net assets at acquisition	(67% x 525)		(351.75)
Goodwill (attributable to the parent)			1,068.25
Fair value of the NCI at acquisition		700	
Less the NCI % of the net assets at acquisition	(33% x 525)	(173.25)	
Goodwill (attributable to the NCI)			526.75
Gross goodwill at acquisition			1,595

Alternative calculation of gross goodwill for Lake

		$000
Fair value of the original investment	(500 + 200)	700
Cost of the investment by Sea		800
Less the indirect holding adjustment	(10% x 800)	(80)
Fair value of the NCI at acquisition		700
Less 100% of the net assets at acquisition	(100% x 525)	(525)
Gross goodwill at acquisition		1,595

Whichever way the NCI is calculated it will be necessary to charge the NCI with the indirect holding adjustment.

W4 NCI

		$000
NCI % in Sea's year-end net assets	(10% x 700)	70
NCI % in Lake's year-end net assets	(33% x 650)	214.5
Less the indirect holding adjustment	(10% x 800)	(80)
Plus Sea's goodwill attributable to NCI		Nil
Plus Lake's goodwill attributable to NCI		526.75
		731.25
Or		
Fair value of Sea's NCI at acquisition.		50
Fair value of Lake's NCI at acquisition		700
Less the indirect holding adjustment	(10% x 800)	(80)
Plus the NCI% of Sea's post acquisition profits w2	(10% x 200)	20
Plus the NCI% of Lake's post acquisition profits w2	(33% x 125)	41.25
		731.25

W5 Group accumulated profits

Ocean's profits do not yet reflect the gain that it will have as a parent company on the revaluation of the investment in Lake by $200,000 from $500,000 to $700,000, thus the first adjustment is being done at the individual company stage.

From a group perspective with regard to Lake what the rest of the statement of financial position reflects is that Lake is a subsidiary, i.e. we have the goodwill of Lake as a subsidiary, the NCI of Lake and its assets and liabilities cross cast, as it is a subsidiary. Accordingly in group accumulated profits we regard Lake as being a subsidiary.

		$000
Ocean's profits per the question		850
Plus the gain to the parent on the revaluation of the original investment in Lake		200
Correct balance of Ocean's profits		1,050
Plus Ocean's % of Sea's post acquisition profits w2	(90% x 200)	180
Plus Ocean's % of Lake's post acquisition profits w2	(67% x 125)	83.75
		1,313.75

Ocean group statement of financial position

		$000
Goodwill	w3 (350 + 1,595)	1,945
Other assets	(700 + 250 + 800 + 100 FVA on Sea's land)	1,850
		3,795
Share capital ($1)		500
Share premium		500
Accumulated profits	w5	1,313.75
Non controlling interest	w4	731.25
Equity		3,045
Liabilities	(150 + 450 + 150)	750
		3,795

In thinking about preparing to do the group income statement, we should remember that Lake will be for 6/12 of the year an associate, and for 6/12 of the year a subsidiary.

When equity accounting for the associate there is no impairment loss or purp to deal with so it is a straight 40% of the time apportioned profits.

There will be the exceptional gain on the revaluation of the associate of $86,000 following the step acquisition.

But on the bright side there are no inter-company transactions, purps, additional depreciation or impairment losses to worry about!

The only additional working as such required is the NCI in the profit for the year.

W6 NCI in profit

		$000
NCI in Sea's profit for the year	(10% x 100)	10
NCI in Lake's profit for the year	(33% x 250 x 6/12)	41.25
		51.25

Ocean group income statement

		$000
Income statement		
Revenue	(3,150 + 2,000 + (6/12 x 2,500)	6,400
Operating costs	(2,300 + 1,820 + (6/12 x 2,000)	(5,120)
Operating profit		1,280
Exceptional gain	w1	86
Income from associate	(40% x 250 x 6/12)	50
Profit before tax		1,416
Tax	(350 + 80 + (6/12 x 250))	(555)
Profit for the year		861
Attributable to parent	Balancing figure	809.75
Attributable to the NCI	w6	51.25
Profit for the year		861

Now that we have just completed the group income statement it is possible to prove the year-end group accumulated profits by reconciling the opening and closing balances as they will have only increased by the profit of the year attributable to the parent.

The profits b/f are the year-end profits less the current years profit. The parent's share of the post acquisition profits of the subsidiary and associate should be included, remembering at the start of the year Lake was just an associate.

Reconciliation of the group's accumulated profits

		$000	$000
Parent b/f	(850 – 500)	350	
Plus Sea	90% (400 – 100 – 200)	90	
Plus Lake	40% (510 – 250 – 100)	64	
Accumulated profits b/f			504
Profit for the year	From income statement		809.75
Accumulated profits			1,313.75

Chapter 19

Answer Rosa Parks

Rosa here has no foreign currency element to its transactions. Rosa functions in $, Rosa lends in $ and is repaid in $.

Parks on the other hand functions in DN but has borrowed in $ and so it is Parks that has a foreign currency transaction to record since when it borrows the $60,000 this has to be translated into DN.

With an exchange rate showing more DN than $ when we move from $ to DN then we shall multiply!

Parks on 10 March has a foreign currency transaction to record.

The receipt of the $ loan will be translated into DN using the exchange rate ruling on the date of the transaction.

10 March	$60,000	x 10	= DN600,000

The transaction can then be recorded in the accounts.

Increase asset of cash	DR	Cash	DN600,000	
Increase liability of loan	CR	Liability		DN600,000

At 31 March Parks has a year-end.

At the year-end the loan is a monetary amount and requires retranslating at the closing rate with the resulting exchange difference being taken to the income statement.

15 March	$60,000	x 10	= DN600,000
31 March	$60,000	x 8	= DN480,000
	Exchange difference		DN120,000

In this case the exchange difference that arises on the retranslation of the liability decreases the liability resulting in a gain in the income statement. Such a gain on a loan would be shown in the financing section.

Decrease liability of loan	DR	Loan	DN120,000	
Recording a gain	CR	Income statement		DN120,000

Assuming that the DN cash balance received of DN600, 000 has not been spent, the extract from the statement of financial position will show

	DN
Bank	600,000
Accumulated profits	120,000
Current liabilities	480,000

On 10 April Parks repays the loan of $60,000 translating the transaction into DN using the exchange rate ruling on the date of the transaction.

10 April	$60,0000	x 9	= DN540,000

The transaction can then be recorded in the accounts

Decrease liability of loan	DR	Loan	DN540, 000	
Decrease the asset of cash	CR	Cash at bank		DN540,000

But note that this transaction wholly extinguishes the loan, which was being carried at DN480,000. There is a further exchange difference arising which increases the loan so is a loss.

31 March	$60,000	x 8	= DN480,000
10 April	$60,000	x 9	= DN540,000
	Exchange difference		DN60,000

To record the exchange loss in income

Recording a loss	DR	Income statement	DN60, 000	
Increase liability of loan	CR	Loan		DN60,000

You were not asked to prepare the loan T account in Park's accounts, but here it is anyway.

Loan account

		DN			DN
31 March	Income statement exchange gain	120,000	10 March	Cash	600,000
31 March	Balance c/d	480,000			
		600,000			600,000
10 April	Cash	540,000	31 March	Balance b/d	480,000
			10 April	Income statement exchange loss	60,000
		540,000			540,000

Chapter 20

Answer Greenland

Let's have a quick translation of the assets and liabilities of the subsidiary at the closing rate.

	DN	Closing rate	$
Tangible non current assets	2,500	÷ 2	1,250
Current assets	3,000	÷ 2	1,500
Liabilities	1,000	÷ 2	500

Let's translate all the income and expenses of the overseas subsidiary at the average rate.

	DN	Average rate	$
Revenue	70,000	÷ 1.75	40,000
Cost of sales	54,250	÷ 1.75	31,000
Operating costs	7,000	÷ 1.75	4,000
Tax	7,450	÷ 1.75	4,257

W1 Group structure

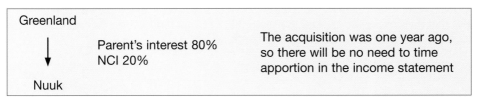

Greenland

↓   Parent's interest 80%   The acquisition was one year ago,
    NCI 20%   so there will be no need to time
Nuuk   apportion in the income statement

Let us as far possible do all the workings as they relate to Nuuk in its local currency of the DN, and only actually translate at the last hurdle.

W2 Net assets

	At acquisition DN	At year-end DN
Share capital	1,000	1,000
Share premium	800	800
Revaluation reserve	200	200
Accumulated profits	1,200	2,500
Fair value adjustment (bal fig)	1,000	1,000
Depreciation		(500)
	4,200	5,000

The subsidiary's post acquisition profits net of the extra depreciation on the fair value adjustment are DN800.

The net assets at acquisition are a given figure, so the fair value adjustment becomes the balancing figure.

The asset subject to depreciation has a remaining life of two years. The subsidiary was acquired one year ago, so the additional depreciation is DN1,000 x ½ = DN500.

W3 Goodwill

The goodwill arising needs to be calculated in the local currency first, it will then be subject to an impairment review and then the residual asset translated at the closing rate. The question gave us the cost of the investment in DN at DN7,500 but this can be proved by taking the $5,000 in Greenland accounts and translating it at the historic rate of 1.5 to give DN7,500.

		DN	DN
Cost of investment		7,500	
Less parent's % of the net assets at acquisition	(80% x 4,200)	(3,360)	
Goodwill (attributable to the parent)			4,140
Fair value of the NCI at acquisition		1,000	
Less the NCI % of the net assets at acquisition.	(20% x 4,200)	(840)	
Goodwill (attributable to the NCI)			160
Gross goodwill at acquisition			4,300

Alternative calculation of gross goodwill

		DN
Cost of the parent's investment (at fair value)		7,500
Fair value of the NCI at acquisition		1,000
Less 100% of the net assets at acquisition	(100% x 4,200)	(4,200)
Gross goodwill at acquisition		4,300

Impairment review

	DN	DN
Carrying value		
Net assets of the subsidiary at year end w2	5,000	
Goodwill w3	4,300	
		9,300
Recoverable amount		(9,000)
Impairment loss		300

The goodwill asset is translated at the closing rate

	DN		
Gross goodwill at acquisition	4,300		
Less impairment loss	(300)		
Goodwill remaining at year-end	4,000	÷ 2 =	$2,000

W4 NCI

Again this is calculated in DN and then translated at the closing rate.

		DN
NCI % in the net assets of the subsidiary w2	(20% x DN5,000)	1,000
Plus the goodwill attributable to the NCI w3		160
Less the NCI % in the impairment loss on gross goodwill	(20% x DN300)	(60)
		1,100
Or		
		DN
Fair value of the NCI at acquisition		1,000
Plus the NCI% of the post acquisition profits of the subsidiary	(20% x DN800)	160
Less the NCI% in the impairment loss of gross goodwill	(20% x DN300)	(60)
		1,100

The NCI translated at the closing rate

DN1,100	÷ 2	=	$550

W5 Group accumulated profits

In accumulated profits the profits of the foreign subsidiary are translated at the average rate, as they are an accumulation of profits that have passed through the income statement.

		$
Parent's accumulated profits		4,000
Less parent's % of the goodwill impairment loss translated at the average rate	(80% x DN300 ÷ 1.75)	(137)
Plus the parent's % of the post acquisition profits of the subsidiary translated at the average rate w2	(80% x DN800 ÷ 1.75)	366
		4,229

The group exchange gain or loss that is recognised in reserves (and so also included within the other comprehensive income section) can be difficult to calculate and will left as a balancing figure and only proved right at the end.

Greenland group statement of financial position

		$
Non current assets		
Goodwill	w3	2,000
Tangible	(15,000 + $1,250 plus the fair value adjustment (DN1, 000 less depreciation of DN500) ÷ 2 = $250)	16,500
Current Assets	(10,000 + $1,500)	11,500
		30,000
Ordinary shares		8,000
Share premium		6,000
Revaluation reserve		2,000
Foreign exchange difference	(Balancing figure but proved below)	(1,279)
Accumulated profits	w5	4,229
NCI	w4	550
Equity		19,500
Liabilities	(10,000 + $500)	10,500
		30,000

The group revaluation reserve is the parent only as the subsidiary has no change in its revaluation reserve post acquisition.

In preparing the group income statement I am going to do a separate working for the cost of sales, and the other workings can be presented as we go along.

Because there was an inter-company sale this automatically creates an inter-company purchase that has to be cancelled out. The transaction was denominated in $ so does not need translating.

The additional depreciation represents an extra expense for the subsidiary that is denominated in DN and so requires translation. All expenses should be translated at the average rate in the income statement.

W6 Cost of sales

		$
Parent		20,000
Subsidiary	(DN54,250 ÷ 1.75)	31,000
Less the inter-company purchase		(1,000)
Plus the impairment loss	(DN300 ÷ 1.75)	171
Plus the depreciation on the FVA	(DN500 ÷ 1.75)	286
		50,457

W7 NCI in the subsidiary's profits

				$
NCI % in the subsidiary's profits as given	(20% x	DN1,300	÷ 1.75)	148
Less the NCI in the depreciation on the FVA	(20% x	(DN500)	÷ 1.75)	(57)
Less the NCI % in the gross impairment loss	(20% x	(DN300)	÷ 1.75)	(34)
		DN500		57

W8 NCI in the subsidiary's total comprehensive income

	$
NCI % in the subsidiary's profit w7	57
Less the group exchange loss attributable to NCI w9	(174)
	(117)

Greenland group statement of comprehensive income

Income statement		$
Revenue	(45,000 + $40,000 less the inter-company $1,000)	84,000
Cost of sales	w6	(50,457)
Gross profit		33,543
Operating costs	(15,000 + $4,000)	(19,000)
Profit before tax		14,543
Tax	(8,000 + $4,257)	(12,257)
Profit for the year		2,286
Other comprehensive income		
Revaluation gain		150
Total group foreign exchange loss	w9	(1,453)
Total comprehensive income for the year		983
Attributable to the parent	Balancing figure	2,229
Attributable to the NCI	w7	57
Profit for the year		2,286
Attributable to the parent	Balancing figure	1,100
Attributable to the NCI	w8	(117)
Total comprehensive income for the year		983

W9 Group exchange difference

The group exchange difference arises on the retranslation of the subsidiary's

- opening net assets (last year's closing rate to this year's closing rate) per w2

- profit for the year (this year's average rate to this year's closing rate) per NCI calculation w7

- goodwill (last year's closing rate to this year's closing rate) per w3.

It is necessary to split the exchange difference between the parent and the NCI. For the net assets and profit that is done in the normal proportions, but not for the gross goodwill.

				Total	Parent	NCI
Opening net assets			$	$	$	$
DN4,200	÷	1.5	=	2,800			
DN4,200	÷	2	=	2,100			
80/20 split				700 loss	560	140
Profits for the year						
DN500	÷	1.75	=	286			
DN500	÷	2	=	250			
80/20 split				36 loss	29	7
Goodwill attributable to the parent						
DN4,140	÷	1.5	=	2,760			
DN4,140	÷	2	=	2,070			
				690 loss	690	
Goodwill attributable to the NCI						
DN160	÷	1.5	=	107			
DN160	÷	2	=	80			
				27 loss		27
				1,453	1,279	174

The opening net assets figure is given in the question at DN4,200, as it is the net assets at acquisition because the subsidiary was acquired one year ago.

The profit for the year is the same figure that the NCI in the subsidiary's profit for the year was based on i.e. DN500.

As the goodwill is not attributable to the parent and the NCI in their normal 80/20 proportions so the exchange difference that arises is not either and it is necessary to separately calculate the exchange differences.

Double entry bookkeeping

Double entry bookkeeping

It is always perfectly possible to prepare the group accounts without any reference to double entry bookkeeping. Nevertheless if you are familiar with double entry then it can provide a further logical explanation of the adjustments that are made in the consolidation process. What follows is a brief recap of how double entry works in case you are rusty. If you are unfamiliar with double entry then please note it is not essential to understanding the book.

Because most double entry book keeping systems are computerised there are fewer and fewer people who actually write up (the) books of account. The double-entry bookkeeping system is well suited to computerisation because the capturing of data and the adjustments to the accounts simply involves the application of rules.

Rule 1. Duality

Every transaction has two effects, one of which will be recorded as a debit (DR) and the other which will be recorded as a credit (CR).

Rule 2. When to DR and CR

This can be summarised in a table – showing the five elements that are recognised in the financial statements.

	Increase	Decrease
Asset	Debit	Credit
Expense (loss)	Debit	Credit
Liability	Credit	Debit
Equity	Credit	Debit
Income (profit)	Credit	Debit

The table is logical in its construction. Starting from the premise that when the effect of a transaction is to increase an asset the entry to be posted to the asset account is a DR, it is appropriate that a decrease in an asset is a CR. Examples of asset accounts include investments, goodwill, plant, inventory, receivables, and cash.

Expenses behave in the same way as asset accounts as they ultimately require being paid for. Increases in expenses are recorded by a DR to an expense account. Examples of expenses include rent, wages, depreciation, impairment losses and purchases, but these are usually categorised into cost of sales and operating expenses.

Further as a liability is the opposite of an asset so it is appropriate that it behaves in the opposite way i.e. that to record an increase in a liability, the entry to be posted to the liability account is a CR. Examples of liabilities include trade payables, loans and tax liabilities.

Equity is often referred to as the owner's interest, or as the company's liability to its shareholders. Although equity is not a liability it does behave in the same way as a liability in that when it is increased this is recorded as a CR to an equity account. For example, when the company issues new ordinary shares the increase in the equity is recorded as a CR to the ordinary share capital account. Examples of equity accounts include ordinary share capital, share premium, accumulated profits, non controlling interest (NCI) and revaluation reserves.

Income is the opposite of an expense and so behaves in the opposite way! Increases in income are recorded as a CR to the income account. Examples of income accounts include revenue (sales/turnover), and interest income.

In the top half of the statement of financial position there will be listed all the assets, which are all debit balances. In the lower half the equity and the liability balances are all listed which are all credit balances. Thus in the statement of financial position the two halves add up to the same total.

To complete our recap of double entry let us consider what the impact is on the financial statements of adjusting for the following transactions.

Shareholders subscribe $200 for 200 shares each with a nominal value of $1	The two accounts affected here are cash and share capital. Both are increased by the transaction.	To record an increase in the asset of cash, the top half of the statement of financial position is increased by the debit to the asset.	DR Cash (asset) $200
		To record the increase in the equity balance of share capital, the lower half of the statement of financial position is increased by the credit to the share capital account.	CR Share capital (equity) $200
An item of plant is purchased for $400 and payment will be made later	The two accounts affected here are plant and payables. Both are increased by the transaction.	To record an increase in the asset of plant the top half of the statement of financial position is increased by the debit to the plant account.	DR Plant (asset) $400
		To record the increase in the payable, a liability, the lower half of the statement of financial position is increased by a credit to the payable account.	CR Payable (liability) $400
The payable is reduced by the payment of $50 in cash	The two accounts affected here are payables and cash. Both are decreased by the transaction.	To record a decrease in the liability of payable the lower half of the statement of financial position is decreased by the debit to the payable account.	DR Payable (liability) $50
		To record the decrease in the asset of cash the top half of the statement of financial position is decreased by the credit to cash account.	CR Cash (asset) $50

The statement of financial position after these three transactions would be as follows

	$
Non current assets	
Plant	400
Current assets	
Cash at bank (200 – 50)	150
	550
Ordinary shares ($1)	200
Accumulated profits	Nil
Equity	200
Liabilities (400-50)	350
	550

All the assets are DR balances.

Equity and liabilities are CR balances.

Because with double entry bookkeeping transactions are recorded in equal measure as a DR and a CR, and one half of the statement of financial position lists all the DRs and the other lists all the CRs, then the two halves of the statement of financial position should always have the same total i.e. balance. That is why they were commonly referred to as balance sheets.

Glossary

Accounting period	The period of time for which the financial statements are drawn up.	
Accumulated profits	The running total of profits that the company has recognised through income. Part of equity on the statement of financial position. This is the same as retained profits.	
Acquisition accounting	The required method of consolidating the financial statements of subsidiaries when preparing the group accounts.	
Acquisition date	The date that the parent achieves control of the subsidiary.	
Asset	An asset is a resource controlled by the enterprise as a result of past events and from which future economic benefits are expected to flow to the enterprise.	Framework
Associate	An enterprise in which an investor has significant influence but not control or joint control.	IAS28
Balance sheet	This is a financial statement showing the financial position of a business listing its assets, liabilities and equity at a specified date. It is the old name for the statement of financial position.	
Business combination	A business combination is a transaction or event in which an acquirer obtains control of one or more businesses.	IFRS3
Business	A business is defined as an integrated set of activities and assets that is capable of being conducted and managed for the purpose of providing a return directly to investors or other owners, members or participants.	IFRS3
Carrying amount	The amount at which an asset is recognised in the statement of financial position after deducting accumulated depreciation and accumulated impairment losses.	IAS36

Complex group structures	A group structure where the subsidiary also has investments in other group companies. This means that a complex group structure will, from the perspective of the ultimate parent have an indirect investment.	
Consideration	The amount paid for the investment in the acquired business e.g. cash and shares issued. The consideration has to be recorded at fair value.	
Consolidated financial statements	The financial statements of a group presented as those of a single economic entity.	IAS27
Contingent consideration	Consideration that may or may not be paid in the future depending on whether some uncertain future event occurs. An example of the uncertain future event maybe achieving a profit target.	
Contingent liability	A contingent liability is a possible obligation depending on whether some uncertain future event occurs, or a present obligation but payment is not probable or the amount cannot be measured reliably.	IAS37
Control	The power to govern the financial and operating policies of an enterprise so as to obtain benefits from its activities.	IAS27
Creative accounting	The manipulation of financial statements by the selection of accounting policies, use of accounting treatments and estimates, with the intent of improving the users' perception of the financial statements, for example by overstating profit, improving the gearing or profit smoothing. Arguably whilst not illegal it is unethical.	

Current asset	Current assets are cash; cash equivalent; assets held for collection, sale, or consumption within the enterprise's normal operating cycle; or assets held for trading within the next 12 months. All other assets are non current.	IAS1
Current liability	Current liabilities are those to be settled within the enterprise's normal operating cycle or due within 12 months, or those held for trading, or those for which the entity does not have an unconditional right to defer payment beyond 12 months. Other liabilities are non current.	IAS1
Credit / CR (as in Debit)	Entry on the right side of a double entry bookkeeping system that represents the reduction of an asset or expense or the addition to a liability, revenue or equity.	
Debit / DR (as in Credit)	Entry on the left side of a double entry bookkeeping system that represents the addition of an asset or expense or the reduction to a liability, revenue or equity.	
Deferred consideration	Consideration that will be paid in the future.	
Depreciation	The measure of the wearing out consumption or other reduction in the useful life of an asset. It is a non cash expense and charged to income.	
Derecognition	To remove from the statement of financial position an asset or liability. Assets are generally derecognised when the risks and rewards of ownership are transferred or the asset expires. Liabilities are generally derecognised when they are extinguished i.e. settled or expired.	

Discount arising on consolidation	This arises when the consideration paid by the parent on the acquisition of the subsidiary is less than the fair value of the net assets acquired. It represents a bargain purchase. Sometimes referred to as negative goodwill.	
Dividend	A distribution of profits to the shareholders of a company. Dividends paid reduce the accumulated profits of the company. Dividends received are recognised as income.	
Double entry bookkeeping	Method of recording financial transactions in which each transaction is entered in two or more accounts and involves two-way, self-balancing posting. Total debits must equal total credits.	
Dominant influence	This is the same as control i.e. the power to govern the financial and operating policies of an enterprise so as to obtain benefits from its activities.	
D shaped groups	A group structure where the parent and the subsidiary both have investments in a third company. D shaped groups are the same as mixed groups.	
Element	The basic building blocks of financial reporting. Assets, liabilities and equity are the elements that are reported on the statement of financial position, and revenue and expenses are the elements that are reported in income.	
Equity	Equity is the residual interest in the assets of the enterprise after deducting all its liabilities. The equity of a company will comprise its ordinary share capital and its reserves. The equity of a group will in addition include the non controlling interest.	Framework

Equity accounting	A method of accounting by which an equity investment is initially recorded at cost and subsequently adjusted to reflect the investor's (parent's) share of the net profit or loss of the associate (investee).	IAS28
Equity share capital	This is the same as ordinary share capital. The equity share capital of the company is recorded at the nominal value and represents capital originally introduced by the owners (shareholders). It is assumed that they carry equal voting rights (unless otherwise clearly stated). The company has no obligation to pay dividends or to redeem equity shares.	
Expenses	Expenses are decreases in economic benefits during the accounting period in the form of outflows or depletions of assets or incurrences of liabilities that result in decreases in equity, other than those relating to distributions to equity participants.	Framework
Exposure draft (ED)	A proposed international financial reporting standard issued by the IASB for consultation and public comment.	
Fair value	The amount obtainable from the sale of an asset in a bargained transaction between knowledgeable and willing parties.	IAS36
Fair value adjustment (FVA)	An adjustment made to the carrying value of an asset or liability to bring it to its fair value.	
Financial instrument	A contract that gives rise to a financial asset of one entity and a financial liability or equity instrument of another entity. Examples include receivables, investments and loans.	IAS39
Foreign currency	A currency other than the functional currency being used by the company.	

Functional currency	The currency of the primary economic environment in which the company operates.	IAS21
GAAP	Generally accepted accounting practice. This is taken as meaning all of the accounting standards together with the way they are interpreted and applied as well and how transactions not specifically covered by regulations are generally accounted for. Best practice.	
Gain	An increase in an asset, or a reduction in a liability.	
Goodwill	Positive goodwill is an intangible asset that can arise in the group accounts on the acquisition of a subsidiary. It is the same as the premium arising on acquisition. It is subject to an annual impairment review. It can be measured gross (i.e. in full) or on a proportionate basis. If goodwill is not positive (i.e. not a premium) then it is negative (i.e. a discount).	
Gross goodwill	A measurement of goodwill introduced by IFRS3 *Business Combinations* when it was revised in January 2008 where in measuring goodwill of the subsidiary at acquisition the fair value of the non controlling interest is considered. This is the same as total goodwill.	
Group of companies	At minimum a group of companies comprise a parent and a subsidiary.	
Group accounts	The financial statements of a group presented as those of a single economic entity. This is the same as the consolidated accounts.	
IAS	International Accounting Standards. These were issued by a predecessor body to the IASB but have been adopted by the IASB.	

IASB	The International Accounting Standards Board is an independent body that develops and approves International Financial Reporting Standards. The IASB operates under the oversight of the International Accounting Standards Committee Foundation. The IASB was formed in 2001 to replace the International Accounting Standards Committee.	
IFRS	International Financial Reporting Standards. They are issued by the IASB.	
Impairment	An asset is impaired when its carrying amount exceeds its recoverable amount.	IAS36
Income	Income is the increases in economic benefits during the accounting period in the form of inflows or enhancements of assets or decreases of liabilities that result in increases in equity, other than those relating to contributions from equity participants.	Framework
Income statement	This is a financial statement in which the revenue and expenses are recognised in order to measure the profit or loss of the period.	
Indirect holding adjustment	A consolidation adjustment necessary where there is an indirect investment i.e. a subsidiary has a subsidiary. The adjustment has the effect of reducing the indirect investment and the NCI in net assets.	
Indirect investment	An investment made by the subsidiary is from the perspective of the parent an indirect investment.	
Indirect subsidiary	A subsidiary of the parent where the investment is held by another subsidiary. This is also known as a sub-subsidiary.	

Intangible asset	An identifiable non monetary asset without physical substance. For example goodwill and brand names.	IAS 38
Inventory	Inventories include assets held for sale in the ordinary course of business (finished goods), assets in the production process for sale in the ordinary course of business (work in process), and materials and supplies that are consumed in production (raw materials). Inventory is the same as stock and goods.	IAS2
Joint control	The contractually agreed sharing of control over an economic activity such that no individual contracting party has control.	
Joint venture	A contractual arrangement whereby two or more parties undertake an economic activity that is subject to joint control.	IAS31
Liability	A liability is a present obligation of the enterprise arising from past events, the settlement of which is expected to result in an outflow from the enterprise of resources embodying economic benefits.	Framework
Loss	A decrease in an asset or the increase in a liability.	
Minority interest	The old name for non controlling interest.	
Mixed groups	A group structure where the parent and the subsidiary both have investments in a third company. This is also known as a D shaped group.	
Monetary item	An item that is cash or very near cash. Monetary assets include cash and receivables but not inventory. All liabilities are monetary items.	

Negative goodwill	An alternative name for the discount arising on consolidation. It represents a bargain purchase. It is accounted for as a profit in income.
Nominal value of equity (ordinary) shares	The nominal value of a share is the minimum value that a share can be issued for by the company. Any excess consideration received is taken to the share premium account.
Non controlling interest (NCI)	The interests of the equity shareholders in the subsidiary companies of the group that are not the parents. The NCI are regarded as part of equity of the group and will have a share in the net assets and income of the subsidiary companies. The new name for minority interests.
Non current asset	An asset that is not a current asset, i.e. is expected to last more than one accounting period e.g. plant and machinery.
Non current liability	A liability that is not a current liability, so generally one that is due and payable in more than one accounting period.
Ordinary share capital	This is the same as equity share capital. The equity share capital of the company represents capital originally introduced by the owners (shareholders). It is assumed that equity shares carry equal voting rights (unless otherwise clearly stated). The company has no obligation to pay dividends or to redeem equity shares.
Other comprehensive income	This presents gains and losses that have not been recognised in the income statement e.g. revaluation gains taken directly to reserves (equity). The other comprehensive income statement together with the income statement forms the statement of comprehensive income.

Parent company	A company that has one or more subsidiaries.	IAS27
Payables	A liability, an obligation to pay cash, normally to trade suppliers.	
Post acquisition profits of the subsidiary	The profits of the subsidiary recognised after the date the subsidiary is acquired by the parent company	
Pre acquisition profits of the subsidiary	The profits of the subsidiary on the date it is acquired by the parent company.	
Premium arising on consolidation	This is the same as (positive) goodwill.	
Presentational currency	The currency in which financial statements are presented.	IAS21
Profit and loss account	The old name for the income statement.	
Proportional method of calculating goodwill	A traditional measurement of goodwill, still allowed by IFRS3 Business Combinations revised in January 2008 where only the goodwill of the subsidiary attributable to the parent is measured.	
Provision	A liability of uncertain timing or amount.	IAS37
Provision for unrealised profit (PURP)	A consolidation adjustment made to eliminate the effects of carrying assets that have been transferred between group companies other than at cost.	
Realised (gain or loss)	A gain or loss can be regarded as realised following a sale or when a transaction generates cash or near cash assets. For example the sale of an asset will cause any previously recognised revaluation surplus in reserves to be become realised.	
Receivables	Debtors, monies that are owed to the business, a type of financial asset. Receivables generally arise from the sale of goods.	

Recognition	Recognition is the process of incorporating in the statement of financial position or income statement an item that meets the definition of an element and satisfies the recognition criteria of it being probable that any future economic benefit associated with the item will flow to or from the enterprise, and the item's cost or value can be measured with reliability.	Framework
Recoverable amount	The higher of an asset's fair value less costs to sell (sometimes called net selling price) and its value in use.	IAS36
Reserves	Part of the equity of the company. Examples of reserves include share premium, revaluation reserves and accumulated profits.	
Retained profits	The running total of profits that the company has recognised through income. Part of equity in the statement of financial position. This is the same as accumulated profits.	
Revenue	The gross inflow of economic benefits (cash, receivables, other assets) arising from the ordinary operating activities of an enterprise (such as sales of goods, sales of services, interest, royalties, and dividends).	IAS18
Share premium	The excess consideration received on the issue of shares by the company over and above the nominal value of those shares.	
Significant influence	Power to participate in the financial and operating policy decisions but not control them.	IAS28
Statement of comprehensive income	The statement that reports all the gains and losses recognised by the company, combining the income statement and the other comprehensive income.	

Statement of financial position	This is a financial statement showing the financial position of a business entity in terms of assets, liabilities and equity at a specified date. It is the new name for the balance sheet.	
Special purpose entities	A separate entity established by a company for a particular purpose. A special purpose entity is to be consolidated if it is controlled.	
Subsidiary	An entity, including an unincorporated entity such as a partnership, that is controlled by another entity (known as the parent).	IAS27
Sub – subsidiary	A subsidiary of the parent where the investment is held by another subsidiary. This is also known as an indirect subsidiary.	
Substance over form	Substance over form is an accounting concept meaning that it is the reality of events and transactions rather than the legal form that should be accounted for.	
Unrealised (gain or loss)	A gain (or loss) that has not been realised in the form of cash or near cash assets. An example of an unrealised gain is a revaluation surplus.	
Value in use	The discounted present value of estimated future cash flows expected to arise from the continuing use of an asset, and from its disposal at the end of its useful life.	IAS36
Venturer	A party to a joint venture that has joint control over that joint venture.	IAS31
Vertical groups	A group structure where the subsidiary company has a subsidiary company.	

Index